AFRICAN
ADVENTURES

BRENDA LANGE

AFRICAN ADVENTURES

REALITY IN THE BUSH

TATE PUBLISHING & *Enterprises*

Published by Tate Publishing & Enterprises, LLC
127 E. Trade Center Terrace | Mustang, Oklahoma 73064 USA
1.888.361.9473 | www.tatepublishing.com

Tate Publishing is committed to excellence in the publishing industry. The company reflects the philosophy established by the founders, based on Psalm 68:11,
"The Lord gave the word and great was the company of those who published it."

Book design copyright © 2008 by Tate Publishing, LLC. All rights reserved.
Cover design & interior design by Lynly D. Taylor

Published in the United States of America

ISBN: 978-1-60604-890-0
1. Church & Ministry: Church Life: Missions
2. Inspiration: Motivational: Biography & Autobiography
08.09.30

DEDICATED TO THE GLORY OF GOD

TABLE OF CONTENTS

STEP THREE | THE MOLDING OF A MISSIONARY

STEP FOUR | BALAMA

FOREWORD

I have always dreamed of going to Africa. The wildness of that amazing continent and seeing the wealth of animals are the biggest draws for me. However, I'm not so actively dreaming that any longer because *African Adventures: Reality in the Bush* by Brenda Lange is written so realistically that the vicious black mamba snakes have scared me away. I do not like poisonous snakes, and that one is deliberately deadly. But Brenda has lived to tell about it, many times over. Reading *African Adventures* is seeing God in action in ways that our western world seldom experiences. Bush Bunny Brenda shares her incredible stories of God's rescues and redeeming love as matter-of-factly as we talk about going to the grocery store. Hardship and heartbreak are daily events of the millions of people living there, but Brenda and her Orphans Unlimited Mission are making a difference. She and her staff are saving children, one meal, one blanket, one school day at a time as they build schools, dorms, and bridges, dig wells, and provide what medical relief they can. One cannot read this book or listen to her speak without feeling like he or she is in the crowd that touched Christ's garment. That God still heals today and that He still provides. The sales from this book and hopefully from its sequel will supply a good portion of the financial support for Brenda's mission. We can all help her by spreading the word about a woman who listened when God called.

—Lauraine Snelling, author of *The Red River of the North* series, *Daughters of Blessing* series, and *Breaking Free*, along with many other titles. I am excited about helping Brenda give children a chance to live.

MY WORLD AND WELCOME TO IT

Picture a delicate deer-like antelope two feet high, with huge Bambi eyes and a mincing step. Now picture a deadly mamba, one of the most dangerous snakes known, relentlessly crawling toward it.

It is no fantasy. I viewed that chilling scene live and up close. With it, I learned a vital lesson about working with God.

God teaches us anywhere, of course—in the dark, quiet room of a nursing home, in a kitchen, in a factory, in a jail. My learning ground, though, is the African bush, with some lessons from Texas thrown in.

The four sections of this book reflect the four main arenas to date of my service and learning: Texas beginnings, early work in Vilanculos in southern Mozambique, and the Village of Love and Balama in Moz's northern states.

It is an incredibly rich and exotic continent, Africa, and ours is an incredibly rich and exotic God, Master of all. I am greatly privileged to be able to serve him and to learn in incredibly rich and exotic surroundings. It is my deepest desire to pass my lessons and adventures along to you, not just to entertain you (though I hope to do that) but to help you reach new, wonderful, unimagined dimensions in your life with Him.

THE FIRST STEP:

1

Brenda Becomes the Bush Bunny

The first real missions assignment for this starry-eyed newcomer to Africa was to help at an orphanage in Vilanculos in the south of Mozambique. The facility consisted of seventeen small houses scattered out across a full mile. It wasn't an easy mile, either. The road connecting the dwellings, like so many roads in Mozambique, was scratched into loose sand. Too, because the country lies within fifteen degrees of the equator, temperatures hover mostly in the 90s F (30s C). And for some reason, the humidity is very high, even in the dry season.

Walking this hot, sandy road at least two times every day was very tiring, to say the least. Now, back in Texas where I grew up, the saying was: "If you can't get there on a horse, it ain't worth going." I had spent a lot of my pre-Africa life riding on, falling off, and caring for horses.

There are very few horses in Moz, but that didn't stop my weary legs from kicking my horsey-minded brain into action. And it came up with the bright idea of riding a donkey instead of walking. It took me two weeks of searching before I finally found and purchased Old Faithful, a rather ragged little fellow. I was on the back of a four-legged critter once more. He was not exactly in the same class as your prize quarter horse, but the small beast served me very well. He eased my life considerably, and I quickly developed an affection for him. He, for his part, developed an affection for garden greens.

Moz is all open grazing for animals, as no fences exist. So I kept

Old Faithful tied with thirty feet of rope to a tree. Each morning and evening I would walk my sturdy male companion to a new tree. It was on one such walk that we met the bush rabbit.

I was leading Old Faithful down a bush path through an area in which waist-high grass lined both sides of the trail. Old Faithful had his own ideas as to destination. He was pulling in the opposite direction, his attention focused on his favorite plants in our nearby garden.

My attention was focused on keeping him headed the right way. So we were both taken by surprise when a huge rabbit squirted straight up out of the tall grass and landed *kerplop!* on the path right in front of us. I yelled and leaped aside while Old Faithful bolted off toward the garden.

Some of the kids who saw this said I jumped higher than the rabbit. Since then I have been Bush Bunny Brenda.

The View from Vilanculos

Mozambique—simply Moz to most people—stretches in a leisurely arch for nearly fifteen hundred miles along Africa's East coast. Look for it across from the huge island of Madagascar. Moz's southern coast, where Vilanculos lies, boasts lovely white beaches and has become a popular resort area. The whole area is lowland, with extensive marshes in some places. Sand, mud, and compacted sand extend well into the interior lowlands. This makes it difficult to build good roads and solid railways. It also, as I just reflected, makes walking no picnic in the park.

Historically this East coast of Africa was a major route by which Arab traders reached the interior. The Arab influence remains strong: Moz is primarily Islamic. The country was also a key outlet for the slave trade. During the colonial era it belonged to Portugal, and Portuguese is still the language to know.

Moz is an extraordinarily fertile ground for humanitarian work because the need is so great. First colonial exploitation and then civil war all but destroyed the nation's economy and infrastructure. They are building now, but the way is difficult.

In the meantime, many children, abandoned or orphaned, need help. They cannot wait for a more favorable economy or some vague, brighter tomorrow. I believe this is why the Lord sent me to this beautiful, beleaguered country. The harvest needs workers so badly.

Most of the stories in this book will come from Moz because this is where I've centered my efforts.

Postscript on the Donkey

It is sad to say that Old Faithful was not to be my longtime companion. About two months after our bush rabbit scare, the farm workers found my buddy dead. We observed two marks on his belly, and it was obvious that he died quickly during the night. We suspect that a mamba bit him.

Moz was still being ripped apart by war at that time. Donkeys were scarce and horses non-existent. I was never able to find another one. Bush Bunny was cast afoot once more.

2

Snakes Alive

Could a snake really kill a donkey with one bite? You better believe it. They are just as deadly to human beings also. These dreadful and amazing serpents are commonplace in Moz, as are the stories about them. You will hear a lot more about them, for we encounter them frequently.

I doubt that the many people who live among them think about it much, but highly venomous snakes subtly shape the very way one looks at life. Security becomes more fragile, caution more constant and automatic. The guard stays up, the eyes open. Always. And yet, after living in the bush awhile, people don't even realize that they are continually on the lookout. So it is important when it comes to understanding the mindset and motives of the local populace that you know just how dangerous and deadly the snakes are.

The Mambas

People the world over hear about the peril of endangered species all the time. They hardly ever hear about perilous species that endanger. Most people don't even realize that there are still places in the world where nature can dish out death at any moment. East Africa is one of those places.

I apologize for sounding melodramatic, and I do not mean to bring back the ugly old myths about "darkest Africa" and great white hunters and all that. After all, automobile traffic dishes out pain and death to the unwary (and sometimes to the wary also!) in Dallas, Texas. You had better understand traffic flow if you want to survive Dallas, and you must understand the bush if you want to survive in my world.

North Americans don't think about the dangers in Dallas because they are accustomed to traffic. It is woven into the fabric of life. They are not, however, accustomed to dangerous, free-ranging snakes. And one of the most common and deadly is the mamba (*Dendroaspis*), the suspected killer of Old Faithful. Nothing in North America comes close.

Cobras and various vipers can all be found in Mozambique. But I would like to use the mamba as sort of a vignette, a specific example to illustrate the more general reality of danger in the bush.

Facts about Mambas

Generalizations: North Americans know basically two sorts of highly venomous snakes, the pit vipers and the elapids. Pit vipers are rattlers, South America's fer-de-lance, and their kin. Elapids are the cobras and coral snakes. Pit vipers usually lie in wait, sometimes for weeks, for prey to come near them. Elapids go out looking for it. Pit vipers, normally big-bodied and stocky, tend to move rather slowly and deliberately compared with the slim, swift, impetuous elapids. Pit vipers usually are ground-dwellers. Many elapids can climb trees well.

Mambas are elapids.

Fact: Two species of mambas occur in Moz, differentiated primarily by color. Both are green when very young. The Green Mamba keeps its youthful color through life. The Black Mamba becomes brownish charcoal as it matures. Both are slim snakes with fairly small heads and no necks. An adult stretches seven or eight feet—a bit short of three metres.

Fact: Mambas are the fastest snake in the world, traveling at speeds up to seven or eight miles, eleven kilometres per hour (for comparison, most people run about twelve or thirteen miles per hour). They climb easily; even tree-dwelling creatures are not safe from them. They are lightning-quick and can accurately strike a target up to ten feet away *from a standing position.*

Mambas do not coil and strike in the same way as North America's rattlesnakes. They raise the front half of their bodies straight up off the ground and plunge forward. I have seen a seven-foot mamba stand up to almost three feet.

Fact: Venomous snakes have two kinds of poisons. A neurotoxic component attacks nerves; a proteolytic component dissolves protein (muscle and most other organs are made mostly of protein). Either venom component can be weak or powerful depending on the snake species delivering it, and most poisonous snakes have at least a little of both.

North America's rattlesnakes are pit vipers, and their venom is primarily proteolytic. Receive a bite on your thumb, and you'll probably lose the thumb as the flesh is broken down.

Being an elapid and therefore a close relative of cobras, the mamba possesses a powerfully neurotoxic venom. It paralyzes muscles not by breaking down their tissue but by shutting down the nerves that tell the muscles to move. As the venom circulates through the body, the victim loses gross coordination and the ability to speak within ten minutes of the bite. When the poison reaches the internal organs, the victim dies of suffocation as the chest muscles quit working, making breathing impossible. Death usually occurs in less than thirty minutes in an adult person.

Fact: The Black Mamba is known as the more aggressive of the two species and is far more so than are pit vipers. Most pit vipers, including rattlesnakes, lie in wait, perhaps for days or weeks, until something ventures close enough to be seized and bitten. Instead of freezing in place or quietly crawling off, as most snakes will do when someone walks into their area, Black Mambas will initiate an attack. And when they are cornered, they will retaliate with vengeance. In short, they are *very* aggressive and easily provoked. Without the Lord's grace and the right knowledge and weapon, the person who corners one of these snakes will lose the battle.

Satan has tried to use both green and black mambas many times to end my life. But God's angels have always intervened so that I could continue taking His love to the people of Mozambique. The stories I tell about these snakes are real faith-builders, but if you are scared of snakes, I don't recommend that you read the snake stories before going to bed. They have been known to disturb people's sleep. You are warned.

Bambi and the Green Mamba

The civil war in Mozambique was taking a horrible toll, with not only death and disease but thousands of displaced persons. Refugees wandered everywhere. Orphans and lost children abounded. At the orphanage in Vilanculos, we found ourselves feeding several thousand malnourished children each week.

Obviously such children need foods that provide maximum nutrition in every meal. One of these foods is soya soup, and we used a lot of it. This protein-rich mixture is just the thing for the children, providing the nutrients essential for growth. It is doubly useful, for it comes in a dried form that is easy to transport and store.

On this particular day, I was asked to drive our Land Rover to one of the soup kitchen sites in order to deliver some large sacks of dried soya soup for the next week's feeding. Just as I was leaving, a man approached me carrying a tiny deer-like creature called a duiker. He had killed its mother for food. Now he wanted to know if I would like this baby. He had no milk, and without help, this week-old fawn would soon die.

If you've ever seen a duiker, you know how cute, cute can be. They are a kind of miniature antelope. The grey-brown adults stand maybe two feet high at the shoulder, give or take. Their Boer name means *diver*, but they don't live near water. Rather, they dive into the brush when they're startled.

When you come upon one, it takes off leaping and ducking, hurdling some bushes, diving down behind others, and changing directions. A single duiker can zip about like popcorn in a microwave, very confusing to predators.

They are absolutely charming, with tiny horns, teeny-tiny cloven hooves, and gorgeous eyes. Now picture an infant one of these. Cute upon cute!

Would I accept it? Heh. So I took it home and began bottle feeding my little Bambi.

After she regained her strength, I placed her in an old chicken pen near my house. Her pen was nothing more than a dirt floor with grass walls and roof. The front of the pen and its door were made of chicken wire. The whole thing measured about a meter wide by one and a half meters long.

Because Bambi was so tiny, with no mother to protect her, and her pen was not predator- proof, I asked the Lord to keep her safe from any creature that might try to eat her.

When Bambi was about a month old, I was washing dishes at 3:30 p.m. when the Lord dropped this message into my head: "Go and feed *now!*"

I normally don't feed until 4:00 p.m., so I argued with him. "Lord, it's too early to feed now."

He repeated the message. Okay. I knew better than to question him a second time. I mixed the milk and went out to feed.

When I opened the door of the pen, Bambi was sitting there looking like a rock statue. Normally at feeding time she always greeted me by running over and nuzzling my leg, but today she never even twitched an ear. Puzzled, I stepped into the pen with one foot.

A loud thump in the back right-hand corner of the pen caught my attention. An off-white tail flipped out of an old, upside-down, cone-shaped chicken nest that had been left in there.

My first thought was *rat.* Then the tail turned over and my mind screamed, *Snake!*

The snake started thrashing around inside the nest, trying to get out. In one swift move, I scooped up Bambi in my left hand and stepped backwards out the door. Freed now, the green mamba struck, but it flew past me and hit the grass wall to my left.

I yelled, "Cobra! Cobra!" which in Portuguese means snake. The workers came running and beat it to death with their long poles.

When speaking in public, I always compare this story to the Bible's story of Daniel in the lion's den. God controlled the lions by closing their mouths so they couldn't eat Daniel, even though he stayed in the pit for a whole night.

I asked the Lord to protect Bambi from predators. He warned me when she was in danger and sent me to rescue her. I realized afterward, once the adrenaline flow had slowed a little, that I was never in danger because God had sent me to get her.

There is no doubt whatever that he was controlling the snake. First, he confused the snake while it flailed inside the chicken nest, giving me the few seconds needed to scoop up Bambi and get out the door. Second, this four-foot green mamba struck at me from a distance of three feet and *missed.* That never happens. Third, as the snake whipped past me, *its mouth was closed.* That is totally abnormal. Snakes strike in order to bite.

A basic, basic lesson was reinforced that day: do not fear to tread where the Lord sends you. Step out in faith. He knows the situation, and he will protect you.

Black Mamba in the Pit

A few months after my green mamba adventure, one of our orphans spotted a seven-foot black mamba slithering toward Bambi's pen late one afternoon. He alerted the workers, but the snake slipped into a deep brush pit before they could kill it. This caused a major problem since, understandably, no one wanted to go near the pit to flush it out, myself included.

The brush pit was basically a big incinerator. Workers would toss in the trash, cuttings, refuse, and other brush that always accumulate when you farm and build.

We were going to burn the pit eventually anyway, so I suggested that we do it now. The workers circled the pit, and the fire was started. The dry brush caught quickly. The flames crackled and roared high.

Everyone watched nervously for the snake to come shooting out. We all knew that the snake would try its escape at full speed. There would be no second chance with the target moving at fifteen miles an hour.

An hour went by, and it was getting dark. The snake never came out, and we all believed it must surely have died, for the fire had been too intense. The workers left for home, leaving only me and two guards to put out the fire. As I was about to go, I caught sight of movement in the pale white sand just two feet in front of me.

My eyes went wide in terror as I realized the snake was lying right next to me. I screamed and jumped backwards into the arms of one of the guards. We all scrambled to get away from it.

Our commotion sent the stunned snake into action. He took off for the nearest cover, a tree with low-hanging branches. One of the guards ran behind the tree, but the snake cleverly altered course toward Bambi's pen.

Without thinking I ran around to block the snake's path. When it saw me, the snake stopped and stood erect to strike. I suddenly realized that my six-foot pole was way too short for a safe kill. This snake could easily strike up to ten feet.

But instead of running, I prepared to swing at his head as he struck. I'd never backed down from any snake fight in Texas, and I didn't plan to start now (not recommended with mambas if you desire a long life). My life was spared because the snake lost its balance and fell to the ground. Before anyone could move, it stood up again.

The guard on my right threw a heavy two-foot stick, entangling the snake and knocking it to the ground. The rear guard rushed in and beat the snake, breaking its back.

But it is very hard to kill a snake in soft sand, and we didn't have a machete—a *panga*—to cut off its head. The fire was still burning, so I told the guards to throw it back into the pit. I thought that a fitting solution for one of the devil's representatives since that's what the Lord plans to do with Satan when he returns.

Those two guards taught me a valuable lesson that day on how to grow old in Mozambique or anywhere else. The number one rule: use wisdom when fighting. Pride and ignorance can get you killed. Number two: go prepared with the right weapons. As you will see, this lesson was well learned and helped me successfully fight many a mamba more in the years to come.

Saved by a Lizard

Entomologists have decided that the body chemistry of some people makes them much more attractive to mosquitoes than other people in the same mosquito-infested place. I have a friend, for instance, whose husband is attractive that way. Mosquitoes by the pound will cross a river and two county lines to get to him while she sits beside him unbothered.

I'm attractive that way with snakes, I guess. However, I am convinced that in my case it is Satan rather than body chemistry. As evidence I point out that, for example, during the first three years of my ministry in the Village of Love near Lichinga, of eleven houses on our property, mine was the only one snakes entered. In fact, I encountered many snakes both inside and outside my hut. Other workers there met few or none.

For example, it was May of 1995 that we first broke ground for our Village of Love. When all you are starting out with is a hammer in one hand and a shovel in the other, you're facing a lot of time-consuming work. And it did indeed consume time. We made mud brick. We laid out a basic plan. We got the garden in—a priority requirement, for that would be our food for the year. We established a water source. We cleared and brushed. We accomplished with a shovel what construction crews in North America use a bulldozer for.

Even as we built using hand labor, we were racing against time. During the rainy season, one cannot make bricks or dig in the sodden ground or build. Once the rains began, construction would end until the next dry season. We had to have the buildings up, roofed, and habitable.

In late November the rainy season arrived right on schedule. The vivid sun faded as blue sky turned to gray. The clouds built up.

The first rains are always welcome after the long dry spell. They wash off the bush, brightening its colors and giving it a feeling of newness. It makes the grass sprout; tiny green blades like peach fuzz become gorgeous green clumps. It lays down the dust and clears the air.

But the rains continue relentlessly. Just when you believe it has ended, it starts up all over again. Eventually you find yourself thinking, *Enough already!*

The heartless downpours forced us from the tents in which we had lived so comfortably just a few days before into our unfinished mud brick huts. These one-room mansions had been fitted with solid wood doors, an essential safety feature. The windows had been installed, but the screens weren't up yet.

Now where I grew up in America's midland, rain brings a cooling-off. A good old-fashioned Texas thunderstorm offers welcome respite from summer's heat. Not in Moz. It's hot and humid all the time, rain or dry. Sitting in a mud hut with the windows closed became oppressively uncomfortable in a big hurry. And yet to open the screenless windows was to invite in bugs and other visitors.

My one-room hut doubled as a store room, for everything we owned had to be kept under a roof, protected from the rain. My dirt floor was cluttered wall-to-wall with cardboard cartons and metal trunks holding our supplies. I had managed to keep open a narrow path through which to make my way from the door to my bed in the back of the room.

About a week after we moved from our tents into the unfinished huts, a loud thump awoke me in the middle of the night. I grabbed my flashlight and got up to investigate. My foot almost landed on a black mamba! A large lizard was jammed in its mouth. The thumping that woke me was the lizard's tail hitting a cardboard box as the snake grabbed it.

For a moment I stood frozen, stunned to see this aggressive, deadly snake just a few feet from my bed. In the next brief moment, though, I snatched up my machete and ended its life.

Killing a snake—or anything else—with a machete makes quite a mess. However, it was too dangerous to go outside to dispose of it before morning. So I scooped it all up and left it by the door. Then I returned to bed, threading my way back through the boxes.

Some time later I told this story to a missionary in Malawi.

He nodded knowingly. "God," he said, "saved my life in a similar way. As I was walking through my home—"

"Dirt floors?"

"Concrete. And thresholds. You would think the house was secure. But I stepped on a poisonous snake in the dark. The only reason it didn't bite me was that it also had a lizard in its mouth."

We both agreed that the Lord sacrifices a lot of lizards to save missionaries in the night.

Just Passing By

About a year later, one evening in 1996, I was sitting on the edge of my bed, taking off my shoes when in my head I heard the word *Look!* My eyes were directed to my right. I froze as a two-foot black mamba came sliding along the wall less than a yard away.

Two feet long doesn't sound like much—a garter snake. The size told me this was a juvenile, certainly nowhere near adult size. But already its venom was every bit as deadly, its speed just as swift as any adult snake's.

This one was taking its time, poking its nose here and there, flicking its tongue. In fact, it seemed to be unaware that I even existed. I was afraid I might upset it by yelling for my nephew, Jason, to bring me a machete. Let's face it; when you're seated immediately next to a deadly snake, you don't exactly remember that snakes are deaf and fail to detect airborne noises. But I yelled anyway.

The sleek serpent never altered its path. With a soft, lethal grace, it glided on past me toward the metal trunk a few feet on my left.

I was concerned that I wouldn't be able to kill it if got behind that trunk, so I did a very dumb thing and threw a shoe at it. The Lord gave me grace, for under normal circumstances that should have sent the snake into a rage, causing it to strike at anything that moved. But it just looked at the shoe for a few seconds and slid on behind the trunk. By that time Jason arrived with the machete. As I pointed my light behind the trunk, the mamba raised its head. I thrust the long blade at it and struck home. The danger was over. Jason returned to his hut, and I went to bed.

It was obvious that the snake never knew I was there until the light shone in its face, because it acted totally out of character for a mamba. The Lord never ceases to amaze me with his protective power.

People have asked me how I could sleep in that room right after killing a deadly snake. It's easy. I say, "Thank you, Lord, for showing me the snake before I slept," and I go to bed. I'd much rather face a known enemy than be bitten by an unknown one in the dark.

God was teaching me to trust him in all circumstances, one lesson at a time.

Touched by an Angel

In March 1997 I was awakened from a sound sleep by someone shaking my right shoulder. Now that made me angry! Sleep is precious, the work days long. I shouted, "What?" as I sat up—not in a pleasant tone of voice either. Then I realized that the room was totally dark. No one was there.

Or was there? I could feel a powerful presence in the room, for the hair on my arms and head prickled. I sensed danger.

I reached over to turn on the solar light at the right side of my bed. As I scanned the room from right to left, my eyes landed on a two-foot Black Mamba crawling past my shoes on the left-hand side of my bed.

With my movement it stopped and lay still. Mambas react quickly and with sensitivity to movement in their circle of awareness. I was certainly inside that circle.

It assayed the near darkness with its forked tongue. I stayed very still and silently asked the Lord to move the snake. I had used my machete just before sundown and had failed to put it back next to my bed. A long table blocked me from getting out of bed on my right, so someone had to move the snake if I was to retrieve my weapon.

Finally, the snake slowly continued over to a log shelf a couple of feet to my left and crawled partially under it. Ever so quietly and deliberately, I slipped out of bed and grabbed the machete.

Now for the hard part. I took a deep breath and asked the Lord to hang onto that snake. It lay stretched out under that shelf with its tail near the corner post and its nose against the brick wall. In order to kill it, I would have to get down on one knee at its tail and, without hesitating, slam the knife behind its head before it could strike.

Again, I tell you that this snake was not behaving normally. If it had been, I would have been bitten the moment I got near it. With all my movement in the room, it had to realize I was there, yet it kept its head pointed away from me. These snakes can swap ends and strike like lightning; a human being cannot out-duck or out-maneuver one. So I *know* that an angel was holding it down, for it never moved until the knife whacked it behind the head.

Now I was socked with another problem. When I hit it, the dirt gave. The snake's neck lay squeezed under my blade, but I had not severed the head. Should I raise the knife for another blow, this bundle of deadly fury could easily whip around and bite me.

What else could I do? I held it in place, pressing down with the blade while its tail thrashed back and forth. In its writhing, it finally wrapped itself onto the blade, allowing me to drag it through the dirt until it was out from under the shelf. I raised the knife a bit and brought it down; that snake lost its head.

I just stood there, my nerves doing jigs, my stomach threatening to flip. I couldn't stop shaking. Through it all, I just kept thanking the Lord for his divine protection.

In the other two instances I just described, there had always been something keeping the snake from being able to bite me. This time I was wide open for an attack. God showed me here that *he was in total control.*

All these unusual faith lessons made me wonder what kind of assignment he was preparing me for.

I mean, let's face it, friends. This is not normal ministry training.

Tree-Top Mamba

I mentioned that some elapids, mambas included, are agile tree climbers. They are important predators of, for example, nesting birds and other tree dwellers. But somehow you don't usually think of snakes up in trees. The following happened at Village of Love (VOL) rather than Vilanculos, but I include it here because it fits.

The day had been busy, busy, busy, as days always are at the Village of Love. During the heat of a Saturday afternoon, I took a break. Understand, rest around VOL was a four-letter word, and I would certainly never use four-letter words. Let's just say that although I'm not real good at simply sitting and doing nothing, on this day it wasn't hard at all. We had a lovely, screened veranda made specifically for resting (excuse me, taking a break). Knee-high brick masonry formed the bottom of its walls. The rest of its four walls was screening stretched between uprights. Its tin roof kept the sun at bay. It was a quiet nine-by-twelve-foot room inside the great outdoors.

And so I sat in the veranda and just vegetated. I watched birds whose names I did not know hopping and waddling about, pecking at things in the dirt, foraging in the trees overhead. The sky burned blue-white.

Suddenly two birds in the tree overhanging the roof started making horrible screeching sounds. They kept at it for several minutes. I figured they were fighting over some tasty morsel or something. A loud *whump!* hit the roof right over my head. A long, fluorescent green water hose came twisting, sliding, sailing off the roof to my right. Curiosity overcame my inertia of rest, and I got up to investigate.

We didn't have a green water hose at VOL.

It was a five-foot-long green mamba! The birds had chased it out onto the limber end of a branch; the snake was too heavy, and the branch broke (thus the *whump*), dumping both limb and snake onto the slippery, slanted tin roof.

The snake was not pleased by this turn of events, and when a mamba is mad, it makes certain that the rest of the world suffers. When it saw me, it raced straight for me, ready to wreak vengeance on whomever it could. The snake struck the screen just above the low brick wall, but thank goodness the wire mesh held. Because the incensed snake would go after anything that moved, I was trapped inside. I was safe, though, so long as the snake didn't happen to notice a small access under the door. I made a mental note that installing thresholds wasn't a bad idea.

In its sinuous, sinister way, the snake started slithering around the outside of the building, looking for a way in. It hugged the wall, but I could still watch it easily. As it passed the door and poured itself around the corner to the back side of the veranda, I raced out the door to my mud hut. I snatched up my snake-beating stick, a six-foot-long hardwood pole.

When I got back out, the dogs were following the snake and worrying it (cautiously!) as it continued to circle the building. Between the distraction of the dogs and its quest for a way into the enclosure, the snake didn't notice me sneaking up behind it. I waited until it was just turning another corner and cracked it across the back with the heavy pole.

The idea is to break a mamba's backbone so that it cannot rear up to strike. The pole connected squarely, and that did the trick. Playing lots of softball had just paid off with a life-saving homerun!

The snake was incapacitated, but that didn't mean it couldn't bite at close range as it lay thrashing on the ground. The dogs closed in, but not too close. I rendered several more hard whacks to subdue it then fetched my machete and finished the job.

Had I stepped outside to investigate the birds' squawking a few moments earlier, I would have had one enraged and deadly snake in my lap or in my hair. You can see, I'm sure, why I am always so grateful for the Lord's protection. A moment this way, a few feet that way, and disaster falls. Bush lore goes only so far. "Street smarts" can do only so much. There is no way to truly protect oneself in the African bush or in the streets of America or on the byways of Europe or anywhere else. In the end, it is only God.

Only God.

3

Stress Release?

I'm sure I don't have to tell you that the civil war in Moz exacted a heavy toll on every person there, missionaries and aid workers included. Missions organizations take that sort of thing into account and compensate as best they can.

Each of us who worked at Vilanculos was given a three-week "stress release" break every six months, an R and R, if you will. Because the Republic of South Africa was, in a sense, our home away from home, on my first break, I went down to RSA.

My traveling companions were certain that any R and R should involve shopping and flush toilets. But I've been an outdoors person my whole life. So while they went off to do their thing, I went my own way, doing mine. Outdoors.

On this particular occasion, I visited a small game park near Margate. Despite its modest size, the park features beautiful hiking trails that wind down the side of one cliff to a bubbling mountain stream and then lead the very adventurous up an even taller mountain for a spectacular view. The park is home to wild buck, birds, and baboons.

I planned to hike the six-mile (ten-kilometer) trail that explored both mountains. When I started out at seven in the morning, the fog hung so thick that it cut visibility down to about ten yards/meters.

But the weather forecast promised that it would clear by nine or so, and you know they're always right. So I decided to walk on down the interesting rock staircase that zig-zagged in giddy switchbacks to the bottom of that first wild cliff.

The first thing I noticed on my way down was that there were no safety rails on the two-foot-wide steps. This gave me particular pause because I had already noticed from the little brochure that the switch-backs traverse a hundred-meter drop to the bottom of the ravine. I proceeded slowly, knowing that if I stepped wrong once, the next step would be many meters long. You cannot walk on fog.

And so I descended from fog into fog in a cool and other-worldly silence. As I reached the last step on the first switchback, some animal screamed a loud warning ten feet above my head. I froze in fear. My head jerked up in reflex.

A *huge* male baboon was jumping up and down in a rage on a rock ledge just above me. I knew that I was well inside his attack zone, and my next move, if any, had better be the right move.

Baboons are highly underrated by people who do not know them. They are not just big, ugly monkeys. They are extremely dangerous, as well as big and ugly. Believe me, I was not underrating this one. A large male is much stronger than an adult man. And I had a close-up look at the two-inch fangs, his canine teeth, which can rip out the throat of a cow.

I closed my eyes and asked, *Jesus, now what do I do?* The Lord immediately dropped this message into my head: *Sit down! You're not in a hurry.* It wasn't an out-loud voice; how can I describe an idea's sudden presence? But it was more than an idea; it was a command.

Actually, I am one of those people who is always in a hurry. He knows that. And never had I felt more like running faster than I had ever run before, right back up those stairsteps without safety rails. But I realized that if I wanted out alive and unharmed, I'd better listen to the warning.

I sat down slowly, casually, on the step behind me as my heart pounded its fists on my breastbone.

The weatherman had it right; the fog was beginning to thin. I saw another baboon now, and another. And others. A whole large family of baboons stared at me from the ledges less than twenty feet in front of me. For the moment at least, they were totally ignoring Big Daddy's persistent screams to *Run for your life!* I doubt that they'd ever been so close to a human being before.

Now, I'm very fond of animals, although this situation certainly wasn't exactly a cuddly moment. So I began talking to them as if we were old friends. They responded by relaxing while Big Daddy continued to scream and dance on his rock. The other baboons and I put him on *ignore* and enjoyed our close encounter in the wild.

Big Daddy was understandably furious, and I don't think I'm just imagining human thoughts in his ape head. He had been caught napping on guard duty. Thanks to the fog and to my quiet footsteps, I had walked right into the center of his family before he realized I was there. Had I been a leopard, which preys heavily on baboons and also possesses a quiet step, some of his kin would be dead. So, of course, he was a little upset.

After about five minutes, I felt the release in my spirit that means, *It's okay to go; the danger has passed.* I wish I could describe that feeling, but I can't. I can't even tell you how I know what it means. But—well, there it was.

The picture certainly didn't look safe. Big Daddy still cavorted there, literally hopping mad.

And here is where I learned to *not* look at the circumstances but to *trust* and *do* what the *Lord* tells me. It was, and is, a difficult lesson, because the circumstances appear so very compelling.

I knew better than to look right at Big Daddy, as eye contact can provoke an attack. So I casually stood up from the step I was sitting on and strolled down the next flight in the rocky staircase.

Not until I reached the trees near the bottom of the cliff did I dare look back. Big Daddy still screamed at me, but he had not moved off that rock. It made me wonder if an angel wasn't holding him by the neck to keep him there. You see, it is totally out of character for a baboon to refrain from attacking when an enemy has ventured so close to his family.

The crucial lesson for me:

When in trouble, *pray, listen, and obey!*

Many remember to pray. Some hear the Lord's answer. But too few *obey.*

Many pay a high price because they didn't heed the warning. Then, of course, they blame the disastrous results on the Lord. I feel sure that if I had not listened—had I panicked instead and run either up or down the mountain—I wouldn't be here to tell you this story. Think about it. I tell this story to groups all over the world because I know the Lord wants and needs his people to *hear* and also to *heed* his voice.

Hung on a Cliff

You would think that the baboon adventure would have been enough for the day. But no. I continued my trek down the cliffside to the mountain stream. It was well worth the hike. Clear water burbled over little stones and between big ones. There was a joy to it, and freedom. It lifted the heart, as so much of God's creation does.

Jumping from rock to rock, I worked my way downstream until I came to the next trail marker. Whoa! Surely someone was making a joke. The marker pointed straight up!

I realized then that it was no joke. Straight up it was. *This trail,* I mused, *is certainly for the physically fit adventurer who is not afraid of heights and stressful challenges. Ah well. Here goes.*

The only way to go was to climb from tree trunk to tree root as you "monkey" your way up the side of the cliff. I love a challenge, so off I went. When the trees ended, the trail led up over a slope too steep to stand erect on. From there I crawled upward on hands and feet until the ground was level enough to safely stand up.

What I didn't see at this point almost cost me my life. A grass fire had wiped out a trail sign that pointed hikers *around* the short, steep scarp just ahead. In fact, the trail appeared to keep right on going up the scarp. The way didn't look too hazardous from my viewpoint at the base. So without the sign I continued up the slope, cheerily unaware of the danger.

Two meters from the top, I found myself doing a vertical climb with a sixty-foot free fall to the rocks below. I was standing with one foot on each of two flat rocks jutting from the cliff face, outcrops so small that only the balls of my feet fit. My left hand grasped a rock near my head. My right hand searched for another handhold.

There wasn't any.

My whole body began to shake with fatigue and fear. My fingers and arms vibrated. I looked down and saw the rocks that awaited me if I fell. Climbing farther looked impossible. Going back down safely was out of the question.

With my head turned to the left, I closed my eyes and pressed against the cliff, trying to relieve some of the strain. For the second time that day, my life was in danger and I cried out to Jesus, "Lord, help me. Don't let me fall."

That small, still voice of his said, *Look.*

I opened my eyes, and just to my left, a rock sparkled like a diamond in the sun. As I saw it, the Lord said, *Step on it.*

Step on it? To do that I would have to move my right foot to the small, jutting rock that my left foot already covered.

How I ever managed it with my muscles quivering like jelly, I'll never know, but I didn't fall.

I reached for the sparkling rock with my left foot and easily found a hand hold above it. I cannot tell you how I got the remaining two meters to the top because I seemed to have blacked out. The next thing I knew, I was on my hands and knees on a grassy slope at the top of the cliff.

As I looked up, a large buck snorted and pawed the ground thirty meters away.

I thought, *Lord, I can't take any more of this. Please get rid of that buck.*

Within seconds two does joined the buck, and the three of them went bounding off over the next rise.

I was so exhausted that I simply lay there for a while. When I could finally stand up, I peered down over the cliff I had just climbed.

It was then that I discovered the trail going around this dangerous cliff. Easily visible from above, it was totally hidden from below.

This was the first time I'd ever gone mountain hiking, and I learned the hard way why you should never go alone. If I had fallen and lived, no one would have been there to help me. My friends would not even have reported me missing until at least 5:00 p.m., which would have meant a long, cold night on the mountain until someone found me.

How I praise the Lord that he never leaves us or forsakes us! Not even on cliffsides.

4

Bush Fire

The United States Forest Service once figured out an interesting statistic. In the first twenty years that Smokey the Bear warned everyone, "Only *you* can prevent forest fires!" the incidence of forest fires went down so dramatically that, in essence, the flat-hatted old bear saved about ten billion dollars worth of timber.

But the tide turned. Ecologists discovered that most forests *need* fire—little fires that burn close to the ground without damaging the trees. If those fires don't occur every few decades, dead leaves and duff on the forest floor build up so thickly that when fire does roll through (and it will!) its intense, tinder-fed heat kills the trees. Those decades of fire suppression were, in some cases, doing more harm than good.

These days forest managers designate some fires as "let-burns" and back off, allowing them to do their thing. In places, the foresters may actually start fires called "controlled burns" to clear off duff and dead materials before they build up enough to endanger trees. It is often more art than science as a forester tries to choose what to do.

None of that is necessary in Moz. There, nature burns off her own forests periodically without so much as a by-your-leave to the people who live there. In the dry season, one stroke of lightning can torch miles of bush. Still, no one thinks much about the prospect of wildfire. And therein lies a tale.

Vilanculos is close enough to the equator that days and nights are nearly equal most of the year. Here the sun paces life. In the bush we live with the sun and march to its rhythms—up with the sun, down with the sun. You work twelve hours, you rest twelve hours. At the orphanage, going to bed when the generator went off at 8:00 p.m. was normal.

Incidentally, it's a fascinating transformation. All day people work, talk, hammer, shout, play, laugh, argue, and make noise a hundred different ways. You know they're around. And periodically in the background, hardly ever noticed, the generator sings its monotonous, two-cycle song.

Come dusk, the noise and bustle die rapidly as people put away the day. What is left undone becomes tomorrow's work. Then that generator goes silent. Almost instantly the night falls extremely quiet. Insects may chirp. Leaves may rustle out there somewhere. But the sounds of nature don't really break the silence; they merely underline it. The orphanage complex, so busy during the day, lies beneath the dark sky as hushed as if it were abandoned.

So I knew something was wrong the night when, after the compound retired, I heard a loud, crackling sound. This was not some bush pig rooting around in the underbrush. It was the crisp, familiar sound of burning tinder.

Looking out my window, I saw a garish red light beyond the trees separating our garden from the open fields. Smoke billowed, orange-bellied, black against the black. A bush fire was being pushed toward us by a strong breeze.

I ran to alert the manager, who immediately grabbed our guards and drove off to the firebreak to see what could be done to protect our compound. If the flames jumped our firebreak, only a hundred meters of garden stood between them and our houses. Wooden, grass-roofed houses.

But this was during the civil war. No fire departments existed in our area. We ourselves possessed no special equipment for fighting large fires. In fact, no one has equipment big enough to stop a full-bore bushfire in its tracks. The best you can do is try to protect buildings by keeping them cool and wet. I felt totally helpless until I remembered what a Christian friend did when a large grassfire threatened her home.

Following her example, I began to pray, rebuking the fire in the name of Jesus and commanding the wind to reverse itself.

Nothing happened.

I didn't give up, though, because my friend had shown me in the Bible that God gave humankind dominion over the earth. I remembered clearly the situation when fire threatened her; I thought at first that she was nuts, yelling at it in the name of Jesus. And then the inferno bearing down on her suddenly changed directions and went around her property.

But that was then. The orphanage and I stood in mortal danger now.

Here came our manager, wagging his head.

"Our firebreak is useless. It's completely overgrown—weeds, grass. All that grass will do nothing but feed the fire."

My heart fell. Still, I found myself strangely confident now that something good was going to happen in this situation. Why? I couldn't say. But I knew that the Bible doesn't make false claims.

Buoyed, I walked away and rebuked the fire again. On impulse, you might say, I asked the Lord to put up a wall at the firebreak so that the flames could not cross.

Suddenly the wind settled and stopped blowing. The roaring noise of this dreadful night began to trickle away. The fire was dying down. The hideous orange light dimmed; the dense smoke thinned. We all stood about in silent little knots, watching. What else could we do?

Some time after midnight, we deemed it finally safe to go to bed. The manager set guards out to watch and to warn, for spent fires smoulder a long, long time and often flare back to life.

The first thing the next morning, one of the guards that had watched the fire approach our area came in with his news. He claimed that the flames had stopped at the firebreak. I lost no time running out to see this thing he described.

Our precious garden lay in the golden morning light hale and healthy; it had not even wilted. The trees beyond it seemed fine. I continued on to the firebreak. I stepped out into the open and stood in utter amazement at what the Lord had done.

Sure enough, the firebreak all around me was indeed badly overgrown, rank with weeds and grass. They were untouched! A few charred sticks and stinking gray ash on bare ground were about all that was left of the brush beyond. The fire had burned hot, right up to the break line, and stopped. Just stopped.

The lessons I learned that night on taking dominion were not a one-time quirk. They would serve me well over and over in the future, for this was only the first of many bushfires that I would deal with.

The lessons serve anyone well. You may never face a bushfire, but you will absolutely, certainly face crises of some sort. Every person does. I beg you to remember the lesson: when in need, *ask!* Don't worry that it's silly or too great or otherwise an improper question. Ask. You must also *believe.* God made the universe; he can handle your problems with it. And then *receive.* The Lord always answers those who believe.

5

Midnight Raid

By 1991 Moz had been at war for more than twenty years. A whole generation of children were growing up never knowing peace in life. For them, war and destruction had become the norm.

Those two decades did not see constant, pitched battle. The fighting waxed and waned periodically during that long, sorry time. Now, as the '90s began, it seemed to be slowing down. Our area, the coast around Vilanculos, had been quiet for over nine months. Our lives rolled along from day to day fairly normally—whatever normal was.

Local officials did their best to maintain law and order. But you can't fight crime without resources. Their hands were tightly tied by a lack of personnel, equipment, money—basic things most public safety forces take for granted. As a result, gangs of bandits still prowled the hills to the west. Now and then, they'd come storming down out of their roosts to raid the agricultural lowlands.

One night around 1:00 a.m., another missionary awakened me.

"Grab your passport and report to the pickup immediately!"

I responded with a swift, intelligent, "Huh? What ... ?"

"Raiders just hit the village! We have to get away!"

I was awake!

The village my colleague was talking about lay only half a mile (about one kilometer) from us. As I ran for the pickup, I didn't even need my flashlight. Raging fires were lighting up the sky as if it were daylight. Every hut and building in that little hamlet beyond the trees had been put to the torch.

A few raiders could employ some pretty sophisticated weaponry while others had very little. It was impossible to tell who was well-armed and who was bluffing, though, because all of them were good bluffers. As we made our escape, flares were being launched from several directions. The raiders were trying to make the people believe they had mortars.

I could hear the basic bandit firearm (machine guns) stuttering in the distance. The fire, the noise, and the confusion churned, surreal in the night.

At the first warning, our orphans and foster mothers ran off to hide in the darkness of the bush. Remember that these kids were born into war. No one had to tell them how to survive. In moments the settlement was deserted.

We missionaries did not have that edge.

The two drivers told us to lie down flat in the back of the pickup. You don't realize how many people are on staff until all but two of you are cramming yourselves down into the truck bed, trying to become two-dimensional. The truck lurched out and rattled away up the sandy road, hurtling through the darkness. The drivers did not dare use their headlights; they would have made us too easy a target.

We would take refuge in the nearby town until the fighting stopped. Larger towns were relatively safe because pillagers knew better than to strike well-populated areas. Too many people could fight back.

The next morning our leaders deemed it safe enough to go home. On this return trip, we could sit up in back, a nice improvement.

As our truck waddled down the soft track toward the orphanage, we passed hundreds of people walking along the roadside. So many had been injured! Again, seeing a movie or televised scene with "blood and guts," no matter how realistically staged, is no preparation for the real thing. A stump wrapped in bloody rags was once this person's arm. That person is using a broken branch as a cane because his mangled leg will never again support him fully.

The movies boast of surround-sound where the noise of their special effects comes from all directions. Here were surround sounds, all of them sad. Surround smells I won't describe. Surround heat and humidity, dust and sorrow and misery.

Old and young, men and women, they carried small bundles of possessions on their backs. These were the fortunate ones in that they had survived the raids. They looked stunned, defeated. Most of them had just lost everything they owned.

Years before an American once asked, "Why don't they just stay home and rebuild? You see pictures of all these people with bundles, walking. Why do they migrate?"

The reason is simple and sad. In many places—America is an example—subsistence farming is an option. The subsistence farmer plants his garden, turns his calf out on pasture to mature for butchering, maybe milks a goat. But if the animals die, and the garden fails in a drought, the farmer simply goes to the supermarket for his food.

In much of Moz, the subsistence farm *is* the supermarket. You grow as much as you can while you can. You both feed your family and put some of that food aside to get you through the lean months, or you go without. If weather or raiders destroy your crops and animals, you have no alternative but to try to find food elsewhere.

Raiders have to eat too, and food was one of first things the bandits would look for. They would seize anything edible, as well as anything of trade value. They would also grab captives. The captives would be forced to carry away the grain, animals, and valuables that the raiders plundered. Many of these captives were never heard from again.

So when I claim the refugees streaming along the roads were fortunate, I say it with a heavy heart.

When we reached home, we found the Mozambican staff of our six-bed hospital busily treating the injured. First a trickle and then a flood of injured had come in seeking aid, swamping the caregivers. We jumped right in to help, of course.

For the most part, our job was to prepare the severely injured for transfer. Men, women, and children lay on pallets or on the floor, patiently waiting for whatever help might come their way. But immediate help was not all that they needed.

In the rural hospitals of Moz, the patient's family is expected to provide the patient's food and drink and most of the patient's routine care. For example, if you come in for an appendectomy, you can expect a family member to feed and bathe you during your hospitalization, and it will be familiar home cooking, too. But many of these patients, ripped from friends and family by the violence of the raids, had no backup, no support. This complicated the situation drastically, for the medical facility was neither prepared nor equipped to feed many.

I didn't sleep well for a week after that. I awoke often, hearing every little noise, wondering if and when the raiders might come back. Because, you see, we were a plum just begging to be plucked; our mission station was the richest site in the area. We had on hand the food and tools that everyone wanted, and we were virtually unarmed.

But not unprotected! God protected us. We well knew that, and we offered him praise upon praise. Not one person living on our property was hurt, nor was a single thing stolen.

Through this incident I realized how quietly Satan can slip in and take you by surprise. Daily prayer coverage is a *must* if you and your family are to be "Jesus Insured" against the attacks of the enemy.

6

Love Conquers All

Anyone can see the obvious, physical effects of war. Buildings lie in ruins. Burnt fields smoulder. Graves abound. You cannot see the inner ravages, the damage to the depths of the human spirit. And it is there that war is cruellest.

Ah, the children!

Children are amazingly resilient little people, but in war, too much is often just too much. Of the many, many children the orphanage took in, a few maintained themselves at something near normalcy. Most suffered varying effects of their losses, often severe effects. And a few seemed virtually unreachable.

One such child we received I'll call Sebastian. At three years old, as other children laughed and squealed and ran around, he stared blankly into space, totally empty. To quote a friend, "The lights are on, but nobody's home."

He made no response to anything said in either his own language or in Portuguese. He did not cry. No one knew for sure why this small child was so devastatingly withdrawn, but rumor had it that he saw his mother killed when their village was raided.

Several months passed. We saw no improvement. Sebastian spent his days staring at the wall of his little house. His only interaction with anyone was to eat when handfed. He did not play. He did not watch others play. Sometimes children who are grieving simply sit on the sidelines and follow the action with eye and ear, not participating. He did not do that much.

As I worked with him one day, I cried out to the Lord for a miracle. Then I held the frail little fellow for over an hour as I sang to him.

Nothing changed. I might as well have been wrapping my arms around a melon.

I went back to my quarters that evening feeling pretty depressed. When adults lose parents, it is tragic, of course. But grownups are, well, grown up. When this child, and the many like him, loses a parent, his world stops turning. Relationships are everything in a child's life, parental relationships especially. Even more devastating, when all but the oldest of these children lose parents, they lose the where-withal for survival. They are too young to make it on their own.

Did Sebastian at all sense that he was in, relatively speaking, the safest possible surroundings? Did he in any way feel the pure, immense love in which we held him? There was no way to know what, if anything, was going on inside that sorrowful little head.

A few days later, I stopped to play with some of the children who lived near Sebastian's house. It's one of my favorite things to do, to play with people who really know how to play, and nobody did it better than these kids. They absolutely loved games. I suppose, in a large way, games were more than just a pastime for them. Play provided a healthy escape from the horrible reality of life. Maybe it did that for me, too. Who knows?

When afterwards I stooped down to kid level to hug my play-mates and say goodbye, a little one pushed through the crowd and sat down on my knee.

I stared in amazement. Sebastian! And look at the radiant smile on his face!

For long moments I was too stunned to speak. Then I hugged Sebastian mightily as I thanked Jesus for healing him. Sebastian just continued to look up at me and smile.

As you well know, normal little boys remain still for only a few minutes at a time, and Sebastian was no exception. He soon got up and walked off toward his house. Even that tiny sign of normalcy was so welcome!

Watching him go, I called out, "*Shaka* (smile)!" He turned to look at me, and his face glowed with the most beautiful smile I've ever seen. There was no doubt whatever that he had been touched by the Master's hand.

The Door

The mission station at Vilanculos could not have provided a bet-ter portal into the weird, unique life I had chosen to make my own.

By doing whatever job had to be done at the moment, I learned with hands-on experience pretty much all the operations of a major mission effort. I learned valuable lessons about dealing with all kinds of people. I learned building and repair and auto mechanics. I learned how to find food for an army. And I learned the bush.

Most important of all, I learned how to trust God. This lesson does not come automatically or easily. It is one thing to discuss trusting God as you sit in the polite, sterile atmosphere of the Sunday school classroom. That's theory. It is quite another when you seem to be standing alone as you are facing down death—and death does not blink. That's scary. God is there, but the circumstances are hiding him from you.

Even though God has always honored his promise never to leave me or forsake me, it seems sometimes that I have to keep learning all over again that he is there.

I didn't realize as I worked with Sebastian and all the other children who were the main thrust of our ministry that I was being prepared for other things. I didn't know when I learned how to repair a disabled Land Rover that this was a lesson for the future; I thought it was simply a temporary fix so that another nurse and I could get home at 2:00 a.m. after an emergency hospital run. I never imagined as I dragged those sacks of dried soy soup around that this toil might be more than just another chore.

And then the Lord spoke, and my life took a sharp turn into new territory. His love, which had lifted little Sebastian and made the very mission itself possible, was about to send me out on my own.

THE NEXT STEP:

VOL—The Village of Love

7

Receiving the Vision

Who is the past? The elders.

Who is the future? The children.

In February of 1992, the Lord clearly showed me his future assignment for me. I was to go into northern Mozambique to build a home for orphaned children. He instructed me to do it the African way, with local material. I was to keep the kids in their culture and make the program as self-sufficient as possible.

That much was clear. What I didn't realize at the time was that I would need several more years of preparation before this vision could become reality. It would be a hard testing ground, as you will see in the following stories. The lessons learned are still helping me through the daily challenges as we train up God's army of children who will help change the heart of this nation.

Cursed by a Witch Doctor

I'd been told in missions school that when God gives you a vision, you can expect a spiritual attack from the devil. Okay. I believed it, but only with my head. And when you think of a spiritual attack, if you think about it at all, you expect something spiritual. Doubts planted in your head, perhaps, or your favorite pastor moving away suddenly, or something.

In March 1992, a month after I received my new orders, I contracted malaria and bacterial dysentery. Both are very serious. Once you get malaria, it's yours forever, because the microscopic *Plasmodium* organisms that cause it are never completely scrubbed out of your body. They linger in your cells and erupt from time to time as a renewed infection.

Dysentery, an especially nasty diarrhea, can kill you if it's not treated with effective antibiotics. You lose fluids out the back faster than you can drink them in at the front. Eventually you are so badly dehydrated that either the fluid loss itself or some opportunistic other disease puts you down.

Contracting both right together was a killer combination, to say the least. Overkill, if you wish.

I was sick for most of March, losing weight rapidly. I am not an especially skinny person, but neither have I any weight to spare. Too, the weakness made me virtually useless. The heaviest equipment I could operate was a toothbrush. I became so gaunt and feeble that I finally had to fly out for hospitalization in South Africa.

After three different admissions, I was only slightly better, and the doctors still had no definite diagnosis. I remained much weakened and seriously underweight. They suggested that perhaps this was nothing more than exhaustion and overwork. I should fly to America for a rest.

A rest? The flight from South Africa to America takes just about an even day—that is, twenty-four hours. The strenuous trip in itself doesn't do a healthy body much good, and my body was anything but healthy. To call the experience grueling was an understatement.

My condition obviously prevented me from being an effective worker. Even so, I yearned to get back out in the field as soon as possible. So the moment I reached the States, I reported to my regular doctor, who is a Christian.

The scene: I walked into his office. He looked at me and immediately declared that I was "covered in witchcraft."

Now that's not exactly what I expected to hear from the mouth of a highly trained medical person, but I knew that something very strange was hiding the real reason for my illness.

The doctor called in a specialist for a second opinion—an evangelist and spiritually aware man who works a lot in Africa. It was the evangelist's questions that led us to the source of the problem.

I had been preaching to over a hundred children every Sunday about the evils of the witch doctors. We'd even taught the kids a song to help them remember the lessons. The song was very popular, and the kids sang it when they played during the week. Of course adult ears would hear it. And if those ears happened to belong to a shaman or the friend of a shaman...

And let's be honest: I was also trying to skate along as a "wimpy warrior." I didn't keep myself covered in prayer like I should have. This pretty much left an open door for the witch doctors to walk through, to attack me repeatedly on a spiritual level.

As this wise evangelist led me in prayer, the curse lifted. I could feel it leave! I started laughing. I laughed until tears flowed down my face. The release from the satanic oppression was indeed that great, and it indeed felt that good.

Within forty-eight hours, my doctor uncovered the reason for my illness. A few simple tests revealed that my pancreas had stopped secreting the digestive juices necessary for processing food. I was living on bananas, because fruit's nutrients are absorbed in such a way that they don't need the pancreas. Once I was put on artificial enzymes and lots of vitamins, my health rapidly improved. The doctors agreed, though, that my pancreas would need at least a year to recuperate.

A year? I was extremely upset! That vision was burning fresh in my heart. Once God lays something like that on you, it doesn't quietly retreat to a corner. I knew I wasn't supposed to be lolling in America for a year. I, the chronically impatient, always-in-a-hurry one, didn't want to sit around!

So I asked God to speed up the process. Know what? I thoroughly believed that he would honor my impatience. And he did! Within six weeks I was well enough to start visiting my churches. Four months later I arrived back in Africa, ready to go!

I've learned a lot about Satan's evil methods since then. I now see that illness is one of the most common ways he uses to pull missionaries off the field, interrupting God's work.

And I warn you, too. Be aware that the devil can blind the eyes of people who are not walking closely with Jesus. My diagnosis was greatly delayed because people, including myself, were not seeing the obvious when it was right in front of them. Be alert to his tricks!

8

Operation Mobilization

January to August, 1993

Once upon a time in North America, when women did all their own sewing, every household attic harbored boxes and boxes of scrap fabric. One never threw away small-but-usable pieces left over from a dress. Party and dinner gowns yielded velvets, satins, and all sorts of lace tag-ends. House dresses, children's clothes, and gardening attire provided calicos, broadcloth, and percales. The women usually made their own curtains, too, so chintzes and damasks were part of the mix.

Then our women would dip into this trove to create a beautiful art form especially our own. Quilts. What a rich melody of colors and textures those patchwork and pieced quilt tops sang! In fact, they still do. The art form is alive and well all over the continent.

Africa is just such a melody, an extraordinary patchwork of many cultures, textures, peoples, languages, and religions. Some blend and harmonize, some clash. Each is individual. There is no one African race or faith. They are many. There is no one African landscape—texture, if you will. Jungles, snowfields, and deserts may occur within a few miles of each other.

This many-parted melody makes Africa endlessly fascinating. It also poses nearly insurmountable problems to those who would bring Jesus to the Africans.

At first, missionaries pretty much ignored the variety that is Africa. One hundred fifty years ago, preachers in conservative European attire would venture out into the patchwork of cultures and countries to declare the Gospel in a context that Europeans understood. Then they expected the Africans to adopt European ways and attitudes, at least as regards the faith. Needless to say, it didn't work, at least not very well. It doesn't work now.

Enter Operation Mobilization into the picture. This training organization based in the Republic of South Africa serves as a gateway and stepping stone for people who want to carry the Gospel anywhere in Africa.

During its six-month training program, its enrolees (referred to as team members, and that they are) learn much of importance about the various African cultures. They learn how to get along in those cultures. They learn evangelism techniques for helping Muslims and Hindus, which are many in Africa, to receive Jesus. They even get useful suggestions for reaching New-Agers! The training is by no means exhaustive; to thoroughly learn the cultures and faiths of Africa would take far more than a lifetime. But it prepares team members to grasp and accept the rich differences they are about to work with.

As does any other school, this one provides a practical examination at the end of the course. After five months of concentrated training, the team members are sent on an extended outreach. It's rather like Jesus preparing and then sending out the seventy disciples. His people returned from their mission amazed, glorifying God. So do Operation Mobilization's team members.

As my first step of preparation to fulfil the vision that the Lord had given me in 1992, I was enrolled in the Operation Mobilization training course. Those five months of study were tough but rewarding. Now came the outreach mission to put into practice all the theory we'd been absorbing.

Because of my previous experience in Mozambique, I was asked to go with a thirty-member team into northern Moz. We would show the Jesus Film in the Yao (pronounced *Yow*) language for the first time (I will explain about the Jesus Film later; it's awesome). I jumped for joy at this opportunity since I knew my future ministry would be in this area! This was perfect! Yesss! Thank you, Lord!

Kaboom

One does not simply drive north from RSA into Mozambique. I mentioned before that you cannot stick a road just anywhere you wish. The best places to build roads are often along highlands and ridges where the substrate is solid and washouts few. These are also often international boundaries. With the roads going where they are easiest and sturdiest and the borders often following lines drawn by people who never saw the countries, you can cross and re-cross borders and traverse countries you have no intention of visiting just to get to the place you want.

That's bad enough when one travels alone. Getting a team of thirty people through eight border posts is a massive challenge. What should have been a five-day trip to northern Moz became seven just to reach Malawi. We're talking about six different border stations to get that far. The main highway, N 1, leaves RSA, taking you through Zimbabwe into Harare then north into Moz and finally to Malawi. We would pause there then head easterly to pass through the final two border stations into Moz.

Malawi is one of Africa's great undiscovered gems. It boasts several very nice national parks and game preserves. Its countryside is lovely, its lakes gorgeous. It is small as African nations go, a narrow little strip-shaped nation situated mostly along the western shore of huge Lake Malawi (which may appear as Lake Nyassa or Lake Niassa on your map of Africa).

We crossed to the lake at Mangochi and finally arrived at our first destination, a mission station overlooking beautiful Lake Malawi. There we were able to relax with a one-day break. Oh, how we welcomed that! By this time everyone was exhausted from the grueling trek.

The mission did not have electricity, but who cares? Their lights were solar powered, and bottled gas (in this case, propane) operated the stove and refrigerator. Having just endured a week on the road of camping and making do, we considered this to be the height of civilization.

Luxury of luxuries, that night we finished the day with cups of hot, aromatic tea. I know that tea is not usually considered a special luxury. But in this setting, after the rigors of our journey, the tea whispered, *Home, friend. You're not that far from familiar comfort after all.*

Few mission stations are prepared to sleep thirty extra people. Neither was this one. But the floor did quite nicely, thank you. We separated out into different areas of the house. The single women, for example, bedded down in the living and dining areas.

Because it looked like a nice, quiet place, I chose to sleep in the dining room near the entrance to the kitchen. A full-length swinging door separated the two rooms. There was no latch on the door since it swung in both directions—you know, like the barroom doors in the old westerns. It opened easily on its hinges so that you could move between the two rooms with your hands full of dishes and pots. As long as no one shoved through the door carelessly and let it swat me, I'd be in a good place.

Thirty people create a lot of rustle and bustle simply by being. The modest size of the building multiplied that busy-ness. As we settled to rest, the busy-ness melted into serenity in the darkness. Motion ceased. Voices stilled. Peace.

Kaboom!

The whole house was shaken by an explosion in the kitchen! I woke up to find myself already on hands and knees in my sleeping bag. What time was it? A little after one...

Did I say, "Nice, quiet place?"

Being the closest to the kitchen elected me to investigate. I grabbed my flashlight, flicked it on, and gently pushed open the swinging door, not knowing what to expect.

The kitchen was a disaster area.

The side wall of the gas stove had been ripped clear off. Two windows were blown out, their curtains all scorched. Empty pots that moments before had been sitting on the stove now lay by the swinging door where I'd been sleeping.

We eventually figured out what must have happened. Normally the gas to the stove is turned off outside at the bottle during the night. This night, however, that little step was forgotten in all the work and excitement of entertaining thirty visitors and serving them tea. The stove's pilot light had ignited, leaking gas. Kaboom.

Marks on the swinging door told us that the flying pots had hit it with great force. The door hadn't budged.

An explosion that powerful should have knocked that swinging door open, allowing the full force of it to hit me in the face, yet it didn't move. Why not? The curtains were badly scorched; they should have burst into flame, yet there was no fire. Who put it out? I was the first one in the room just seconds after the explosion, yet I saw no sign of smoke, much less fire. There is only one answer: the Lord and his angels. Praise the Lord that they never sleep!

9

Double Donkey Trouble

Because of the way the roads of East Africa wind among the highlands, just about the easiest way to travel between RSA and Moz, and sometimes even between distant points in Moz, is through Zimbabwe, which lies inland immediately to the west. Much of Zimbabwe is upland, with elevations of 3,000 to 9,000 feet or more, but for the most part it is gently rolling grassland—not particularly mountainous. It's the solid spine of East Africa.

The Zambezi River makes a spectacular northern boundary to the country, starting with Victoria Falls in the extreme western tip of the nation then swooping in a majestic arc up and around the central highlands. By the time the Zambezi enters Moz on its journey east to the Indian Ocean, it is a vast, sprawling, muddy watercourse worthy of singing songs about.

Those of you who are older may remember when Zimbabwe appeared on maps as Rhodesia or Southern Rhodesia. It was, these readers will recall, named for Cecil Rhodes, a pioneer in the mining development and politics of southern Africa when the British controlled the area. But a thousand years before the world ever heard of Cecil Rhodes, Zimbabwe already boasted a long and colorful human history. The ruins of Great Zimbabwe rank as one of the wonders of the world.

I would like to say we were traveling in Zimbabwe in order to soak up the exotic charm of the country. In truth, though, we were there because that was where the paved highway went.

My traveling partner on this occasion was Frits, a pastor with whom I would be working in northern Moz. It was a nice arrangement. My pickup pulled his trailer, and he and I shared the driving. Between all his belongings and supplies and mine, both the truck and the trailer were loaded to the gunwales. We were in absolutely no danger of breaking any speed laws.

Pickup trucks are not the favorite mode of transportation in many African countries, however. Single-axle donkey carts are, particularly outside of the cities in remote hamlets and villages. It's logical. Donkeys don't require expensive petrol. Donkeys will take you home, even if you fall asleep at the "wheel." And donkeys make more donkeys. Pickup trucks can't do that.

On the down side, the slow, leisurely donkey carts are also a common cause of accidents along the excellent modern highways stretching across Zimbabwe.

Frits happened to be at the wheel as we came tooling over a gentle hill. He was doing about fifty miles per hour (eighty kilometers per hour), which, considering our load, was pretty much flat out. At the bottom of the hill, the highway crossed a small drainage. The narrow, two-lane concrete bridge there was made even more narrow by sturdy railings on both sides.

And my heart stopped.

On the far side of the bridge, here came a donkey cart pulled by not one but two donkeys. A boy about twelve was driving the cart, and a boy a few years younger rode in the back.

Like nearly all such donkeys, these two were not closely controlled with reins. They wore no bridle of any kind—not even a halter. The driver might guide them with a switch. A more direct method is simply to jump out and shove them to change their direction or stop.

When those donkeys entered the bridge, they naturally took their half out of the middle. They did not at all appear upset by the prospect that a large oncoming vehicle was about to hit them. With the trailer and the heavy load shoving us along, there was no way we could stop in time.

The cart driver didn't even try to redirect his donkeys. He was over the bridge railing in one clean jump, leaving the ten-year-old and the donkeys to fend for themselves. The boy, frozen in fear, never moved.

There was only time for a quick, *"Jesus, help!"* before it was all over.

The donkeys were jerked to their side of the bridge by an invisible force. We rushed past them with two inches to spare!

As I think about it in retrospect, I suppose the donkeys could have realized their danger and leapt aside. They can be quite agile when they care to; ask anyone who has tried to catch a loose donkey who doesn't want to be caught. But donkey carts do not share that agility. The cart was lumbering down the middle of the bridge; then it was not.

I thank Frits, who is one skilled, cool-headed driver. But most of all I thank our guardian angels for pulling us out of that mess. What a tragedy it could have been!

Nothing is impossible for God. And he hears loud and clear when you scream, *"Jesus!"*

10

Moonlight Mission

February 1994

I was now living in Cuamba in northern Mozambique only sixty or so crow-flight miles east of Malawi. The roads, of course, did not follow crow paths, so the actual travel distance to, say, Blantyre was much farther. The railway that linked Malawi and the interior with the Indian Ocean's ports goes through Cuamba, so it is one of Moz's more important cities.

And as I lived and worked there, I chafed; I admit it. The vision I had received two years before was still not realized. Remember, I am one of those type-A people who wants everything to happen *now*. But the project was getting closer. That buoyed my spirits somewhat. And in the meantime, the Lord gave me many opportunities to serve in other ways.

For example, one afternoon around 4:00 p.m., a man came to my house to beg a ride for his very ill and pregnant daughter. She was in a small village nine miles (seventeen kilometers) out of town on a road that was little more than a washed-out foot path. He had to get her to medical aid, and soon.

Pastor Frits and I discussed it briefly and agreed that we should try to help. As it turns out, this man had already been refused by all the other transport options he'd tried. We were his last hope.

It would be dark by 6:00 p.m., so I quickly grabbed some snack food, water, and a flashlight. Rule number one is *always*: never go into the bush without basic survival needs, for an accident or breakdown can mean walking hours or even days to the nearest help.

The man, Frits, and I climbed into the pickup. We had another passenger along that evening. An American woman wanted to join us "for the adventure."

She got the adventure, all right. It took us four grueling hours to crawl those nine miles to his village.

Twice, boulders weighing up to a hundred pounds blocked our way. As the old camp song says, "Can't go over them, can't go around them, gotta go through them."

Both times I told this Mozambican man, "I'm sorry. There is no way we can pass here."

Both times he jumped out of the truck, begging, "Please, wait!"

Now not only was this man short, he weighed about the same as one of the boulders. But he was determined that nothing would stop him from getting help to his daughter.

Picture this modestly-sized man putting every ounce of strength he had into rolling those rocks aside. Within minutes the way was cleared enough for us to get the truck through. I was embarrassed by how easily I was letting simple obstacles (a few rocks, for crying out loud!) defeat our mission.

My mind kept telling me, *This is an impossible situation, so give it up*. But this man showed me that a positive attitude and lots of determination can move worlds. As we came upon still other obstacles, I no longer took it as defeat. I got out and helped look for the solution.

At 8:00 p.m. the man called for us to stop. The road had trickled from a two-rut track down to an overgrown footpath. With much gesturing, the father explained that we must leave the pickup and walk about a mile into the bush to his village. A full moon lighted our way, so I saved our one and only flashlight for the medical work ahead.

A fifteen-minute walk brought us to a mud-and-grass hut so typical of that rural area. Fritz and the woman remained there. I was escorted deeper into the bush to another hut.

We entered a cleared area and approached a group of people sitting around a campfire. The villagers froze in terror. It took me a moment to realize what they were seeing. Imagine a white-skinned person arriving unannounced in an African village in the dark, illuminated only by a distant, flickering fire. To these very superstitious people, the vision screamed "Ghost!" Come to think of it, I doubt that a white person had ever visited them, especially due to the uncertainty and turmoil caused by the many years of civil war that had troubled the area.

In a rapid, tumbling torrent of words, the father explained my presence to them. That out of the way, I was allowed to examine the young woman.

She lay inside the hut in total darkness, curled up, obviously miserable. Very weak, she was racked with fever and abdominal pain, but the pain was clearly not contractions. The pregnancy aside, very bad things were happening inside her.

We couldn't make a stretcher; no one owned a blanket. Ever inventive, the woman's husband borrowed an old bicycle. The father and he lifted her onto the bicycle seat. Supporting her as she moaned and teetered, they pushed her the mile through the bush to my pickup.

On the way the husband continued with the patient. The father stopped briefly at his hut to get us a gift of thanks for our help. He apologized for not having a chicken, the gift of highest gratitude; his last one had recently died. So he hurried out into his field and came back with an armful of mandioca root (manioc) and corn on the cob (mealies). We reached the pickup just as the bicycle ambulance arrived with our patient.

I mentioned before that in most hospitals, patients must supply their own food and a bedside attendant. After getting the girl settled, we loaded family members and some supplies for her stay in town. At last, greatly wearied, we crawled back through the ruts and holes to Cuamba. However, with all the major obstacles out of our way, we made the nine-mile trek in a little over an hour. We delivered our patient and her family to the hospital.

Midnight was breathing down our necks as we rolled into our familiar old parking space. We were greeted by a very worried group of friends who feared we might never return. In the African bush, that's not necessarily an idle fear.

Two days later we had to leave on an assignment in Malawi. We never learned what happened to the young woman and her noble husband and father. I can say, though, that our mission of mercy made us a lot of new friends.

I believe you can see the lesson here as clearly as I, and it applies in any circumstance. When challenged, I learned to never be defeated by the situation. Ask the Lord for a solution. It may be given to you, or you yourself may be the solution. But for the sake of love, never give up.

And I see another lesson in this as well. Perhaps the girl would have died had we not intervened. Perhaps she died in spite of our help. Her welfare was and is and will always be God's province alone. We were called by him to help not so much to save her but to please him. The outcome to the situation was in his hands. It is always in his hands. Answering his call is in ours!

11

The Mud Bunny

I have mentioned before about the log bridges that are such a common sight in many African countries. You will find a picture of one in the center section. Please believe me, I am sure not bad-mouthing them! On the contrary, I praise them and thank God for them. In rural areas where the usual building materials are very expensive and cement and girders are out of the question, those bridges, however rickety, serve a vital function. Without them the smallest stream would present an insurmountable barrier.

The simplest bridges are nothing more than rough-cut logs laid lengthwise from shore to shore. These can span streams up to about three meters wide—ten feet, give or take. To bridge larger streams or rivers, small logs and limbs are laid crosswise over a wood-and-rock frame that extends out into the riverbed. Ideally the cross-members are tied down, but don't bet real money on it.

Now God does not make a lot of straight trees in the bush. Therefore the logs are not always straight. Also, they tend to move around on their supports even when tied, for the ropes work loose. Some of the resulting gaps could swallow a refrigerator. Okay, I'm exaggerating. But they can leave spaces big enough for a fourteen-inch tire to fall into.

As you look at the photo, you will realize why rule number one on these bridges, never to be ignored, is: never ever cross until you've done a safety check.

Oh, the tales I could tell about the vagaries of those charming log bridges! For instance, in 1995 I was driving alone on the dirt road leading to Lichinga in far northwest Moz. As I topped a hill, I could see the seven-meter log bridge at the bottom. It looked solid, but I felt a check in my spirit about crossing. So I stopped and got out for a look.

Sure enough, there was a three-foot gap where four logs had broken and fallen through to the riverbed fifteen feet below. The hole was not visible from a distance. Had I driven merrily on, the gap would have completely swallowed up my front end.

No calling up the Department of Transportation on a handy cell phone. The only solution was to fix it. And it appeared that I would have to fix it by myself. Very little traffic traveled that road in those days, so it could be a long wait before helpers arrived.

Looking through the gap to the river below, I could see several logs that might be used to fill the hole. The sandy riverbank was very steep. It was also very red. Forget about your gleaming white sand on coral beaches or the glittering black of Waikiki. This stuff was dark and dirty, more mud than clean sand.

I took the fast way down inadvertently when I slipped, causing a landslide that took me with it to the edge of the river. My sweaty body was now covered from head to foot with sticky red dirt.

Once the dust settled and I could breathe again, I found out that the logs I wanted were more than my hundred-and-fifteen pound body could move up a steep hill. Looking around, I saw logs on the other side of the river that might work, and that far riverbank was less steep than this side. So, after all that, back up the sandy slope I went.

Thirty minutes later I finally had the bridge repaired enough for my pickup to cross, but I was one filthy, red mess. Covered in dirt. Really covered. I was too tired to climb down for a bath in the river, so I just drove on to Lichinga.

My friends had a good laugh when I arrived, but then, what are friends for? They now called me the Mud Bunny instead of the Bush Bunny. Oh well. Such is life in the bush.

Afterwards I wrote the mission school leaders at my church and highly recommended they add a bridge-building course to their curriculum.

12

Life in the Bush

On May 15, 1995, my nephew Jason, three Mozambican workers, and I climbed down from our dented, dusty pickup truck and waded out through tall grass to look around. We stood in the middle of bush. That was all it was. Wild, remote bush. Some people accustomed to green lawns and tidy farms would call this scrub desolate. Ragged trees studded fields of unkempt grass and weeds. The only sounds in the sullen air were those of buzzing insects. You could smell the dry, the dust. You could almost smell the heat.

Ah, but we five were standing in the midst of five hundred acres of land that had been granted to us for building the Village of Love Children's Home. The vision was finally taking form! I who am so impatient and constantly wanting to go, go, go could see real progress. I could not be more elated!

I could, however, probably have been a lot more comfortable.

Now in the eight years between the time I stood on that undeveloped site and the time this book went to press, rural Africa has changed in startling ways and has remained exactly the same in unexpected ways. Much of our lifestyle described here in 1995 still goes on. Much has changed. But at the time of my life described here, daily living was grindingly primitive.

From the hour of our arrival, in the very beginning, we kept two guard dogs chained to trees near us. They were watchdogs in the purest sense of the term, serving as our ears to detect approaching wildlife.

And wildlife abounded. The area is home to elephant, lion, leopard, hyena, jackal, fox, hippopotamus in the nearby river, and lots of poisonous snakes (incidentally, here's a factoid for you: the large animal that causes the most deaths in Africa is not the lion or leopard but the hippo. It spends its days in the river and comes ashore at night to graze. Should your boat or dugout startle it in the river during the day, it will send you off one way or another. Possessed of good ears and a very short fuse, a hippo is even more dangerous when you come upon it ashore at night).

We camped out in the open in two-man dome tents for the three weeks that it took to build our bamboo-walled "fort." The bamboo pales would hardly keep out a strongly determined predator, but the wall effectively deterred most animals.

Our days began and ended with the sun. That meant getting up at 4:30 a.m. in the peak of summer (December and January; remember, the seasons are reversed in the southern hemisphere). Sundown comes around 6:30 p.m.

Life was rugged and very basic—no electricity, refrigeration, or running water. Meals were cooked over a campfire. Candles provided light at night. The toilet was a hole in the ground surrounded by a grass fence for privacy.

We built grass shade covers over our tents, as the temperatures stay in the 90s F (mid-30s C) most of the time. The added shade made a great difference in the tents' comfort, though I use the word *comfort* loosely.

A good spring about five hundred yards away downhill provided us with a dependable water supply, but it wasn't easy to obtain. After we cut an access path, one of our men would trundle our wheelbarrow down the hill to the spring and haul water back up in twenty-liter containers. Twenty liters is a lot if you're making soup. It's a drop in the bucket if you're taking a bath.

Indeed, taking a bath was quite a project. Would you like to try it? First, get a large plastic cup for dipping, your towel, soap, and a bucket filled with water warmed over a campfire to the temperature you prefer. Find a nice private spot outdoors where you can bathe while enjoying the sunshine and the singing birds. We set aside a small grass-fenced area just for bathing. You might stand in a plastic baby bathtub while you take this "bucket bath." Otherwise your feet will end up dirtier with splashed-on muddy water than when you started. If you want to water your garden with the bath water as we did, then you'll need to stand in a second bucket in order to catch the water as it runs off your body.

Dip the cup into your bucket of water and wet down. Soap up. Remember, the more lather, the more rinse it's going to take. Now rinse off with the remaining water in the bucket. Watch out; if you use too much water to wet down, you'll be sorry at the end! There's no tap to turn on for an extra rinse.

Clean? Good! Now it's time to go cook over the hot, sooty, dusty, open fire.

Our biggest challenge was not the little inconveniences of living in the bush. It was gaining the acceptance of the locals. As you can imagine, some of them weren't too keen on a bunch of Christians moving into the neighborhood. Their distrust was compounded when they found out that a woman was running the program.

In that part of Africa, women are not without a powerful voice, but it is a hidden voice. They are powers behind the thrones, if you will. They are not recognized as out-in-the-open leaders. So I had two strikes against me before I even started.

But then, who ever said it would be easy? God was on my side. He was the one who sent me out here. With his grace we would prevail!

The Village of Love was off and running!

13

Exciting Life?

I've heard it said that sailing is hours of boredom punctuated by moments of sheer terror. But isn't most of life that way? We talk about the exciting events in our lives, but they are interspersed among long, long stretches of unremarkable routine.

And that's the way our ministry unfolds, too. I have been telling you about exciting times and the wonderful ways that the Lord's hand held us. But then there is all that other time. Our adventures certainly have been both exciting and challenging. That's life in the bush.

Life in the bush can also be grindingly lonely.

The loneliest times are generally the evenings. That was true particularly during our early efforts at our well-loved VOL, the Village of Love.

As you can well imagine, in a home for orphaned and abandoned children, the days were always busy. Besides the ordinary care our children needed, there were also the inevitable little (and not so little!) emergencies to handle. Anything from snakebites to ruffled feelings might seize your attention at any moment. You make certain every child is attended, every child fed, every child soothed. And finally, as the sun rides lower and lower, you assure yourself that every child is safely abed.

Then the busy day unravels and invites the darkness to your side. The night closes in tighter and tighter, for there are no lights other than those that the Lord provides, the moon and stars.

By candlelight or (later) lamplight, you read. You write letters. You play games. Playing games means you have to find someone else who wants to play also. That doesn't always happen.

My guard dogs quickly tired of playing Scrabble. We finally settled on playing chase or tug-of-war. Limited intellectual challenge.

Just as oppressive as loneliness is the isolation. For my first three years, I lived totally without immediate communication with the outside world. Getting to a telephone or mailbox meant a ninety-mile (160-kilometer) drive. That's an hour and a half by freeway. The rough, rutted roads were not freeways, and a trip to the mailbox could take upwards of four hours one way!

I cannot stress too strongly how much every missionary, no matter where he or she is, needs letters from family and friends. A letter is like getting a long-distance hug. A letter tells infinitely more than just the news from the past, familiar life out there; it says, "Someone cares." What a lovely voice is a letter from home!

In 1998 I was able to purchase a small two-way radio that could at least reach the local South African farmers in case of an emergency. This was a giant step forward in bringing the tyrant isolation under control.

In fact, it's worth a chapter of its own.

14

Radio Days

A friend of mine in Dallas made this observation: "When I was a kid back on the farm, not every house had a telephone. People without could make a call by going to a neighbor's or sticking a dime in the payphone in town. Today my grandchildren are growing up thinking a telephone in the car is normal.

"Half the people in the grocery store, it seems, have cell phones pasted to their ears. I read in the paper about an abused wife who summoned police by e-mail when her husband threatened to beat her up if she touched the telephone. They arrived within half an hour. Now you can be connected to the whole world twenty-four hours a day, anywhere. It's scary."

Scary, maybe. But it's definitely not Moz.

Moz is scary in the opposite way.

As I mention elsewhere, up until very recently, we and many other people working in the bush were routinely out of contact not only with the greater world but even with our own partners in service.

Regular mail? Surface mail takes the back half of forever. Packages from overseas may be in transit for months, occasionally years. It sometimes seems as if most of postage is storage fees.

Many parcels never make it. Air mail has to shed its wings and walk partway to reach its destination.

Hardwired phone service? Only in major population centers, and few missions set themselves up in cities. The same with telegraph. Cell phone? It's starting to come in, but service is very spotty. E-mail service is limited because phone signals—even wireless signals—are, as they say, dirty. Static causes glitches in transmission. Up until very recently, this problem was compounded by the fact that e-mail, especially on a solar laptop, is very slow. It may take ten minutes to bring down four messages, and servers have been known to cut off senders who are careless with length or volume. It's better, but still not great.

Most communication that does not involve standing in a doorway and yelling still happens via radio. Even radio has its dead spots.

Often it's difficult to get out of deep valleys and thick forests. But radio, reliable or not, is usually the only game in town. It is every person's way to conquer isolation. An incident during my VOL service brings this out vividly.

Just call me Bush Bunny Brenda's shuttle service. As often happened, I was called on to make a series of sixty-mile (one-hundred-kilometer) supply runs for VOL, transporting goods for the children's home in-bound and a mission family out-bound. A visiting worker assigned by his church to assist us on a short-term tour of duty was supposed to accompany me in on the first run, for I would otherwise be alone.

As they were loading my bakkie, the pickup truck I might as well have called *home*, the visiting worker arrived.

His first announcement: "I'll not be going with you after all."

My mouth dropped open. Arguing that one does not travel alone through this area did no good. He simply did not grasp the safety issue, or rather the lack of safety. I would be on my own.

Now that particular stretch of bush through northern Moz is known for its bountiful and exotic wildlife. It can also be quite dangerous wildlife, for it includes baboons, jackals, lion, leopard, and elephants. I know a couple Mozambican acquaintances, for example, who tried to bicycle the route. They were treed by a lion overnight.

Experienced off-roaders don't go through there alone for several reasons. Not only do the wild animals pose a danger, a breakdown or accident can leave you stranded for days. Two pickup trucks a week is considered heavy traffic, and not one solitary human being lives out there.

And that's not considering the infrastructure itself. Because it is so rarely used, the road is not kept up. Two of the rickety bridges are nothing more than two-inch logs laid crosswise across two iron spanner rails. The cross-members are not secured in any way, so they shake and rattle mightily whenever vehicles use them. The cross pieces also tend to drift around. Sometimes they drift far enough apart to swallow your rear tires. Bare air makes poor traction. Standard operating procedure requires the driver to get out and examine the bridge, adjusting cross pieces, before actually using it.

Radio to the rescue.

The moment I learned I would be taking the bakkie back alone, I got on the radio to the only mission station that usually monitored their radio during the day. Most stations, you see, leave the radio off unless the generator is running, to save the batteries. And most stations don't run their generators unless they need the electricity for an immediate task, such as communication.

I praise God that they heard me calling, because the signal from there is not always very good. They promised to monitor for the three and a half hours that it would take me to get through the danger zone. Should I call for help, they would instantly send a rescue team. However, the station was over sixty miles away, so "instantly" was a very relative, flexible term.

Away I went.

I managed all the rickety bridges. I daresay the bridges were in better shape after I passed than they were before I reached them. Living in the bush, you get pretty good at mending bridges, literally as well as figuratively.

I got past all the fallen trees. In that area trees do not simply drop dead on the road. Elephants push them over. Ecologically speaking, elephants are browsers. That is, they eat

leaves out of treetops, hundreds and hundreds of pounds of leaves daily. To reach the tenderest morsels in the growing crown, they simply lean on the tree until it topples. The goodies, once very

high, now lie at comfortable trunk level. No fools, elephants. But it doesn't help travel a bit.

I arrived at VOL betimes without undue incident and delivered the supplies. And of course I notified the monitoring station that their bird had come safely to roost.

So you can see that the radio has been a real blessing. That trip went smoothly by bush standards. Had something gone wrong, though, I would not have been stranded or endangered, alone and totally without resource.

15

Travel

The nearest city to our Village of Love was Lichinga (pronounce the *ch* like *sh*), only about forty miles (seventy-five kilometers) east of Lake Malawi and the Malawi border in the state of Niassa in far northern Moz. The merchants of Lichinga could provide many of the things we needed, but they could not provide everything we needed. Therefore, twice a year I had to drive down to Johannesburg for building supplies and groceries that weren't available in our area.

I just said *far northern*, remember? Lichinga is very nearly as far away from South Africa as you can get and still be in Moz. The trip of two thousand miles from the Village of Love to Jo'burg takes three to four days each way, not to mention several weeks to do all the shopping, packing, and loading.

Each trip thus chops about thirty days out of your life if you are very well organized and nothing goes wrong. Do you want to guess whether perfectly organized, all-goes-right trips ever happen?

What supplies? Since meat was hard to get in our area, we bought it canned or used soya mixes to give us a break from the local food—rice and beans. They get a little old as a steady diet over six months, but I am not complaining in the least. Rice and beans, when both are served, provide complete protein, and children need complete protein for adequate growth and development.

Jo'burg is the place to obtain construction supplies and hardware.

I also used this time in South Africa to visit the churches that support us. Too, the pickup always needed something, and I tried (not often successfully) to time repairs and major maintenance for the Jo'burg trips.

Routine maintenance, of course, was done at VOL because most of our driving consisted of getting around Lichinga and the local area surrounding VOL. In fact, therein lies a tale.

In mid August of 1999, I was driving to VOL with Elias, a Moz pastor. We were using what we call the back entrance, the Revia Road.

This back way in is the very road I just described when I was talking about the value of radio to monitor for possible emergencies—the area in which lions and elephants figure prominently.

The timing was such that we would end up spending one night in the bush. Not a problem; we are always equipped to stop anywhere. Elias would sleep in the back of the pickup. I would pass the night in my rooftop tent.

But first, we did a snappy oil change just before sundown. This was one of the very few spare moments I'd had lately, so to speak, and an oil change was not a problem either. I have become remarkably experienced in basic mechanics—of necessity, not always by choice. Out went the old filter, in went the new. Out dribbled the old oil, in poured the new.

Then we retired, because tomorrow would begin early. The next morning around 6:00 a.m., we were due to meet with the VOL missionaries about an hour's drive away in order to trade supplies.

Well before the sun came up the next day, we hopped in the truck to hit the road, in good time to make our rendezvous. The moment I started the engine, though, oil spewed out of the motor. I quickly turned it off, but not before two and a half liters of new oil lay puddled on the ground.

I hadn't bothered to start the engine the night before. And so I had not known that the new oil filter was faulty.

I got physically sick.

We had a little new oil yet, but not nearly enough to refill the crankcase, and I'd tossed the old filter into the bush. We were stuck a long way from nowhere with too little oil to safely run the motor. I prayed for guidance.

Then the Lord brought the old oil to mind. I had saved it; we paint fence posts with used motor oil to keep termites from eating them. I found the old filter, still clean enough to use, and installed it in place of the faulty one. Then I put in the small amount remaining of new oil, along with a liter and a half of the old oil.

I touched the ignition off again very carefully. It ran just fine. No leaks. Off we went.

I learned two valuable lessons that day: never throw anything away, and don't choose a remote spot to do normal maintenance work.

16

The Split Inferno

My nephew, Jason, had a little trouble getting started in life. By the age of eighteen he was on parole for grand theft and remanded to my care. He was one of these kids who is certain the world is there to serve him and he can do what he wants. And with the attention span of a butterfly, he was constantly flitting from thing to thing that he'd want at any given moment. His moral structure was, shall we say, far from solid.

And yet he had such wonderful qualities. Still does, in fact. He's a very bright young man and always has been. When he wants to learn something, he learns it. When he wants to do something, he finds out how and does it. Those are valuable traits in any person.

For example, when he arrived in Moz, he instantly fell in love with the country, its people, and their way of life. Always the avid outdoorsman, he went bush with flair. He learned Macua; he moulded himself into the local culture.

Moral and religious training took a bit longer. In fact, I don't mind saying that for the first year and a half he lived with us, he was an obnoxious brat. However, God provided enough intense, vivid lessons that Jason caught the message. One of the most vivid was God's lesson about the power of prayer.

Now one of the best building materials in the area of our VOL is grass. That sounds strange to people who equate *grass* with *lawn*. But grass here is not lawn. Bush grass occurs in loose, broad clumps about six feet high. It's really quite elegant. It grows rapidly during the annual wet season, which ends around April. From then on its green fades, until by August it's a pleasant beige. Its texture turns from soft to stiff. It whispers and rasps on the hot, dry air.

The individual blades are scratchy, tough, and durable. They are strong enough that you can weave them into a kind of coarse mat. Often builders tie the grass into bundles to use as thatch—on roofs, for example. So it's not unusual to see a house with beams and corner posts made out of a couple of poles tied together and the walls and roof fashioned exclusively from grass. Flimsy as it sounds, a home thus constructed is actually quite comfortable and serviceable.

Need I mention that these dwellings are extremely flammable, should a spark of fire touch them?

One day Jason and an American family of four were working near the compound. The family had only been with us two weeks, but their twelve-year-old son had already become Jason's little buddy. As the others worked, the boy wandered down by our mud-brick pit east of the tent camp, exploring and playing. His parents knew he was around, of course, but not exactly where.

Jason and the three heard crackling in the distance. They looked up to see in the east a massive bushfire headed straight for our camp. The flames stretched six hundred yards out across our east boundary from the road to just about forever! Ugly, boiling smoke turned the blue sky gray. A steady wind was pushing the terrible wall directly toward us at a rapid pace.

Our homes were canvas tents. Tinder. The bath house and some outbuildings were of grass. Tinder. We were surrounded by scrub woods, brush, and dry grass. Tinder. And we certainly had no practical way to stop the flames—no equipment, not enough water, not enough time to build an effective firebreak.

They began instantly and fervently to pray.

Suddenly Jason remembered where his little buddy had gone, and he could see that wildfire closing rapidly on the brick pit! He took off running and shouting. Until the boy saw Jason coming and heard the call, he had no idea wildfire was bearing down on them. The tall grass blocked the sight of it, and he didn't realize what that crackling sound was.

Away they raced, Jason and the boy, with the fire roaring high behind them.

The fire, still westbound, reached the bottom of the hill on which our tents were pitched. Another seventy-five yards, and it would engulf our settlement. Then for no discernible reason, it abruptly shifted ninety degrees and headed south.

Our tent camp was spared. But now the fire was aiming itself straight for our garden and our grass bath house.

When it reached the garden, it split. It burned on either side of the cultivated area, but it missed our plants. It missed the bath house, even though it sat directly in the way of the fire.

The fire continued out across the open field, reducing everything in its path to smouldering black and white ash.

And then, along came a sudden downpour, drowning the fire. The burning bush hissed and stank. That hideous crackle faded.

It was over. The danger had passed. All was safe.

Only with time have I come to realize how much the Lord showed his power that day. After living there for four years, I could begin to see the multiplied miracles in his feat. For one thing, very rarely do the winds ever blow toward the south. The tents and the bush in which they were pitched should have been totally destroyed. There was no reason the wind ought to have turned and re-directed the flames.

Second, the garden was not even scorched despite the heat so close by. And the bath house ... ! The grass surrounding it had burned to within a foot of its walls. The leaves in the tops of the nearby trees were also burned. A fire that close to a grass building would normally ignite it simply from the heat.

Third and most bizarre, *it never rains in August!* Never! This is the height of the dry season, the one time of year you can be absolutely sure no moisture will fall.

The only thing to say is, *"Thank you, Jesus!"*

This lesson was not lost on Jason. I suspect that because he was so bush-wise, he realized sooner than I how immense was the work of God that day in response to prayer.

How did the flames start? Our workers told us the next day that three men had been seen setting fire to our eastern boundary line. We never found out who they were, but every year someone would set that boundary on fire, and every year the Lord would stop it before it could do any damage.

Large firebreaks didn't help, because our enemies just started the fires on the inside of the break. Believe me, we are very grateful for the Lord's fire brigade angels. And I am grateful also that Jason was given these vivid lessons teaching him to rely upon the God of Africa and America.

Come to think of it, it was a vivid lesson for me, too.

Postscript regarding Jason:

Jason's impetuous and successful run saved his little buddy, but it was a very close brush with death. They barely escaped being engulfed by the flames. At the moment he did it, it never occurred to him that his own life was on the line. Afterwards, though, the incident so unnerved him that it was over a year before he told me about his heroic act.

Did those two years in the bush produce any good effects at all? When he returned to the states, he bounced around for about a year from job to job, getting his bearings back. Then he decided to pursue his life's dream: to become a police officer. I think I mentioned that when he puts his mind to something, he sees it through, and that includes the law enforcement training program.

Today he is working for the same police department that once upon a time arrested him.

17

A Bridge Too Far?

The road leading from our project to Lichinga, ninety miles away, has a good many of those single-lane bridges on it. One of the hairiest of them is also one of the most sophisticated, so to speak. Called the Lacoovy, it is a rickety old metal bridge lying in wait for you at the bottom of a very steep hill.

The use of metal in its construction did not confer safety. The

Lacoovy is far from the widest of bridges, and it lacks any guard-rails whatsoever. Too, traction on the bridge is minimal. A heavy rain could give a bridge-crosser gray hair. First, the road down that steep hill gets very slippery as the sandy dirt turns into a muddy sluice, slicker than a slug in mayonnaise. You venture out onto the bridge and find its surface is also quite slick—at least much slicker than you had anticipated.

October 1995 I had to drive into Lichinga. When I arrived at the Lacoovy bridge, I encountered a dismaying situation that had taken place the day before. A tractor pulling a trailer loaded heavily with corn—that is, mealies, in the local parlance—was coming down the hill when the driver lost control. The tractor and trailer slid sideways right out onto the bridge. When the rig came to rest, the tractor was hanging off one side of the bridge, its frame on the bridge surface and its front wheels parked on bare air. The trailer dangled down over the other side.

The driver's horror did not end when he climbed out of his rig. The load of mealies was someone else's, but the tractor belonged to him. And he was terrified that if the trailer disconnected, that precarious balance would be lost and his tractor would tumble into the river below. Wreck the tractor, and his livelihood was gone. He had no money to hire local men to work for him. No one could, or would, help him get off the bridge.

Fuel is very valuable there, so I decided to stay the night. Surely they would remove the tractor the next morning, right? After all, it was totally blocking the road. With time on my hands, I made a lot of acquaintances and handed out tracts and talked to people about Jesus. I finally went home the next morning after it became clear that getting the road opened again wasn't going to happen for several more days.

Over a week went by, and the tractor still hung there, blocking the bridge, dangling on the ends of its poor owner's nerves. I made special petition to the Lord, asking him to please send someone to move it. We were running out of essentials; I needed to get to Lichinga.

That night I awoke from a dream in which I was told to remove the tractor from the bridge.

Whoa! *Me?* I didn't have the knowledge or the equipment needed to do the job. Confused but still weary, I drifted back to sleep.

The incident was unusual in part because I rarely remember my dreams. But that night a second dream came. In it I saw how to use logs as rollers, doing the lifting with jacks. The next morning I realized that it must have been the Lord giving me the plan.

I was excited, but I was also scared spitless. The first step was to release the trailer from the tractor. The trailer would fall into the river, but what if the tractor, no longer held back by the trailer's weight, plunged off the other side of the bridge? What if it destroyed itself in the stream below?

I gathered up the materials we would need. Off I went with one of my workers, who would help me organize a local work crew.

The driver was elated that we wanted to help him, but we had to talk like Philadelphia lawyers to convince him to let us release the trailer. We hired six men to cut the big logs needed for rollers once the tractor was jacked up.

Showtime. As the first step, we freed the trailer. It fell away into the streambed below with a mighty thump. Everyone watching agreed that it was quite spectacular.

And the tractor stayed put on the bridge!

That turned out to be the easy part. We struggled with that beast for six hours. We'd jack the tractor frame up a bit, wedge a support under it, jack it a bit farther. Finally, the front wheels had been raised until they hovered within four inches of being back up on the bridge. One rear tire was flat, making it virtually impossible to move the tractor even when the roller logs were in place.

Our hired people were tired. "This isn't working," they said in effect. "We quit."

I prayed, asking the Lord to send me some strong angels to help us push. I begged the workers, "Let's try just one more time."

Even before I could organize that one last try, a ten-ton truck pulled up with a forty-man work crew in the back. I explained to the supervisor what we needed. With shouts and waving arms he directed his men. Within fifteen minutes they lifted that tractor by brute force the remaining distance onto the bridge.

Even though the engine wouldn't start and several tires were flat, that marvelous crew of angels shoved the tractor off the bridge onto solid land and left it by the roadside to be repaired.

The owner's truck was saved.

The road was clear again.

At last I could go to Lichinga.

In retrospect I see that I made many friends among the truck owner's people and in the nearby village during the time I spent there. This later opened the door for me to witness and give a Bible to the Muslim chief. What I felt was wasted time, God had used to plant seeds in the hearts of many people whom I would otherwise probably have never met. His ways are not our ways. His patience is not my patience.

So why did the Bush Bunny end up clearing that bridge when any number of capable men might have done the job? I don't know. It was certainly not some extraordinary knowledge or skill or even piety on my part. I do know that, however reluctantly, I obeyed when the Lord showed me what he wanted done. I seriously doubt I am the only person to whom he called. Apparently, though, I was the only person who stepped forward to answer.

18

The Reason for Being

I believe one of the biggest and best reasons I love Moz is the people. They have been through so much in the last thirty years, and yet they give so freely.

The trials and triumphs of our Village of Love more or less illustrate in a microcosm the nation's struggle.

There are certain factions in Moz, as there are anywhere else, that are convinced there should be only one religious belief (theirs, of course) and no outsiders. Other factions welcome outside help as they seek to stabilize the country. The ideologies may be strong, but nearly everyone is acting from selfless motives.

And so, when I speak of men on our eastern boundary trying to burn us out or kick us out of the country, that is only one small faction. Many more times I stand in awe of the people who work so diligently for so little reward to help us and the orphans we serve.

One such was Crispo.

When I first met Crispo, my initial thought was, "Is this guy accident prone?" The answer to that was, "No. He just looks that way." Like so many Mozambicans, he was battle-scarred from the war. A bullet wound in his leg has left its permanent mark, and he sported other scars from a variety of reasons—spills from a motor bike, for instance.

About five-foot-seven, he was powerfully built. If you need a hippopotamus lifted, he was your man. A skilled outdoorsman, he could capture wild pigs or bucks in rope traps. These traps, then, required him to dispatch the angry and dangerous game without himself being dispatched. How he managed to do that time after time, I don't know. I don't want to know.

And he was brilliant. He spoke five tribal languages fluently in addition to English and Portuguese. He wrote and typed clearly in both of those European tongues. His knowledge of how the Moz government works matched his keen business acumen. For example, I helped him set up a small store out of his home and it prospered. Too, he worked with orphans during the war, so he came to us with a solid body of experience behind him. In short, Crispo was invaluable to us.

The best of all was his dedication to God. Because he studied the Word so diligently, he grew steadily in the Lord. On the other hand, the Lord in turn took care of Crispo; I don't know any other explanation for how Crispo managed to return unscathed from some of his hunting expeditions.

The focus of the Village, though, has never been the adults of the area but the children. They are, ever and anon, its reason for being.

In 1996 our first full year of operation, the Village of Love received over eighty children. Some were true orphans, bereft of parents. Most, though, were refugees, lost or abandoned during the political turmoil.

Please keep in mind that when unrest or problems in some remote place cease to make the newspaper anymore, that doesn't mean they've ended. The problems still exist, still need attention. And most are very long running. Long after the news-making war ended, the refugee children still appeared in our area. A lot of them simply needed temporary assistance until their families could be located. Therefore, those eighty children that I just mentioned were not all housed in VOL at one time. They came and went. Little Tiago's story, for example, is fairly typical.

Reunited

Crispo and I were driving through the village of Mecaulo (Mekwa-loo) one day. Typical of such villages, Mecaulo consists of clusters of simple buildings. The main noises are not traffic but crowing roosters and laughing children. Someone fresh from the streets of London or New York would call the place primitive. It is anything but. The so-called simple buildings are perfect for the climate, quite comfortable. And at a political level, the elders and head man keep life running smoothly. New York and London should be so lucky.

On this particular day, the local school director waved for us to stop. We exchanged pleasantries. Then he asked for our help.

He brought Tiago, six years old, out to us. Tiago, he explained, had been separated from his family when his village was raided during the war. He was just a toddler at the time. A family in that village took him in. They had been caring for him for the past four years. But now that family was having problems of its own and could no longer feed him. No one from his own family had returned after the refugee camps were emptied, so everyone assumed that his immediate blood relatives must all be dead. Could we please take him to the Village of Love?

Of course!

Tiago was hoisted up into our bakkie right then and there, and away we went.

Again, Tiago's case was typical; you will notice there was no transfer of possessions and luggage. He had nothing. Rarely do our orphans and refugees possess anything.

About two weeks later, we were driving through Mecaulo again. The same gentleman came running out to the road to stop us.

He greeted us. Then, "Little Tiago is still with you, that is true?"

"Yes," we answered.

"You will not believe this," he said. "Tiago's mother walked in yesterday from Malawi. The poor soul is exhausted, not to mention in sorry health. Hers was a journey of many days. She is rejoicing to know that her little son is still alive, but she is upset to hear that he is so far away."

VOL lay about thirty miles (fifty kilometers) from Mecaulo. To a sick and weary woman on foot, that would certainly seem a horrendous distance.

The school director asked, "Would you take another woman with you who would escort Tiago back here to his mother?"

And our answer was, again, "Of course!"

A few weeks later, we happened to see the director.

He beamed. "It was such a very happy reunion, Tiago and his mother! The poor woman lived these last four years not knowing if her son had survived the raid. She had been sent to a refugee camp in Malawi. As you well know, there was no way of tracing anyone during the war, certainly not across national boundaries." His voice softened. "Ah, the joyous smiles."

Tiago's story, so typical in many ways, is not typical in one very important regard: many, many children do not live to see his happy ending, reunion with at least one parent. A whole population of orphans and displaced children are growing up in Moz today without parents, trying to make the best of a horrible situation.

It is moments like this and children like Tiago that make all the long hours of work well worth the trouble. When the burden grows heavy and Satan throws his worst at you, you sometimes wonder. You doubt. The most dedicated of God's servants doubt, believe me. But after the ups and downs and all-arounds of that first year, I realized that I could never be happy living in America again.

I do not mean to sound melodramatic or terribly pious or better than anyone else. None of that is true. I'm not any of those things. But as a simple fact, I knew then and have become increasingly convinced since, that my heart's desire is to continue helping these kids in difficult circumstances until Jesus takes me home.

19

Mud Hut Delivery

The very first thing every worker in the bush learns to do is: lots of other things!

In the western world, we become accustomed to specialization. One doctor treats ears, nose, and throat while another across the hall sees only feet—a podiatrist. A few doors down, the proctologist treats...you get the idea. Construction companies may build nothing but roofs. Some electricians limit their practice to commercial jobs.

Not in the bush.

For instance, Vernis, an elder in our church, awakened me at 5:00 a.m. one morning in February 1997. His wife was giving birth and seemed to be having problems. Could I please come and help?

Me? I was totally unprepared for something like this!

My past training as a nurse kicked in (that's another thing about work out here; everything you ever learned comes in handy sooner or later—even some stuff you never thought you learned!). As I ran out the door of my hut, I grabbed as many of the essentials as I could think of.

That close to the equator, the air is never frosty, but this particular pre-dawn felt about as cool as it ever gets. Pleasant comfort floated on the silent breeze. Somewhere the sun was yawning, preparing to rise. Its first light was warming up the eastern sky.

It was still very dark inside Vernis's hut. I gave my eyes a few moments to adjust, but there was hardly any light to adjust to.

Problems indeed. The birthing bed was a soiled feed sack on the dirt floor. Their brand new baby boy lay uncovered between his mother's legs. The placenta had not delivered, and the umbilical cord was still attached to the baby.

I am not an obstetrics nurse. True, I ended up doing five emergency deliveries back during my hospital nursing days. But none of those deliveries was accompanied by any complications, and trained hospital staff were not far off, available if expert help was needed. Out here in Vernis's hut, it was me and the Lord. Of necessity, I was totally dependent upon the Lord to guide me in this procedure.

Now, as most readers know, the pre-born baby develops inside a living sac, the placenta. This container absorbs nutrients from the uterus in which it is housed, and those nutrients are then passed to the baby through the two-foot-long umbilical cord.

Obviously the placenta must rupture before the baby can come out, and it does so. The placenta normally delivers in one piece shortly after the baby comes. But if any tiny bit of the ruptured placenta remains inside, the woman almost always suffers a fatal infection. In a hospital setting, the placenta is carefully examined to make sure it is intact. If there be any doubt, the attending physician or midwife takes immediate steps to ensure that no piece is left behind.

Many women in our area die each year from simple complications that would be handled routinely in modern hospitals. The needed drugs and equipment are simply not available in these remote areas.

So I had no backup. I was scared, but I didn't dare show it. I trusted the Lord to help me where my own scant knowledge was lacking.

First thing, I covered the baby to prevent any further chilling. Newborns cool off quickly, for their temperature regulation isn't cranked up yet. Then I tied off the cord and cut it with a sterile scalpel.

The baby was breathing easily and appeared fine except for being cold, so I bundled him well and placed him on the bed.

I had no sterile gloves and no water with which to wash my hands. I did have a pair of reasonably clean gloves. That left no choice but to put on the clean gloves and ask the Lord to please help me to deliver the placenta.

It's tricky. You dare not pull on that cord and hope the placenta pops out. Even if you don't rip it, you can cause fatal hemorrhaging. God was going to have to do this part. With a sudden strong contraction by the mother, the placenta delivered in one piece without complications! To say I was *soooo* relieved is understatement.

I gave the baby to his mother, and he eagerly took to the breast. A very good sign! You see, a great deal of blood is spilt in birth, and the mother can easily bleed to death postpartum. The physical act of suckling, of drawing milk from the breast, helps the uterine blood vessels close down and slow bleeding.

I had been praying as I worked; desperately begging the Lord to help out is a pure form of prayer. Vernis and I then applied prayer in a more deliberate dimension. We specifically asked the Lord to please protect the mother and baby from infection. I had medicated and covered the cord, but you never know. Tetanus kills many a baby out here when less-than-sterile procedures allow infection to enter, particularly through the cut cord. And tetanus germs are everywhere.

All went well, praise God. The baby seemed healthy, and the mother did not experience any problems. I was very grateful for that.

That very day, back at my hut, I put together a kit of needed items just in case this situation should ever happen again. Actually, I had quite a few things appropriate for an O.B. kit. But they were scattered here and there through my baggage—things I packed when I left the States in 1991 because I thought they might come in handy.

For instance, among my other nursing gear, I dug out a DeLee suction for infants. This is a very simple device, a pair of tiny tubes connected into a small trap bottle. The nurse inserts one tube into the baby's mouth or nose and gently sucks on the second tube. The gizmo draws the baby's nasal or oral secretions into the bottle. It is used to clear the airways of newborn infants.

At 8:00 p.m. a week later, Vernis was back at my hut, yelling,

"The baby can't breathe!" The infant, he said, had choked and turned blue after breast feeding.

I grabbed the DeLee suction and raced to his hut in the dark.

The baby was struggling to breathe and starting to lose the tussle. Thick mucous blocked its airway. I carefully suctioned his mouth and then his nose. The problem quickly subsided. Would that all medical emergencies could be so easily relieved!

So simple, if you have the right equipment and a little knowledge. Yet this problem would have killed him if we hadn't been there, because the nearest medical help was twelve miles (twenty kilometers) away. I was glad to be able to respond, but obviously this area needed a real clinic. In a near sterile setting, mothers could be delivered of their babies with far less chance of crippling or fatal complications.

You guessed it. In September 1997, eight months after the birth of Vernis's child, the Lord told me to build a clinic in that village. By now I knew better than to argue, but a few minor little details stood in our way. Money, for instance.

Even the simplest clinic takes money. We didn't have the funds. *Nada.* No matter. I had long since learned that when God speaks, it pays to get busy. So we started making the bricks anyway. You can make mud bricks without money.

In October I received a letter from a businessman in Pennsylvania. He said the Lord had told him to help us build a clinic.

"How much," he asked, "do you need?"

The funds were in the bank by November, and the clinic opened on December 25, 1997.

No longer do mothers have to bear their babies in the bush. I thank the Lord for his love toward these people. And what a powerful testimony he affords! His people here have suffered so much and have known such want. Believe me, they are truly grateful for his help. Most gratifying of all, they know well from whence that help came.

The day after we attended to Vernis's baby's choking problem, my nephew, Jason, told me that they named him Lazarus. I had, you see, raised him from the dead. As I write this book, Lazarus is a healthy, active two-year-old with the most mischievous grin.

20

This is No Documentary!

The favorite relaxation of one of my acquaintances in the States is to watch nature documentaries on public television. From the comfort of her armchair, she observes hyenas and lions fight each other for pieces of zebra. She watches cheetahs run in slow motion and admires their magnificent, spring-loaded strides. She chuckles at the antics of a troop of baboons.

Real life in the bush is not a nice, safe, tidy filmstrip. Real life is slaughtered goats and savaged dogs. In real life those "cute" baboons pose a very great danger.

In fact, at VOL, baboons were the biggest nuisances we had. During the rainy season from December through April, when the crops in our fields were coming into fruit, we had to keep guards on duty from sunup to sundown, or the baboons would steal all the food in the garden, even before it was fully ripe. Normally they are chaseable. They run if a person comes near them, but if they think their young are being threatened, they are not the least bit afraid to attack.

When we moved onto the VOL property, the area was overgrown with six-foot-high grass. You would be amazed at how many things can hide in there, even if it's in clumps with open dirt between. Until we got the mud-brick buildings up, our living quarters were canvas tents. A canvas tent is pretty flimsy protection in country with major predators. So we built a sturdy bamboo fence around the compound.

And we kept guard dogs. These were not pets. They served a vital purpose, for they could detect danger long before any human being knew what was coming. One of our dogs, Scout, turned out to be an amazing escape artist, the Houdini of hounds. We kept him chained to a tree inside the fence.

One afternoon when Jason was alone in the compound, he decided to go for a walk down the path leading to our spring. It wasn't all that far. He closed the bamboo gate behind him, leaving the dogs chained to their respective trees.

He'd walked only a short distance into the bush when he startled a female baboon and her baby foraging near a tree. I had impressed upon Jason that he must freeze if confronted by a wild animal. I thank the Lord that he remembered that lesson, even though he'd been in Africa only a short time, because the huge male baboon, which posed an even greater danger than did the female, sat hidden in the grass off to his left.

The male started barking at Jason. Jason remained frozen. He had no idea what to do. He hadn't been in the bush all that long, and those two adult baboons acted terribly angry and vicious. Jason could see no escape.

Suddenly, from out of nowhere, Scout came racing down the path, barking for all he was worth! The terrified baboons bolted and ran off. We will probably never know how Scout not only slipped his collar but also opened a locked gate. But his talent definitely paid off that day!

On a different day, Jason and Scout were walking together down by our spring when they saw three hyenas catch a small baboon. Now, hyenas are usually portrayed as scavengers who slink around stealing morsels from lions or whatever. Once in a while, I suppose, they do, but they are also efficient predators in their own right.

When two of the hyenas spotted Scout, they must have decided that he'd be a dandy snack, so here they came, running right toward them. Scout, a wise mutt, bolted for the safety of our fence, and Jason was right behind him. The hyenas gave up as these two reached the safety of our camp. The close call underlines the danger.

At different times we were visited by lions or leopards as they roamed the area looking for food. Goat happens to be one of their favorite delicacies, so their visits became more regular once we bought our first goat herd in late 1996. To protect the goats at night, we built a solid log barn for them to sleep in. Also, a guard in a nearby hut had to keep a fire going all night. The combination of fortress and fire worked well. Although the cats would come, they never got in. Our guard always managed to scare them off with fire.

Then in March 1998, while I was visiting in the USA, a large male leopard stood on his hind legs and got one of the goat pens open. That night he killed seven goats before the guard could summon help to frighten him away. Seven goats was a major loss.

Everyone knew that he'd be back for another easy meal, so half a dozen of the best hunters in the area said they'd come by and try to kill the leopard the next night. They did so. But the leopard outsmarted everyone. He came through just before dark, slaughtering the remaining eight goats, as well as most of the ducks and chickens.

The third night our people were ready for him. They erected a strong log pen and put one of my guard dogs inside to draw the cat. For bait they killed a chicken and laced it with a strong poison, placing it on top of the dog pen. Then they sat down to wait.

Deep in the night, the leopard came prowling. Fire didn't frighten it away. Instead of melting back into the darkness when confronted by humans, the cat crouched and snarled at the hunters watching it. Then it bolted down its free lunch, the chicken.

There is no free lunch. The leopard started to scream as the poison began its work. He wheeled away and in one great stride vaulted over the six-foot fence then collapsed and died about fifty yards into the bush.

My men skinned and tanned his skin. The government wouldn't let us keep the hide, though. The leopard is an endangered species.

Leopards are counted among the great cats, but they are not really all that big. For instance, a typical male leopard weighs somewhere around 150 pounds; a male lion will top 400. This particular animal turned out to be the largest leopard on record for our area. He measured over four feet (1.3 meters) from his nose to his rump, which does not include the long, graceful tail. The left front paw was gone, probably lost in a trap of some kind.

We believe that this lost paw is what caused the leopard to abandon its fear of man and fire. Reduced to three running legs, he was no longer fast enough to catch normal prey. Too, he now lacked half his front claws, the tools with which he could grasp a fleeing animal. So he had to resort to the easier meals of confined goats and poultry.

We received some grief for killing that poor endangered animal, not from local authorities but from people in the United States. The local authorities understand all about survival and about the peril in rogue predators. They know what loss can mean to subsistence farmers. Believe me, I do not condone killing animals except for food or protection. And that's a very big *except*. In this case, my people did what must be done. A major predator that has lost all fear of humans is too dangerous to remain at large.

It wasn't just the slaughter of our precious livestock. The cat had proven it didn't bother to wait for dark in order to attack. Our children work and play in the bush. They walk through the bush to and from school. What a tasty morsel one of them might have been.

21

Crispo and the Black Mamba

I have mentioned before the hunting prowess of Crispo, our right-hand man at VOL. He didn't have to expend costly ammunition or drag out heavy artillery. He could achieve hunting success with nothing more than his incredible bush savvy and a rope. You would be amazed at what he could catch with simple deadfalls and snares. With such snares, he and others captured wild pigs so that our orphans could have fresh meat occasionally.

In July 1997 Crispo and two other men ran a line of rope snares in tall grass near the Lugenda River, about a mile (1.6 kilometers) east of our VOL project. Like so much of enterprise in Africa, the materials are cheap, the time and labor are intensive. The procedure in this case is to arrange a number of looped snares in places where one thinks animals will be moving, such as game trails, for instance. Periodically—usually at least once a day—the hunters retrace the line. They re-set snares that were tripped without catching anything and retrieve any animals that have been captured before wild predators and scavengers find the free meal.

On this particular day, they were out checking the line. Without warning a large Black Mamba stood up in the grass next to Crispo and bit him on the back of his hand. All three men ran, knowing that an irritated Black Mamba will bite anything that moves in its territory.

In that part of Africa, all snake bites are usually fatal because no antivenin is available near enough to be administered in time. Besides, mambas' venom is so powerful you could have a syringe of antivenin in hand as the snake strikes and you might die anyway.

The three men ran the 150 yards to the road near the river bridge. Crispo was already losing coordination as the poison circulated through him doing its evil. One fellow helped him to sit on a log while the other jumped on a bicycle and raced to my house.

As the cyclist slid to a stop in front of my gate, all I heard him say was, "Crispo snake bit!"

My heart skipped a beat. Then I immediately cried out to God that Crispo must not die! I grabbed my pickup keys, tossed myself behind the wheel, and raced for the river.

When I pulled up next to Crispo, he was still sitting on the log. Even as I flung myself out of the bakkie, I could see that his arm was already swollen to the shoulder. It felt hard to the touch, a bloated piece carved crudely from wood. His eyes had already glazed over, and he was unable to speak. With considerable help he was able to rise to his feet, tottering and swaying, but we had to lift him bodily into the pickup seat.

As I wheeled the truck around, I told him, "Start thanking Jesus for your miracle healing!"

No response.

"Crispo, I know you can hear me, even though you can't speak. Thank him in your head, and I'll pray for you as I drive." I then rebuked the poison, asking the Lord to cleanse Crispo's blood with the blood of Jesus. I rebuked the spirit of death and commanded life back into Crispo.

You're right! That was heady stuff, ordering life and death around and virtually insisting upon God's help. This was a terrifying and extraordinary situation, and it never occurred to me that I might be acting just a wee bit pushy, spiritually speaking.

But! There is no entity in the universe pushier than Satan when he thinks he can get away with it, and there is no being in the universe more powerful than our Lord. Those extremes require that the person in prayer not hesitate or hem and haw about. Wishy-washy does nothing of value in an arena of such power as God and Satan wield. And so, yes. I rebuked and begged, knowing that no matter how forceful my petitions, I was dealing with circumstances infinitely more forceful than I could ever be.

Thirty minutes had passed since the bite. Crispo was struggling to breathe as his muscles and diaphragm, increasingly paralytic, began to close down. His lips and fingernails had turned blue. All I knew was that the Lord told me to take him to Lichinga. That was a four-hour drive away! I clearly remember thinking as I shoved the truck over the rutted track, "Glory! The Lord is going to raise him from the dead, because without a miracle, he'll be gone in another five minutes."

As I approached Malanaga, our nearest town with a clinic, Crispo turned his head toward me and spoke in clear English, "I feel better."

I started jumping up and down in the seat as I drove, filled with the most vivid joy! I almost hit a tree in my excitement.

I asked him to draw a deep breath. He did so without difficulty. More or less experimentally, he started moving his good arm and leg.

His right arm, understandably, was terribly painful, for it was still swollen hard and huge. The Lord had nullified the poison, though; that showed clearly enough. I knew therefore that the life-threatening danger was over. My only concern focused on possible infection and the massive swelling, so I diverted into the Malanaga clinic. Perhaps they would give him a shot of antibiotic before I took him on to Lichinga, as divinely instructed.

The pickup fishtailed a little as I slid to a stop in front of the clinic. Now everyone there knows that I don't normally drive that way, so many people came to see what was wrong. Before I could get out and run around to the passenger side of the truck, Crispo had opened the door and climbed out! There he walked, a bit weakly and wobbly, up the four steps into the clinic!

I gaped, astounded. His rapid recovery was beyond incredible. It was miraculous.

In the little examination area, the male nurse scowled at Crispo's arm.

I explained why we stopped—that Crispo had survived a direct hit but needed antibiotic to stem possible infection.

"Snake bite? No!" The nurse shook his head. "No medicine for him. He's going to die."

"He's not dying! He—"

"Medicine is precious. We don't waste it on a dead man. No."

"He hasn't died yet, and he's not going to! I insist he receive penicillin."

"No! We can't waste."

Now, you don't argue with someone who has just been ordering death around. She isn't about to back down for a mere mortal, not when she has God in there pitching miracles. After some serious back-and-forth, the nurse finally relented and gave Crispo a shot just to get me out of there.

By then Crispo was becoming shocky from the ordeal. I wrapped him in a blanket and headed for Lichinga.

It would soon be dark, and ahead of us loomed one of those treacherous log bridges. This particular span was 130 meters (a little over 400 feet) long. I asked the Lord therefore to please help me through the next four miles of road. To drive that area in the dark was asking for trouble. However, the Lord's hand prevailed, and we got through the bad part just as the final rays of light disappeared behind the mountains.

We arrived at the hospital in Lichinga about 8:00 p.m. The town had no electricity that night, so the emergency room was using only a few solar lights. I helped Crispo out of the truck, and he doddered into the emergency room still swathed in the blanket.

By the blue-gray light of the solar lamps, we looked at Crispo's arm for the first time since 5:00 p.m. From the shoulder clear down to the wrist, the swelling had disappeared! Not just eased. Not down a little. Gone!

Massive swelling still stretched the skin tight and glossy across his fingers and hand, however. The fang marks, vivid punctures with discoloration, were plainly visible.

The doctor, a Russian, came immediately when they told him that a snakebite had just walked in. When he saw Crispo's hand, he assumed the bite had just occurred.

"No," I told him. "It happened at three this afternoon."

"What?" he screamed, his eyes wide. "That's not possible! No one lives five hours after a mamba bite!"

"You don't understand," I explained. "Jesus just performed a miraculous healing. God saved his life."

He threw his pen to the floor and stomped off in a rage. Some folks have trouble accepting miracles.

A few minutes later, he returned with an injection and a prescription. "Well, I guess you'll live. Go home and go to bed and get this filled in the morning."

What a night! The emotional stress as much as the physical stress was starting to make itself felt. We crawled into the pickup and started the long, dark journey home.

"You realize," I pointed out, "your family assumes you're dead. Like the doctor said, no one lives."

But we had no radio at that time, so we couldn't tell them the good news.

I believe I mentioned before that ghosts play a highly important part in those people's lives. And it is not a cheerful, welcome part either. When we drove up to Crispo's house, we found the people there preparing his funeral.

Crispo stepped out of the truck, and I thought the whole group of workers were going to die of fright! What a scene.

Quickly he showed them the bite marks. Eagerly he told them how Jesus had healed him.

It was a powerful, intense witness, the first unquestionable miracle that these people had ever seen. No one doubted it, either. Crispo was the first person in memory ever to live after such a snake bite. It just doesn't get any more miraculous than that.

The next morning all the swelling had left Crispo's hand except for a small area around the fang marks. He hopped aboard his motorbike and roared away to Malanaga.

When he returned I asked him, "Why did you go to town?"

He grinned gleefully. "I wanted to show everyone that I lived. They all thought I was a ghost as I rode through town. It really shook them up!"

I'll bet.

For the next thirty days, Crispo was a celebrity, a star of the first magnitude. People would come to us, friend and stranger alike, to ask if he was the man who lived after being bitten by a mamba. The fang marks remained visible for that whole month before finally fading away.

It was a total, vivid, glorious testimony of the healing power of Jesus, and it reached many.

And the doctor who treated Crispo that night? Sad to say, he did not fair so well. Crispo heard on the radio a few months later that the man had committed suicide.

The Lord used us to reach out to him with a medical miracle, a palpable, delicious miracle, and he refused to receive it. He did, you see, have the choice.

Obviously none of us knows when our time of death will come. Should we reject Jesus, we buy a one-way ticket to the hell. The Bible assures us that the Lord doesn't want anyone to perish, but should a person reject him, he can do nothing to help that soul. He gives us each the power of choice.

As I think about it, that wild ride to Malanaga with Crispo dying on the seat beside me was not the only occasion when I rebuked death. I did so also in the moment I accepted Jesus. It was a conscious decision, choosing life in Jesus and thereby banning death. That same decision falls to you as well.

In the end, the doctor chose death.

Postscript

There is an interesting postscript to Crispo's horrific adventure. It could be titled, "How I got invited to Canada."

I was invited to a five-day missions conference in Burlington, Canada, as a key speaker. I assumed I had been asked in to the church because Les Reynolds, from that area, had been sent over by his family to assist me in 2001.

When I got there, I learned quite a different story.

The missions director, Ron Oatman, is an intercessor, a serious prayer warrior (for those unaccustomed to this term, an intercessor is a person in agreement with God to offer up prayer in any circumstance, at any time, about any matter, as directed). In January of 1997, the Lord showed Ron that a man would be bitten by a snake somewhere in Africa. It would be a grave situation, and it would happen that July. He was to pray for this man. Ron knew nothing other than that tiny tidbit. Of course, he prayed fervently and consistently.

At that time God didn't happen to let him in on how the situation turned out. When he saw the *Guidepost Magazine* article about Crispo that appeared in February of 2001, he realized he was looking at God's answer to his prayer. He decided, "That's the one we should ask to our missions conference, because we want to set these people on fire and motivate them for missions."

So it was that I was invited in. It was the first I knew that anyone was praying for Crispo and me, backing us up on that amazing day.

And the conference? Awesome! I remind you that it was God's doing, and Ron and I were his instruments. I'm certainly not claiming any glory. My assignment was to go and to speak as I was led. It was the first such missions conference I'd ever done.

I made nine presentations in the five days of meetings, speaking to everyone from six-year-olds to adults twice my age. God really worked in a serious way. At an altar call, all but four people came forward. Fifty came forward to receive anointing for missions. They had accepted God's challenge in their lives—*his* will in their lives, not theirs.

How about you?

So what happened to Crispo? The story ends sadly.

The incident with the mamba occurred in 1997. Around 1999 Crispo, I think, got a little bored with mission life and wanted to go out and make his fortune. So he quit our job and started a transportation business. We lost direct contact.

But stories drifted back to us. We heard reports of drinking. He apparently was also, to use the vernacular, getting around.

In January of 2002, I was driving near Nampula when he saw me and flagged me down. We talked for maybe five or six minutes. I was glad to see that Crispo, appearing hale and hearty, was still his usual exuberant self. I don't remember the exact conversation, but the salient parts went something like this:

"You're looking good, Crispo. How is your transportation business coming?"

"Aa," he said and shrugged. "Think I'm going to go over to the coast—Nacala or somewhere—and try to find a good driving job."

I asked the important question, though I feared that I knew the answer. "How is your walk with the Lord?"

"Good. Good! My pastor is counseling with me, and I'm getting back to where I was. I'm getting my life right again."

"That's wonderful!"

And wonderful it certainly was. Occasionally the best and noblest fall away, and I can imagine angels weeping when it happens. But Crispo was back.

Nine months later, missionaries at the VOL mission station received a message that Crispo was in the Lichinga hospital. He was extremely ill and emaciated, and doctors were unable to decide just what was wrong. The infections with which he suffered were highly resistant to treatment. Bad sign. When that is happening, you rather assume HIV and probably full-blown AIDS, although as I mentioned elsewhere, there are no tests in our part of rural Africa. Our missionaries were able to visit him briefly the first week of September. He looked terrible. Absolutely gaunt.

On September 15, Crispo died young, presumably of AIDS.

It is such a sad finish to his blessed life. However, in his story and its end I can see lessons.

I am confident that he truly did get back with God following his wild spree in the world. Genuine restoration is really hard to fake when your friends know you well. So I am convinced that he is with our Lord now. But look at the price he paid for falling away!

Yes, but what lessons? Consider: Crispo was alive because of a genuine miracle. Yet even after this miraculous intervention, God did not coerce him into walking the straight and narrow. It was still his choice.

That choice is yours also. No matter how charmed your life, your future depends on the choices you make now. Right now. Like Crispo.

He deliberately stepped out from under the wings of God's protection, as Christ so beautifully put it with the example of a hen sheltering her chicks. It's easy to do, and it can happen to any of us. You, me, Crispo. None is perfect or exempt.

That, you see, is why Jesus gave us the privilege to ask for forgiveness and to start again. Being forgiven does not mean we no longer have to take responsibility for past actions.

Even though he was right with God in the end, Crispo was not divinely healed when the virus invaded. Why? Only the Lord can answer that.

The observation I would like to pass on is this: I've known people on death row who truly found Jesus and repented of the murders that they committed. They were forgiven. But God did not miraculously deliver them from their death sentences. However, he did give them the "peace that surpasses all understanding." They could then go on to a beautiful eternal life with Jesus.

Our Father loves us, but he does not control us. So be prepared for the consequences if you step out of his will for your life.

22

Roadside Bandits

Not many people today recognize the names Martin and Osa Johnson. Some of my old friends (by "old" I mean "up in years") remember them. In the 1930s the Johnsons made a career of wandering around Africa taking many, many pictures and writing articles. They appeared regularly in *National Geographic*, for example. Martin, stalwart and handsome in his pith helmet, looked every inch the Master of the African Bush. But it was Osa—perky, pretty little Osa—who stole readers' hearts.

"When I was growing up in the forties," a friend told me, "the pictures, all in black-and-white, which the Johnsons sent home *were* Africa. The sum of my opinions and dreams and impressions of the continent came from them. And I think that was true for much of my generation."

The pictures she is talking about were of vast herds of gnu (called wildebeest in those days), elephants, and spring-loaded Thompson gazelles thundering across unending veldt, often filmed from a low-flying airplane. Those uniquely shaped acacia trees studded sparce grassland, usually shown in silhouette against a sunset sky. Black men with spears posed on top of termite nests. Photos showed the Johnsons lounging at the front door of a canvas tent, surrounded by wooden crates. In the celluloid world of these early chroniclers, there was no urban development, no civil unrest, no death and mutilation, no crime or bribery, no dust—not even dirty clothes. They didn't sweat on camera. In black and white, they portrayed an Eden on the equator.

Africa in full color is much, much more real than that. Infinitely more! The veldt does not really go on forever, but when you make the long haul from Jo'burg to Lichinga through Zimbabwe, it sure seems to. Herds still thunder, but they are smaller herds. The land is as flat as ever, and widely spaced thorn trees still dot sparse grasslands.

And it is so very beautiful, the land. Photography cannot capture it adequately. When the equatorial sun pours down out of the blue, the whole country shimmers. "Heat waves," you say. "Most areas get them." Yes. But it's not just the heat. There is a golden vibrancy to it beyond mere heat waves. The dirt itself changes colors as you drive across the plains. So do the termite mounds.

Game, though, is not nearly so numerous or visible as the Johnsons' photos would lead you to think. During the heat of day particularly, you're lucky to glimpse some creature afar off. But you do glimpse them, and looking for wildlife is a constant pleasure.

When the Johnsons did their work, very few motor roads penetrated the interior. Only the hardiest souls ventured into the bush. Land Rovers, the British version of the American Jeep, so to speak, were the only vehicles that could negotiate the dirt tracks. Now a network of good roads has opened up the interior. Not the kind of roads you'd want to travel in a sports car, but good roads. These roads make journeys of a thousand miles or more at least feasible, if not comfortable. And Africa is so vast, it takes a thousand miles to get you from place to place.

But it is not Eden. Death, misery, and unsavory characters abound. The Johnsons never mentioned that part of it.

Bandits, for instance.

The civil war in Moz did not confine itself to that country. It disrupted the whole region. When the war ended, a generation of fighting men suddenly had no war to fight and no cause to which they ought be loyal. The various government factions no longer paid them money to take up arms. Many became outlaws, simply because there was not much else for them to become.

Even as disenfranchised soldiers sought a place in the sun, floods of starving refugees washed back and forth across borders. The homeless, the shell-shocked, the orphaned all wandered around without regard to whose country this might be. Chaos. It was pure chaos. That chaos spilled over heavily into Zimbabwe to the west of Moz.

Government leaders in Zimbabwe did their best to handle the extraordinary conditions. They found themselves combating thousands of outlaws and trying to feed tens of thousands of refugees and wanderers. I'm amazed that they handled the hopeless task as well as they did.

The situation is settling now. Conditions have improved. In fact, by September of 1997, as I was leading a four-pickup convoy from RSA to Lichinga, travel was considered reasonably safe.

As always when travelling from the Republic of South Africa to northern Mozambique, we took the road that runs straight through the heart of Zimbabwe. Zimbabwe's capital, Harare, is in the north of the country. Once you cross the border, you drive through an awful lot—I mean an awful lot!—of high plains to get there. From there we would angle up to Blantyre in Malawi then northwest to home.

There is only one public campground between the southern border and Harare. I am not much at night driving, but it was too early to stop there. So we elected to push on to Harare, an additional four hours away.

We had travelled two of those four hours when I simply became too tired to safely drive any farther. I was knackered, and so were my travelling companions. We stopped at a roadside park, not much more than a wide spot in the road. The party contained nine of us, and we drove four vehicles, so we never guessed that the roadside bandits would bother us. Were we ever wrong.

Around 11:00 p.m. a Land Rover pulled in front of my pickup and ten men got out. Fortunately, I am an extremely light sleeper. I awoke immediately, alert for trouble.

I grabbed my flashlight and shown it into some very scary-looking faces. I shouted in as gruff a voice as I could, "What do you want?"

The leader moved out of the light and walked over behind our camp while a second man circled to the other side. The leader started urinating right behind the head of one of the women.

I knew we had to show our numbers quickly.

"Intruders!" I yelled. "Everybody up!"

When those cheeky outlaws saw nine bodies rising out of sleeping bags, they ran back to their Land Rover, piled in, and peeled rubber getting away.

But we weren't safe. We knew they would come back bringing

reinforcements, so we hastily broke camp and pushed on to Harare. It was a long, long, hard, hard night, but we thanked the Lord that he helped us bluff our way out of a bad situation.

You see, I'm sure that the bandits didn't realize that there were only three adult men in our group. The other two thirds sitting up when alerted were women and children.

23

The Village of Love Gets Closed down—Sort Of

Gabriel

The civil war pretty much resolved itself in 1992. I can't exactly say that normalcy returned to Moz, but little by little, life settled down. People returned to farming and herding. Children began again to laugh, to sit in the evening listening to the old ones' tales, to learn the ways of their parents and ancestors. Little boys dreamed up mischief. The older girls fell in love.

I am repeatedly amazed by the resiliency of the people. Many of these folks drove through hell with the windows rolled down, to quote a friend. Yet they are able to pick up the threads of their lives as soon as that is possible. And they can build new lives.

Unfortunately, that is a generality, a swath painted with too broad a brush, because not all is normal and ordinary, by far. Healing has occurred, yes, but not everywhere and not for everyone. There are still wide, wide cracks in the social fabric, holes not yet mended. Through those cracks fell a horrific number of children.

Gabriel's story illustrates what I am trying to explain as well as any. And remember as you read about him that there are scores of similar stories I could tell.

Gabriel walked into the Village of Love in December of 1997, at the beginning of the rainy season. This was five years after the official end of turmoil. In theory the war was over and everything was now okay. He said he was ten years old.

I have never seen a skinnier child. "Bag of bones" may be a cliché, but it was a thoroughly apt description of him. His eyes were vacant in a way I cannot describe. If you have ever seen it, you know what I'm talking about. But few, especially where life is bountiful, have seen that tortured, distant look. In addition, he suffered with a large ulcer on one leg.

The dull facial expression, the lack of muscle and total lack of body fat, the ulceration, all bespoke starvation. And yet, although he was indeed starving to death, he only asked for medicine for his leg.

He spoke no Portuguese, but I managed to round up an interpreter who could communicate with him. Through the interpreter we learned that the boy lived in the Lugenda village just one mile from us. But his mother refused to feed him. According to her, the child was simple-minded and not worth the food. Food was too scarce to waste. Giving it to a mental incompetent, naturally, would be a waste.

The child therefore was left to forage in the bush, eating whatever he could find. It was obvious that he wasn't finding much.

We tended the ulceration, and I gave him some rice and beans left over from my lunch. I told him to return the next day.

At 6:00 a.m. the next morning, he appeared at my door as instructed, to get his leg rebandaged. Could I simply dress his ulceration and send him back into the bush? Does a concert pianist play only one note?

So Crispo and I loaded him into the bakkie and drove him to his village. We intended to ask his family if he could come live with us. The grandfather greeted us, for the mother was gone off somewhere.

The grandfather's attitude apparently mirrored the family's.

"You want to take him? Do so! We don't want him."

Through the interpreter I asked Gabriel to fetch his things. There were no things. He possessed nothing but the rags he was wearing.

Crispo took Gabriel home to his own house and fed him breakfast. By that afternoon, Gabriel had been wormed, bathed, fed again, and put into clean clothes. In just those few hours, he was looking a little better.

And he was bubbling over with joy. I don't know where he got the energy, as emaciated as he was, but he effervesced. He kept thanking us for the food. He said he had never before eaten three times in one day.

We took him to the district clinic the next day and had some basic tests run. For starters, he was severely anemic. There was little we could do about that except pump him full of iron tablets and good food. The clinic staff claimed that his was the worst case of malnutrition they had seen since the war ended.

To make a long story short, Gabriel turned out to not be nearly as simple-minded as his mother thought. After a few weeks of nutritious food, he started school. Did just fine there, too.

You see, biochemically speaking, the human nervous system needs fatty building blocks. You've heard of fatty acids and lipids. I'm oversimplifying, but if there is no fat in the diet, the brain cannot function well. A child's brain and nerves cannot develop well. Adequate protein and fatty substances were God's means of working his miracles in Gabriel. The lad blossomed.

But Gabriel didn't just get smarter, so to speak. According to Crispo, he was always a grateful child, ever ready to help around the house. Every so often he would go to the village and pick fresh fruit for me as a thank you gift. To say that he touched the hearts of all of us is a gross understatement.

Gabriel has advanced to the second grade now, and he is growing at a rapid rate.

I have already mentioned that Gabriel's story is only one of many. So many children's stories have no happy ending. And when I think of Gabriel's recovery, it brings to my mind a story about a little boy picking up starfish that had washed up on a beach after a storm.

A passer-by happened to see the little boy fling a starfish back into the surf to save it from dying on the sand.

"Here now!" the man told him. "Look at the hundreds of stranded starfish here. There must be thousands along this coast. It is impossible to save them all. You're just wasting your time. What you're doing doesn't matter."

The little boy simply picked up another starfish and threw it out into the sea as he replied, "It matters to that one."

That's how I feel about our work.

True, I get very frustrated seeing so many children needing help and not having the means or opportunity to help them all. But then there is Gabriel. It mattered to that one.

So I praise God that I can make a difference in the lives of those whom we are able to reach!

Did I say frustrated? Let's talk about frustration.

Closed Down!

In July 1998, half a year after Gabriel came to us, government officials closed down the Village of Love. Their reason: the facility was no longer needed. After all, the war was over.

We had thirty children under our care. Whatever could we do with them? Simply turning them out and closing the doors was unthinkable.

Thirteen of them we returned to their villages. In theory, at least, a village takes care of its own. And they do try. But many villages are too poor, live too close to the edge to be able to take in another hungry child. The fate of those thirteen was uncertain despite their villages' best intentions.

We were able to hastily place the others in church families. The officials allowed them to stay where they were put.

Although we were no longer an orphanage, with a lot of wheeling and dealing and finagling, we managed to open a mission station across the road from the old VOL. This mission station was not an orphanage and therefore could not actively accept children. And we certainly could not go out asking to take in children as we had done with Gabriel a few months before. But if a child comes in and sits down waiting to be fed, why, what could you do? Feed him, of course. And if he does not leave at sundown? Well, I guess he'll just have to stay the night.

Ten of those thirteen sent out into villages returned to us within thirty days. One boy walked for four days through lion country to get back to VOL because he had no remaining family in his village, not even extended family. Too, he wanted to continue his education.

The three children who did not return were too young to travel alone. However, they have been placed with a family that is taking good care of them.

And so the Village of Love is still caring for children, but we are doing so unofficially, without the formal sanction of the government. As a mission station, we operate under different rules from orphanages, and those rules are in some ways more amenable to what we want to accomplish. The long and short of it: when Satan sets a stumbling block before us, he trips and falls on his face.

Although we operate unofficially, the very same people who closed us down have now officially sent us a child for whom they could not find a home. The local government leader has also sent us many children from the area. Cholera and malaria are still far too common, and those diseases far too often take mothers, leaving their children orphaned.

So we are closed. As of this writing, our "closed" facility is caring for fifty-four children. Fifty-four starfish being thrown back into the sea.

They have nowhere else to go.

STEP THREE:

The Molding of a Missionary

24

Texas Horse Lover

Before I continue with this narrative of my African adventures, I would like to fill you in on how I got there. It is also instructive, I believe, to show what God had to work with in order to create a missionary, and how I was changed.

Like so many "horsey" girls, I grew up with the childhood dream of becoming a veterinarian. I dearly loved all animals, not just horses. But horses were it. And because I lived in Texas, horses and cowboys and all were a tradition as much as a dream.

My family loved to rodeo (yes, rodeo is officially a verb; it means to take part in rodeo events, especially competitively). So I grew up on top of a horse. I was riding independently when I was three, and I was breaking and training my own horses by age twelve. That in itself was a dream come true.

And then there is my competitive nature. I've always been that way, wanting to excel and accepting challenges I shouldn't. That spirit of competition led me into many sports, but horses remained my first love.

Then I was sent off to church camp during my twelfth summer. There I learned how much Jesus loved me, and I accepted him as my Lord and Savior. Two years later, I vividly remember, I was looking at the sky as I was riding in our car when I sensed that Jesus had something very special that he wanted me to do for him. I had no idea what it was, and the incident soon faded into the background.

Actually, it was pretty much crowded out. My teenage years were filled with horse shows, sports, and academics. What more could a horsey girl want? Oh, sure, I was a Christian in the way so many young women are. I didn't just go through motions. I really did like Jesus. He was my best friend. But that was all he was. I was not totally committed or even devoted. Loving Jesus was the right thing to do, so I did it.

And then that good old competitive nature paid off. I always strived to be the best that I could be in whatever I put my hand to. These efforts were greatly rewarded when I graduated second in my high-school class. This earned me an academic scholarship to Texas A&M University. Now to those of you who don't know, Texas A&M is *the* dream of anyone wanting a vet degree. It is as good as a school can get in several fields, and that is one of them.

On top of it all, I was also honored by being chosen to go to Europe as a People to People Ambassador with the national 4-H Club. It was my first overseas experience. Life was wonderful beyond words. Things were going better than I ever imagined they could.

Then reality hit. This small-town girl, scholar though she was, met the rough grade of a major university. It's like throwing a guppy into Lake Erie and saying, "Sink or swim."

I adjusted well to the academics. I kept my grades up. They weren't perfect but pretty close. Nearly all As. That part was all right.

But spiritually? I began to waiver. The excitement and busyness of university life soon drew me away from the Lord. My days were filled with agricultural classes, a part-time job, and a boyfriend. I trust you remember how much time a serious romance erases from each day.

During my second year, things began to unravel. For one thing, my childhood dream of going to vet school was shattered. Even though my grades were high, that wasn't good enough, especially for a woman aspiring to veterinary medicine in the mid '70s. Discouraged and angry, I changed my major to commercial production of poultry. My boyfriend and I married, but even that fell apart by the time I graduated in 1977.

There are not a whole lot of openings for a commercial poultry producer.

By now my life was pretty much a mess. A failed marriage was still a severe stigma then, and my education seemed a waste. Today I can look back and see how the Lord used the disappointments to change my medical interests from animals to people. But then, as I was living those days, my attitude was even more a mess than was my life story.

In 1976 a new concept began in the field of pre-hospital emergency care. The idea was that trained medical professionals who were not doctors would be first on the scene to handle emergency calls. The pioneers in this movement envisioned qualified emergency care in every corner of every county, no matter how rural.

In addition to transporting patients, these trained personnel would do the preliminary assessment and render immediate aid. Today we take these professionals for granted. Emergency medical technicians (EMTs) and paramedics are an accepted part of every city and town's emergency response. The pioneers' dream is a reality. Even all-volunteer fire departments can render excellent aid quickly. But back then it was a new thing, and not everyone thought it a good idea.

I sure did. I became increasingly interested in emergency medicine. It was an exciting line of work with lots of adrenaline rushes (and lots of boredom waiting for the next call). And it certainly fed into my competitive need to be the best possible—nothing is more needful than to provide lifesaving service quickly.

After four months of training, I became an emergency medical technician and began working ambulance for a county hospital. Assisting during my spare time in the emergency room (ER to most folks) and intensive care unit (ICU) of that hospital gave me the idea and initiative to go on to nursing school. In 1980 I began a new career, not in poultry but as a registered ICU nurse.

And my spiritual growth? Don't ask.

During this time I was badly backslidden, to say the least. I was living with a lover. And my only goal was to buy enough land to start an Arabian horse ranch, so I could enter the world of endurance racing.

In an endurance race, a horse and rider must cover a hundred miles in less than twenty-four hours. There are mandatory vet checks along the way, and other devices ensure that the race is conducted humanely. But is it ever grueling! It requires ultimate fitness of both horse and rider, as well as perseverance and determination. You can see how that would appeal to my basic nature.

By the age of twenty-eight, with the help of my lover, I had obtained my prized stallion and an eighteen-acre ranch. True, I was $95,000 in debt, but hey! Dreams aren't cheap, and mine were coming true.

Yet I felt a void in my life. I wasn't happy, and I couldn't figure out why. I was getting everything I wanted. What was wrong with me?

As I walked toward the house from my barn one afternoon, I looked up at the sky and remembered Jesus. He'd been my best friend as a teenager. Back in those days, I talked to him as if he were walking next to me.

So I struck up a conversation again. I asked him what was wrong with my life. Why did I feel so empty inside?

A few days later, I got his answer.

25

Why me, Lord?

You've read the poem "The Village Blacksmith" by Henry Wadsworth Longfellow, haven't you? "Under the spreading chestnut tree the village smithy stands..." Most people get it in grade school. The blacksmith it describes is a spiritually honest man who has lost much but still values life. There really are such blacksmiths.

A few days later, after I started talking to Jesus again, I met a spirit-filled farrier and his wife, Dee. He was out to shoe my horses. As you know, farriers are essentially blacksmiths who do shoeing.

They saw my live-in lover situation, and I think they saw the emptiness, too. He and Dee began a quiet and very subtle persuasion.

Nine months passed. By then we were pretty good friends. One day Dee invited me out to her house. There she dropped the bomb, so to speak, when she showed me 1 Corinthians 6:9 in the Bible. This verse lists ten sins that shall not enter heaven. When she read "sexually immoral," I flew into a rage and stomped out of her house.

I realized that Dee's message to me was this: I was born again since childhood, and I thought that I had a ticket to heaven no matter what happened later in my life. I didn't realize that by deliberately living in sin, I was cancelling that ticket. Now some theologians claim "once saved, always saved," but eternal life is nothing to take chances with. What if they're wrong?

From childhood I'd known that the Bible was the truth, and now Dee had used that Bible to confront me with the fact that I might not be going to heaven. By the time I drove home, I'd cooled off a bit. At least I had the sense to ask Jesus to please confirm to me that I was living wrongly.

Over the next nine months, he did just that. My lover was laid off work and had to move to another town to get a job. Our "love" weakened and finally ended. Finally, I admitted I was wrong. In my own living room, I asked the Lord to forgive my sins. I rededicated my life to him.

I remembered the message he'd given me at age fourteen, too. So I told him I was ready to do whatever he had planned for me.

No immediate answer came to that one. I called up Dee and asked if I could ride with them to church the next Sunday. The closest spirit-filled church was in another town sixty miles away. She readily agreed, and God's plan was in motion. It's amazing; it's absolutely amazing how all sorts of strange threads, each different and diverse, weave together into God's plan.

Two months later as I sat in Tree of Life Church, New Braunfels, Texas, a missionary spoke about smuggling Bibles into China. As she ended her talk, she said, "If you feel called to missions, you are welcome."

My stomach suddenly jumped as if I'd gone down a steep incline in a roller coaster. I didn't understand what it meant until Dee passed me a note, saying, "I just had a vision of you training as a missionary and using your medical skills as well." The message didn't just impact me. It slugged me. I thought my heart would stop.

My immediate thoughts were, *Lord, you've got to be joking! Me, a missionary! Hah!* I don't remember anything after that. I love to eat, but I could hardly touch my food. I was in shock, plain and simple.

Driving home I asked Dee where a person gets training to become a missionary. She named off several schools, but when she mentioned Oral Roberts University, I sensed that this was where the Lord wanted me to go. I agreed to call them the next day for information.

After Dee and that saintly blacksmith let me off at my pickup, I asked the Lord, *Why me? I have everything material I ever wanted. I earned every bit of it with blood, sweat, and tears. Now you expect me to give it all up and become a missionary! Why do I have to go?*

This time he responded immediately by giving me this message in my thoughts. *I will use your agriculture, your nursing, and your ability to rough it.*

I am a practical person, and he gave me a practical answer. I appreciated that then, and I still do. From that moment, I accepted my assignment and drove on home. I wasn't sure what I had just agreed to, but I had given him my word.

I grew up loving the Old West and the cowboy code that states that a person's word is something no man can take away from him or her. When you give your word on something, you stick to it until the job is done. In fact, as a youngster I told God that I was mad at him because he had allowed me to be born 150 years too late! I wanted to be a pioneer in the Old West. Little did I know that he was about to fulfil that particular desire of my heart.

The fun began at 2:00 p.m. that Sunday afternoon, July 28, 1988. I was hemming a pair of blue jeans at my dining room table and listening to a John Michael Talbot tape. I had fallen in love with that tape and listened to it constantly. Suddenly the words on the tape seemed to jump out at me, saying, "The spirit of the Lord is upon you, the spirit of the Lord has anointed you."

This was followed a few minutes later by the line, "Father, I give my life to you."

That last sentence was exactly what I had said to the Lord in that very room just two months before.

As I sat there puzzled by what was going on, I heard a man's voice speak to me over my right shoulder, "I want the afternoon with you."

I jumped up and looked around, but no one was there. I checked every room in the house. *Nadie.* I began to think I was losing my mind.

I sat down, nervous and uncertain, and started sewing again.

The voice came again but more firmly, "I want the afternoon with you."

I froze. *This has to be the Lord,* I realized, *because no one else is here.* So I said aloud, "Okay, Lord, you've got it. I understand you want me to be a missionary. Mind telling me where I'm going?" A beautiful picture came before my eyes of a golden wheat field ready to harvest. It was surrounded by mature oak trees.

All he said was, "Africa".

I got excited then, because I had always liked the idea of Africa. Its exotic ruggedness appealed to me. It was dark. Mysterious.

Even though I was a baby Christian, I knew that the golden wheat field represented the harvest of souls waiting to hear the Gospel. But what did the oak trees mean?

Six months later, Anne, the lady who discipled me, would show me the answer. In Isaiah 61:3 the Lord describes the righteous as oak trees, planted for the display of His splendor. I was to become an oak tree.

That vision was only the first of many things he showed me over the next two hours. At first I would ask a question aloud, and he would drop the answer into my head. But as I became more comfortable with our conversation, I would only have to think the question, and the answer was there before I could open my mouth.

First, I was told what I could keep, what I was allowed to sell, *and what I had to give away!* That was the killer! Everything on the givea-way list was something I treasured. They were things that I either idolized, putting them before God, or obtained in my immoral rela-tionship with my lover.

My stallion and his dam, worth over $10,000 together, were first on the list. I loved my horses as if they were my children! How could I give them away? My prized ranch, the TV and VCR, and my pickup (cowgirl's status symbol) had to be traded for a small station wagon (no status at all, at least in my eyes).

I was crushed, but I had given my word. I would do it no matter how much it hurt. I shed many a tear before it was over.

Please realize that the Lord did not have to actually mark everything down on each separate list. As I would look at an item, I would just know somehow which list it was on.

His final instructions came as an even bigger shock. I was to move to Tulsa, Oklahoma, and attend church on the ORU campus *before* September first. That gave me only a month to get rid of everything.

I cried out, "But Lord! You know I've tried to sell this ranch for eighteen months! There's no market. How do I do it?"

He responded, "Let it go."

I argued, of course. "I have always paid my debts. Dumping the ranch and not paying it off is going to ruin my credit rating!"

He replied, "*Let it go!* Where you're going, you won't need a credit rating."

Now that *really* upset me! My whole life thus far was solidly based on materialism and credit ratings. You can't survive without that stuff in this day and age, right? My head was spinning with the shock of all this.

Ah, but as I said, the fun was just beginning.

26

The Fun Continues

The morning after my heart-shaking chat with God, I called the saddlery shop. I had just purchased a $7,000 custom-made horse trailer with living quarters. I told the owner of the shop that the Lord wanted me to become a missionary and asked if I could return the trailer. I thought sure he'd think I was a nut case. Shucks, *I* was beginning to think I was a nut case!

But instead he asked, "How fast can you return it?"

"Huh?"

"I have a buyer who wants that exact design."

He tore up my check, and I lost nothing on the deal. That was my first lesson in seeing God's plan in action when one follows his orders. Apparently I wasn't a nut case after all.

This is not to say that everything went like peaches and cream. That Monday night at work, I explained my experiences from the day before to my Christian boss. A non-Christian nurse overheard our conversation. She reported to the medical director of our ICU that I was hearing voices and selling everything I owned to go work for God in Africa.

That Friday, when I walked into the ICU, I was escorted by two doctors to a private room for counselling. They ordered me to use tranquilizers and sleep for the next three days. They said I was overworked and not thinking rationally. If I didn't report to work on the following Monday looking rested and thinking more clearly, they would sign me into a mental hospital for a thirty-day psychiatric evaluation.

I just stared at them in stunned silence. The whole time they were talking, I felt wrapped in a warm blanket. I didn't get mad or upset at what they said. I accepted the prescription and calmly walked out to my car.

Once inside my car, that "blanket of peace" dissolved. I suddenly realized that they thought I was crazy! I was furious! How dare they call me looney! I drove straight to Dee's house and told her the story.

She rolled on the floor with laughter. Well, not literally, but you know what I mean. Here I was, mad as a cat in a bath, and she was laughing! What was going on?

When she finally got control of herself, she explained, "Brenda, when you are stepping out of sin into the will of God, Satan comes against you with anything he thinks will stop you! God protected you by keeping you calm in front of the doctors. If you had shown your anger in front of them the way you spilled it to me, they probably would have committed you immediately!"

And I could see then that had that happened, it would have messed up God's time schedule for my training in Tulsa. So I relaxed and enjoyed my three-day paid holiday!

As I thought about it, I realized I needed that time to get the garage sale together for the following Saturday. It was amazing to see people coming from everywhere, asking for my cats and dogs. Everything I had for sale was gone in seven days! Within three weeks, the giveaway items were gone also.

I drove up to Tulsa the third Saturday in August and attended church the next morning at Oral Roberts University, as I had been instructed to do. His plan was unfolding as scheduled.

Actually, until I got there I didn't realize that Oral Roberts didn't have a church. The church in question was Victory Christian Center with Pastors Billy Joe and Sharon Daugherty. I had just walked into the start of their week-long "Word Explosion." Speakers from all over the world come to share the Word of God with thousands of Christians from throughout the United States.

Quite an eye-opener for this baby Christian! As I sat in the sessions, I not only learned about the Lord but about Victory's Bible and Mission school program. It didn't take me long to realize that this was the church and school the Lord wanted me to attend.

The next day I called the City of Faith hospital and inquired again about a job interview. I had already called once from Texas. At that time they didn't have any openings in ICU. This time they not only had an opening, I could choose which shift I wanted! I worked there until the hospital closed nine months later. It was here that the Lord began to show me how to combine medicine with faith for healing.

In May 1990 I graduated from Victory's Bible school and applied for missions school. I was now debt-free and had the required tuition and living expenses that would sustain me through the ninety-day missions course.

But I had a problem. I didn't know what country in Africa I was going to. One of the school's requirements is that you write a research paper on the country the Lord is calling you to. So I asked him to please tell me where I was going.

His answer: "Buy a TV."

"What?" I couldn't have heard that right!

He repeated it.

Well, okay. If you say so, Lord. So I went out and purchased a television set. Talk about TV remote roulette! What was I supposed to see? I landed on a Christian channel and found that I was strongly attracted to a program showing starving African kids in an orphanage in Mozambique.

That night I couldn't sleep. I kept seeing those kids' faces. Finally, I sat up and asked, "Lord, are you trying to tell me that I am supposed to go to that orphanage?"

No answer; just a sudden peace. The faces went away.

The next day I called that ministry and found out how to get an application. I knew I was going and put out the word in my newsletter long before I was accepted.

Five weeks after graduation, I landed in South Africa. In March 1991 my real training began as I entered war-ravaged Mozambique.

27

Welcome to the Real World

Mozambique was a fertile ground for sacrificial ministry. I have said more than once that its needs are very great. Basically, the country had been at war since the 1960s.

First, they struggled long and hard to gain their independence from Portugal. They finally accomplished that in 1975. Then a civil war broke out between political factions. Who would rule? Whose vision of the future would prevail? That fighting went on for another seventeen years.

Moz received a double whammy when a severe drought hit the southern part of the country in the early 1980s. By the time Moz's plight became known abroad, the country's food supply was basically gone. Many children were left homeless and starving. This orphanage was started to help alleviate the suffering for some.

It was a large complex, as I described at the beginning of the book. I was assigned to be the children's supervisor for the 127 orphans who lived there.

During my first year of service I learned the many do's and don'ts of operating a Mozambican orphanage. I also gained experience in children's ministry when I planted the first children's church in that area. I have already related how, every Sunday, over a hundred kids would come sit under a huge shade tree to learn about Jesus. The local church pastor's wife and I worked together, as most of the kids did not understand Portuguese. The lessons had to be taught in the local tribal language. One thing we strongly emphasized was the evil of the witch doctor's medicine.

As I also related before, in February of 1992, the Lord clearly showed me his vision for my life. I was to go into northern Mozambique and build a home for the orphaned and abandoned kids. I have described how the witch doctors, whom I had so severely offended with the Christian message, placed a curse on me, which a wise doctor in the United States eventually recognized and lifted.

I already told you in the chapter Kaboom about the trip into northern Moz under the auspices of Operation Mobilization. We had many other challenges also, some of them rather interesting.

For example, the road leading from the Mozambican border to Lichinga, our target city, was heavily trenched and rutted. The distance is only about ninety miles, but it took fourteen hours to traverse.

Darkness fell too soon. The road was not one you could negotiate by headlight. The shadows and ruts were too deceptive. So we made camp thirty miles from the border in some old deserted brick buildings.

Well, we thought they were deserted. The next morning we awoke to find ourselves surrounded by soldiers armed with machine guns. We were camping in their regional headquarters! To avoid imprisonment, our interpreter and leaders had to have a quick peace conference with their leaders. A few hours later, the problem was finally resolved, and we were allowed to leave. Even though the war was officially over in 1992, this area had not yet been disarmed by the United Nations.

The incident points up the fact that nothing I had so far experienced in the United States could be depended upon in Moz. And that is still true. I don't think that when people in North America think of culture shock, they realize how profound such differences are. The cultures of Moz are totally, fundamentally alien to North American ways. Certainly not wrong. Not bad. Just very, very different, from the core on out. It took me a long time to develop a real understanding and appreciation of the differences—to be able to freely adapt to Moz attitudes and ways.

On our return trip to South Africa, I was dropped off in Zimbabwe to attend a week-long bush survival camp operated by Christian friends of mine. I knew beyond a doubt that the Lord wanted me to attend this camp but didn't understand why I needed such extensive training.

And it was exotic, if I do so say so. We learned how to prevent and handle wild animal attacks from lion, leopard, elephant, hippo, and snakes. We received lessons in identifying and using edible and medicinal plants. Tracking and bush survival were also included. Until the Lord showed me where to put the Village of Love in 1995, I had no idea how significant this training would be. I can't tell you how many times I've thanked him for the knowledge I gained during that week in survival camp.

Although I started out at O.M.'s base camp in RSA, I was assigned to go to their facility in southern Moz. But as I was having my quiet time with the Lord one morning, he clearly impressed on me that I was to go north now and fulfil the vision.

I responded, "But Lord! You know I have another year's commitment to O.M." There I was arguing again, so I amended it. "I'll gladly go, of course, but I need you to tell the leaders."

A few days later, the Mozambican leader asked me, "Brenda, are you still wanting to go into northern Moz?"

I responded with a big "Yes!"

He nodded. "The Lord told me that I am to release you to go north now to fulfil a vision." Then he phoned the leader for southern Africa, but before he could say much, the leader informed him that Brenda was to be released now. "She is to go north to fulfil the vision that God has given her, and we will not stand in her way."

I was dumbfounded, to say the least. Without saying a word, I had just been released from my commitment. I was free to go north. But how, and with whom? I knew no one working up there and had no pickup. The area we were talking about was very remote, and there was no reliable public transport.

An O.M. leader gave me a tip on whom to call, and I was soon on the trail of a missionary couple in northern Moz. Frits and Nicky, who were praying for a nurse/children's evangelist to join them. A week later they and their family flew into Port Elizabeth, RSA, for a month's rest. The Lord confirmed to all of us that I was to join them. The *who* question was answered. The transportation problem remained to be resolved.

That problem too was solved a few days later when I received a $3,000 check from the USA. Five months before, you see, the Lord had told me to close my savings account and use the money to buy equipment. But he never told me what equipment. I'd sent for the funds, but due to some paperwork hassles, the sum was delayed in arriving.

Now the money was here, and there was no questioning what equipment I needed to buy with it. I soon found a bright yellow 1984 Isuzu 2.2 diesel pickup. My own bakkie, to use the local term. Within a few weeks, money had been donated to fix it up with a canopy, bull bar, trailer hitch, off-road tires, and the necessary repairs it needed before going into such a remote area.

This elegant rig was infinitely more than a cowgirl's status symbol! It was a bright yellow symbol of God's providence.

Nicky and the two children flew to Malawi to await the arrival of Frits and me in the yellow bakkie. Frits bought a small trailer for his family's things, so we were heavily loaded. The 2,500 kilometer (1,200 mile) trip to Malawi would take us at least four days. We made it, but not without a little excitement, as I have related in Double Donkey Trouble.

A week later we left Malawi with all five of us crammed into the pickup. Two adults and one child could sit up front, while one adult and one child sat in the back on top of one of my metal trunks.

Travel was incredibly slow over the badly rutted and potted roads. Darkness caught us ninety kilometers (fifty miles) before we reached their home in Cuamba. One of the last bridges we had to cross sagged badly in the middle. As we crossed, the undercarriage caught on the bridge, damaging the brake system. Frits worked for an hour to free the jammed handbrake. We drove the last thirty kilometers (fifteen miles) without much brake, but the terrain was flat and, praise His name, we made it safely.

So there we were, experienced missionaries and the raw young recruit from the States who took everything as a competitive challenge and had lots and lots still to learn.

28

Final Training

During World War II in America, the men went out to fight and the women took over the jobs men had left. We became riveters and tractor operators. We built ships that sailed as well as any built with masculine hands and airplanes that flew quite as nicely, thank you. Then the men came home.

A generation later women again moved into occupations once considered masculine pursuits. Today we are as likely to be found designing airplanes as riveting them. We've fought persistently for the freedom to work in the occupations of our choice, and that war is not yet won. But in Africa it has hardly begun. In most African cultures, women are not recognized as work leaders outside the home.

This proved to be something of a hindrance to me, because during my eighteen months in Cuamba, I had to supervise Mozambican work crews building a mud hut compound. The problem was multiplied by the fact that my Portuguese needed a lot of improvement. Communication was difficult at best and hilarious at worst.

But the problem became a challenge, which became a lesson. By not shrinking back or shirking labor, I earned the respect of the better workers. I fired the rest. The arrangement worked out. The workers and I learned from one another, and we always managed to get the job done.

It was not an easy task. It was made harder by the fact that raw materials for building were extremely hard to find.

This, though, turned out to be my final training stage before plunging into the bush to begin bringing the vision to fruition.

But where was I to plunge? All the Lord had revealed to me was that the orphanage was to be built in the area where the Yao (Yow) and Macua (Ma-coo-ah) tribes mix. I had no idea where that was.

It didn't take Him long to show me.

In July 1994 I worked as interpreter for a Jesus Film team that was taking the film into the remote area of Majune (Ma-june-y) District. As they oriented me to the work, I was shown a map that divides the entire Niassa (Knee-ah-sah) Province into tribal language groups. Majune District is where the Yao and Macua tribes mix! I was ecstatic since the Lord was using this trip to show me my new home.

In October 1994 the Lord impressed me to write a proposal for a foster parent program and present it to the government. It was well received, and I was asked to begin immediately. I explained that I would first have to visit the USA and acquire the funds. A ninety-day stateside tour raised $12,000, and many signed on as monthly sponsors for the program.

The government wasn't nearly as impressed as I would have hoped. The available funding wasn't enough to do the job, they insisted. I finally convinced them that if I built the homes from local material, it would indeed be enough.

They finally agreed to give me the 200 hectares (550 acres) of land that I requested in Majune District. I was sent to find the land.

So how do you find one particular plot of less than a square mile that lies somewhere within many, many square miles of wild, un-surveyed bush? At first it seemed a daunting task. But all I had to do was ask. The Lord had already it picked out, and he guided me right to it.

The Administrator of Majune, the top government official of the area, must give permission for anyone to use land in his district. He told me I could pick out a place in the Lugenda River Valley, since I needed such a large area. This river is one of the largest in northern Mozambique, and the area is habitat for many wild animals. Elephant, hippo, crocodiles, hyena, lions, leopards, baboons, fox, jackal, different types of antelope, and many kinds of deadly snakes call it home.

Now I knew why God sent me to that bush survival course. I was being planted in an area where one mistake could be your last. This was no place for the inexperienced and untrained. Once I had chafed because training and preparation were taking so much time. I now understood why.

It was too late to start the land search on the day I arrived at the Lugenda River, so I camped at our guide's hut in the Lugenda Village. Supper was fresh fish roasted over a campfire. As we prepared for bed, Bernardo, our guide, brought out his only piece of furniture, a bed made from palmetto stems.

It touched me deeply to see the hearts of these forgotten people. They had been cut off from the world by thirty years of war. Their only possessions were things they made from local materials. Cooking pots were native clay, fish traps were of bamboo. And the bed, very simply wrought. They have to guard their few chickens inside their small mud hut at night. They had so little, yet they willingly gave up their bed so that I could sleep off the ground.

The next morning I explained to Bernardo that I was looking for two hundred hectares of land with a good water source and rich soil for farming. I explained why we needed it.

"Ah!" He knew just the place. The piece we were looking for was less than a mile up the road. It has an underground spring that has run for over thirty years without drying up in the peak of the dry season. Its source is an underground river, which runs under a low area that is perfect for growing rice. Two small plateaus on the land were perfect for building houses and growing the crops we'd need to help make us as self-sufficient as possible.

By May 18, 1995, we had obtained government approval for this land. My Mozambican work crew broke ground for the Village of Love, and the vision became reality.

29

It Ain't Easy

It is not easy to start a remote mission station from raw bush. With my eighteen-year-old nephew, Jason, three Moz guards who had come with me from Cuamba, and a work crew hired locally, we set to the task.

For the first three weeks, we slept in small tents that we placed around the building equipment. We tied our two guard dogs to trees nearby to alert us to any dangers.

The work crew cleared a living area about thirty by fifty yards, walled in with a bamboo stockade. Our fort had an open kitchen under a grass roof, a log storage room, and a good-ole outhouse with a separate bathing area for a private bucket bath. This, our home for the first nine months, gave us some security from thieves and wild animals.

By December 1995 we finished a small missions compound and five children's homes complete with outdoor kitchens and outhouses with bathing areas. All our houses were made of mud bricks sun-dried on site, homemade wooden doors, and windows cut from our own trees.

The floors were hard-packed dirt, and the roofs were made of grass and plastic "shingles." I learned how to make these shingles from a missionary in Malawi. With a few modifications, they have worked very well. During the five months of the rainy season, December to April, the constant precipitation can destroy a mud brick house in a couple days. With a good roof, though, a house will last indefinitely.

We accomplished much in that first year, and all the challenges were worth it once we saw the kids start flowing in. Some were refugees returning from camps in Tanzania and Malawi, while others were abandoned or misplaced kids who had been found in villages near us. All of them were suffering from malnutrition and intestinal worms.

The first thing I did when children were admitted was to give them wormer medicine. I would tell people, "I don't feed worms, just kids." Their clothes were mostly rags that they tied around themselves. To a person, they were a pitiful sight when they arrived, with little life in their eyes. Constant hunger and lack of love cause depression and hopelessness.

Words cannot describe the looks on their faces when they received two sets of clothes and a blanket! Most had never slept with a blanket, for even the flimsiest blankets cost a month's labor, about sixteen dollars American. Receiving three meals a day was also a first for all the kids. It was pure joy to see how rapidly they changed once they realized that they could stop worrying about their next meal. We enrolled them into school, and within a few months, most had settled into a "normal" lifestyle.

In 1996 we assisted about eighty children. Thirty of them ended up staying on permanently. Our goal, though, was to help any child in a difficult situation for as long as he or she needed it. Some stayed only a few months until their families were located, while others needed assistance until they could care for themselves as young adults. We soon built four more housing complexes.

Each house was run by Mozambican foster parents who had received Jesus. The children were raised according to Bible standards, and most came to church. By Easter 1997 most of our older children had accepted Jesus as their Lord and Savior. The changes in their countenance told us that they had truly been reborn by the love of our Lord.

By 1999 we were serving fifty-plus kids who were living at the Village of Love. I was doing what I wanted to do in the place God had planted me. I was satisfied.

And then he transplanted me.

STEP FOUR:

BALAMA

30

Balama or Bust!

In the United States, we drive around and stand in line a lot to obtain permits and papers and jump through all the legal hoops daily life puts before us. If, for example, you get a traffic ticket, you learn what frustration and long lines are. Or something as simple as a driver's licence renewal. They don't tell you this when you're young and rosy-cheeked and in high school. Well, you can't escape the paper hassle in Africa, a fact you don't appreciate when you're young and rosy-cheeked and in missions training.

If I were to go into exact detail about obtaining permits and papers and about the waiting and traveling that goes into it, this book would be eight hundred pages long, and the reader would be sound asleep. I will, of course, spare you all that. The bottom line is, it was time to renew my residency papers.

The easiest way to do this was to first travel up to the embassy in Malawi to get a new Moz residency visa. Malawi, you'll recall, is the lovely little country nested to the northwest of Moz on one of the world's great rift lakes. Blantyre, the major city at its south end, is most pleasant also.

So here I was, sitting in the embassy wondering where to go next. Our facility in Majune (VOL) was on its feet and running, serving the needs of the people around it. It appeared that my work there lay behind me and it was time to move on. But where? When I took up residence in Moz, in what area would I next hang my hat?

The word *Balama* dropped into my head. That's all I can say. One moment it wasn't there, and the next moment it was. Now I caution you that it may not always be the Lord speaking when something like that happens. Sometimes our brains do things our flesh desires when it's not God's plan at all. But this time I wasn't worried that it wasn't God speaking, because I had never heard of the place. I didn't even know if it was a place.

Still in waiting mode, I ambled over to a map of Moz on the wall. Let's see. I was in Blantyre, so I started surveying northern Moz, the area closest to Malawi, simply because that was what my eyes first scanned.

Moz has ten states, and I started at the top, the north end. The first one I studied, Cabo Delgado, is wedged into the extreme north along the coast. Whoa! Right there it was, in the western part of that state, in a western district (what we would call a county).

Balama.

Now I knew there was such a place, and I knew that was where God was sending me. But not instantly. This was March of 1999, the tail end of the rainy season. For all practical purposes the roads were still closed. I had a couple of months to get my act in gear and my necessary papers together.

By late May the rains were over and the roads again passable. My papers were all in order. Time to go home to a place I'd never seen.

Getting from Malawi to Cabo Delgado takes about two and a half days, maybe three, on the road. A pastor friend, who acted as interpreter as well as traveling companion, joined me, and we headed off up there. The last large town before Balama is called Montepuez.

We first sought out a missionary in Montepuez named Isenminger, with the Wycliffe translators. He was the only foreigner and Christian that I knew of out in that area. The man was shocked to see me. He was even more shocked when he found out what I intended to do.

"It is horribly isolated," he informed me. "When you leave Montepuez, you leave tar behind; the sealed roads end in town. There are no white people out there. The locals all speak Macua, and many don't even know Portuguese. It is highly dangerous, extraordinarily dangerous, for a woman to live alone out there," he insisted.

Hey. I knew that was where the Lord was sending me, and whom he sends he protects. Truly, I entertained no qualms. So off we went across another thirty-five-plus miles, and this leg of the trek was dirt road.

The dirt was in good condition considering that the rainy season had just ended. This was because the state is largely agricultural and the principal crop is cotton. Cotton growers have to get their trucks in and out, from the fields to the shipping points. So the farmers themselves do a lot of road and bridge repair to maintain access for their vehicles.

When I reached Balama, I presented a letter of introduction to the Assembly of God man out there, Pastor Joao (pronounced *Jow*). That part was simple. The church was easy to find. We drove right up to it, got out, went in, and handed the man my letter.

But how would it be received? After all, here was a stranger popping in, and a woman at that.

We were received with open arms. How awesome! We learned that this church had been praying for a year—a whole year!—that God would send someone to help them spread the Gospel. Although a few outlying churches existed, Balama and the district around it remained largely untouched.

Oh, and there was so much need! Devotional and explanatory literature such as believers in the States find helpful (and totally take for granted) did not exist. Worse, the people had no Bibles. The pastor had one or two. Nine churches out in nearby villages possessed not one Bible among them.

I had a few Portuguese editions in my truck. I gave them immediately to the pastor, still in awe.

Praying a whole year!

As is polite and customary, I was introduced to the top local government officials, including the county manager, or administrator as he's called there. The meeting with this man was amazing.

Even before we sat down, the first thing he asked was, "If you move to Balama as you say, what are you going to do for us? How can you help us?"

Now my heart, as you know, goes out to the country's many orphans. But that's a difficult program to simply walk into. So on the drive out from Montepuez, I had asked the Lord, "What do you want me to do? Where do we start?"

He had said, *Go in and tell them you want to start a boarding facility for students from outer areas so they can come in and receive an education beyond their village school.* Again, I recognized that this was from the Lord, because it was unusual and quite out of line with what we normally do.

I told the administrator what the Lord had given me.

His mouth dropped open. He walked over to his desk and picked up a sheaf of papers two inches thick. He said, "It must have been God who sent you. For two years we have been trying to get some organization to build us just such a facility. Our children finish the fifth grade in their village schools, but most can go no further unless they have relatives in Balama. Village parents are poor and can't afford to board their children in the towns. The students without family have nowhere to stay and no food if they leave their villages. Most of my district's children are limited to five years of schooling."

Can you imagine? Two years trying to get someone to help.

He promised us land to build on and asked, "When can you get started?"

On impulse I replied, "The first of August."

This was June.

Disaster

There were a lot of logistics involved in moving permanently to Balama. I had to find a pastor to go there with me. I had to register in Pemba, the state capital, and get all the many documents needed to register a church, myself, and other stuff (I started this chapter discussing paperwork, remember? Believe me. It never ends).

It took two days of constant pushing. And here is an amazing aside that shows what the Lord can do when He's eager to move: the Wycliffe leaders told me that they had *never* been able to get anything or anyone registered in only two days. They had professionals doing it, and they lived there!

I finished all that on August 1. On August 2, I drove to Balama and asked permission of the administrator to buy a house.

He was astounded when I walked in. "So many people promise us things," he said, "but they leave and never come back. Buy a house and get settled in. We'll go from there."

The next step was to meet with the director of education in that district. She was a lovely woman, enthusiastic about her work, and frustrated by the walls that the area's poverty had erected in front of her. I told her my plans, and she said, "Show me a diagram. What do you have in mind?"

I rolled my simple blueprint out across her table.

"Building with mud brick alone is going to be difficult, and mud brick has a limited life span. As I discussed with the administrator, we want to build with a concrete foundation and floor, mud brick walls, and a tin roof. We'll seal the mud walls in concrete to waterproof them. We can gather materials and be ready to begin construction after this next rainy season."

She was so excited she vibrated. "We have four hundred children who finished fifth grade this year. They desperately need a place to go. Can't you build something right now? Please?"

What could I say?

Okay, this was a massive project to move forward with instantly, but I had about ten thousand dollars to work with. I organized a construction crew, received leasehold of the land, and we got started. It all came about without serious delays. Everything just fell into place. As anyone who has built a major project knows, this kind of progress is unheard of. We completed the exterior structure by the end of December. The rain didn't seem to bother the fresh mud-brick walls, especially after we got them roofed over and plastered. We dug the latrines.

I had a fundraising trip scheduled in January when, as usual, I would tour around the United States telling our story and helping to generate the needed revenue. But I had to leave Moz before our final inspection. So I left all the instructions with the people who were trained for the job. They could talk to inspectors as necessary. Pastor Benjamin was going to oversee the program. He already had in hand the food, the school materials, the clothes, everything. Save for the final inspection, we were ready to roll. Let the children move in! But the inspectors repeatedly failed to appear.

On March 14, I received an e-mail message followed by a phone call.

Disaster.

A hurricane-force storm had hit the northern coast of Moz and veered inland. For three solid days, torrents of rain driven by howling winds ripped through Balama, 135 miles from the coast. Areas that had not seen standing water in a hundred years flooded, including the land where our brand new dorms stood. The foundations buckled. The walls cracked. Exposed and inundated, the mud-brick eroded rapidly.

Sorrowing workers salvaged doors, windows, roofing tin, and whatever else they could. Then they watched the rest melt away. Our dreams dissolved into the thick flood.

Many, many places were destroyed in that cyclone, not just ours, and many people died. Basically, the whole area suffered total disaster. Crops and fields were ruined. Thousands of people in the district were already living on the edge. They had no resources left with which to repair, to rebuild, to recover. None.

I was in tears. Devastated. It had all gone so smoothly! It had all turned out so well! It was all so desperately needed! And now...

What do you do when disaster strikes? You pray, of course, even before the tears have ended. And whatever else you talk to God about and pray to him about, you ask for guidance and you praise him. Yes, praise, in the midst of ruin. It works in Moz. It works in the U.S. a world away. It works in the daily life of you, the reader.

As I was praying, the Lord planted this command very clearly: he said, *You will go back and rebuild bigger and better than before.*

Yes, but...

But nothing.

He knew what was going on over there. He was there. And he was here. I resigned myself to the fact that we would indeed go back and do it bigger and better, and that simple fact—we would!—assuaged my discouragement.

But how? There I sat, a world away, unable to see or do anything. But wait. I was in the United States. I hope that during the millennium, when historians write the history of the United States, they call it the Land of the Generous. These folks opened their hearts to children they would never meet, in a land they would almost certainly never see.

The people in poor, stricken Moz had few or no resources, but I did. We had the book, the modest first edition of this book you're reading now. In part by selling the remaining copies, we were able to raise another ten thousand to rebuild. When in May I returned to Moz, I had the necessary resources in hand.

The first thing I did when I got back was to petition the local government for a better piece of land on higher ground. Sure, the cyclone was a freak of nature. It wasn't going to happen like that again for another century, right? I wanted the better location anyway.

And we got it, good land right beside the junior high school. Construction began again. This time we made the whole thing of concrete, which can't buckle or melt. We ended up with strong, permanent buildings.

We built in two phases. Of first priority were the dorms, a place for the students to live. We built two dormitories, one for boys and one for girls. Each building was thirteen feet wide by sixty-five feet long, divided to provide two long rooms. Each of those two long rooms could house eighteen children. Peak capacity, therefore, was thirty-six boys in one dorm and thirty-six girls in the other. Seventy-two children. Already the capacity was insufficient, but it was a start.

The first phase called for a temporary kitchen and cafeteria. These were little more than crude, tin-roofed barns. Each of the bathrooms, girls' and boys', was divided by a wall. One side of the wall provided a bathing area with a concrete floor. The other side was the latrine. It was all roofed, and the concrete potties had lids to keep the flies out.

All was improved over the original plans. I don't mind saying that we boasted quite a nice facility when it was finished.

In 2001 we completed the second phase, which included a 20' x 60' permanent kitchen and cafeteria, a 13' x 69' warehouse, and a 13' x 69' wood storage area with a small office. The whole complex cost us about $50,000 American over the two years.

Our facility is now the model for such projects in Moz. Government officials from the national capital even came up to check it out. This was the first time anyone in the country had built a private boarding facility in which children did not have to pay anything.

People in the United States and other first-world countries understand the concept of free use, but you may not appreciate how absolutely essential that free access is in Moz. Many of the students have no money. I mean none. Their parents can barely afford the clothes on their backs. But they are not poor in other, non-monetary ways. They do work projects and participate in programs to help out. They grow gardens and haul water and wood. In this way we get along without a lot of the ancillary personnel most facilities require.

The government, however, asked us to somehow make the facility totally self-sufficient. Okay. We put in a maize mill. Cornmeal mush is a staple food, the main carbohydrate source in that area (it's quite tasty, too!). The corn must be ground into a fine meal. All the local farmers have to grind their corn one way or another. So they came to us. We provided a basic service, and the modest profit from the mill supported the boarding facility.

The first year we took in thirty-two sixth graders. This was what you might call the shakedown cruise, serving half of the full number of children possible while we got all our ponies trotting in a straight line. The logistics are horrendous when you've never done anything like this before. The second year those thirty-two advanced to the seventh grade, and thirty-six new sixth-graders came in to complete our capacity.

Just think! God took a disaster and made it into a beautiful success story. Our facility, which once melted away in a flood, was now the talk of the nation. I take no credit for it. It is God who directed, and his vision is always the way to go.

Incidentally that flood that happens maybe once in a century hit Balama again the very next year. Another cyclone roared inland from the coast along virtually the same path as the previous year's storm. It destroyed the area and ruined the crops all over again.

This time, though, our facility emerged unscathed.

The Flood Damage

I would like to comment a little further on those floods.

When you see flood results on television or in news photos, typically the houses will be up to their windows or eaves in water. Then the pictures stop, and the next big news event takes over the world's hearts and minds. But in Balama and the other places like it, the flood damage was not simply houses temporarily inundated. It went on and on and on. Somehow people outside the affected area don't think about that.

When heavy rains fall, as for example during cyclonic storms, tremendous quantities of water rush down off the mountains and get channeled through our narrow valleys. Torrents rip out buildings and destroy the corn, peanut, and bean fields all over the county. The violent flooding totally takes out everything near the rivers. Manmade structures like buildings and bridges and God's structures—trees and soil—all go.

No one took any official surveys, but the best estimates claim that our district lost forty percent of the crop in 2000 and forty percent again in 2001. Now remember that these people are subsistence farmers. They grow and store barely enough food to get from harvest to harvest. Under normal conditions, by the beginning of the next harvest, nearly all the food from the previous harvest is used up. They cannot grow and store forty percent more than they need. So when forty percent is lost, that is a month's worth of food gone.

But the world no longer notices. It has gone on to other things.

Building problems are greatly exacerbated by floodwater. The local soil is mostly sandy loam. When it is saturated, the sand loosens up and shifts under weight. There is even a term for it—solufluction. Buildings without foundations are toast; they simply sag and collapse. The first set of dorms we built had cement foundations going down two feet. Surely that would suffice and our foundations would not fail.

It did not suffice. They failed.

The second set is built on foundations going a full three feet deep. So far there are no cracks, shifts, or sinks. That extra foot has helped a lot. You can, however, see the district-wide problem these floods have caused. A terrific amount of rebuilding is required, and most people will not be able to afford deep foundations. The district's infrastructure—roads and bridges, especially—was particularly hard hit, because the roads follow the valleys. With limited tools and resources, the government simply cannot make a swift response.

But the world no longer notices. It has gone onto other things.

Most heart-wrenching and disastrous is the loss of crops. The best fields, here as elsewhere, are bottomland. The bottomland was scoured. What was not washed away was buried in mud and sand. One day you look out across your farm with satisfaction, knowing your needs will be met for the year. The next day everything is gone. You see bare, glistening mud and maybe a few broken-off trees.

In any circumstance, the loss would be severe. But a lot of our local farmers are single parents, usually women without husbands, victimized by war, disease, or abandonment. Often they'll be raising from three to eight children. Life for them is particularly precarious. Any flooding, but especially those two massive, back-to-back disasters, causes a horrendous starvation problem.

Hungry people without other recourse can gather mandioca root, a tuberous root in the bush. The leaves are edible, and the root is starchy. But the plant provides no protein. It fills the belly without offering any real nutrition. Children cannot survive on it. Adults last only a short time. The only food that many people had to eat were leaves and mandioca.

Some of these folks heard of us and came in for help. What a sad, sad sight as these severely malnourished and fragmented families came seeking anything at all! Not something specific. Anything at all.

Typical of these famished farmers was a father whose wife had died. He was doing the best he could, but by the time he came to us, much damage had been done. His son, aged three, weighed twenty-two pounds and did not walk yet. Worse, the boy had been blinded by a complete lack of vitamin A in his diet. After a few months on our high-protein food, the child started walking. But the blindness is not reversible. When he is older, we or others may be able to train him in the skills that will make him self-sufficient.

We see, over and over again, severe problems with nursing mothers. We normally think of a mother's milk as being the very best food for her baby. But when women are starved, their breast milk is deficient in crucial nutrients. Formula is costly and rarely available in any but the largest towns. Besides, most of the women who find us do not even have jobs.

The world doesn't notice, of course. It has gone onto other things and other crises.

We deal with crisis daily. When the baby is malnourished and the mother emaciated, we get them both on a high protein diet. Sometimes it improves her milk. Sometimes it does not. The body may just shut down altogether and her breasts cease producing. We will put a baby on formula until it is three months old. Milk is very expensive, and ordinarily formula is out of the question. But formula delivers more concentrated nutrients than does straight milk, so we give it out to the youngest clients, those three months old and younger. So as soon as we can, we start the little guys on baby food that we make right here. We mix up a cereal of sorghum, corn, and rice. When the babies master that, we cook crushed, powdered peanuts into it. Peanuts are a nearly complete protein source. Ripe fruits, especially bananas and papayas, add other nutrients.

When the child is six months old and eating well, we can start giving ground, cooked beans. Beans help tremendously; their protein is very nearly complete. In short, we make do with what's available.

You'd be surprised how well the babies thrive on what American mothers would consider inadequate or indigestible. As the kidlets gain weight and get chubby and their moms regain their health, we teach them how to feed and care for their children, trying to break the cycle of malnutrition.

For example, most first-world moms know that the human body cannot make its own amino acids, the building blocks of protein. They are aware that complete proteins are made up of all the amino acids the human body requires daily for growth and maintenance. They usually know that meat, eggs, and milk products contain all the necessary amino acids, and that beans and peanuts contain most of them. In fact, many moms know that a combination of corn, rice, and beans provides all the required nutrients because what one source lacks, the other provides. Our moms hardly ever understand anything about proteins or vitamins.

It's not a college-level course, naturally, but we do provide lessons in balancing the diet so as to get all the required nutrients.

Come November and the beginning of the rains when the crops are planted, we give seed to the people we serve so that they can start their fields over. Those who lost everything in the floods had no seed to plant. You see, the farmers in our district don't go out seeking the latest variety and the greatest hybrid purchased in colorful packets. They get their seed by holding back and drying next year's seed out of this year's produce. No harvest, or reduced harvest, means no seed to plant for the next crop.

Am I boasting about all we do? Nope. Because we're not doing it. Our good Lord is. God said he would do this, and no man can stand against it all the days of our lives. We take Joshua 1:5 very seriously around here!

But floods are actually the least of the problems brought on by water and the nature of it in this rural area. Just plain old water itself can cause grief.

Water and Women

There are two reasons why you don't drink water from the tap in our women's home villages. 1) The water is polluted, and 2) there are no taps.

There are no pipes either, or water systems out in the villages where we live and work. The water does not come to you. You go to the water, scoop up a containerful, and haul it home.

Every drop you use must be carried from a well somewhere. Remember that the next time you leave the tap running while you brush your teeth. And don't fuss about the nasty chlorine in your water at home. It is helping prevent the dysentery and cholera that could kill you and your children.

I have described wells elsewhere—shallow seeps that are indescribably dirty. And I have mentioned that toward the end of the long, dry season, many of these wells dry up, leaving people to walk long distances for water. Almost always it's the women who haul the water, and often as not, they do it on foot.

Women and water are inexplicably tied together in this part of the world. Women do the washing and the cooking. Both require water. Women tend the children. Jesus' comment about giving a little child a cup of water takes on a whole new dimension in this country where Momma has fetched that water from who-knows-how-far to give it to her child.

And women take the brunt of the poverty that is so much a part of this area. Wash clothes? They buy a tiny bar of soap at the market for a nickel or so. Vendors don't sell a whole bar of soap, which comes in foot-long, inch-wide, rectangular bars. They chop up that long bar into five or six pieces and sell the pieces. Make your own soap? Soap is made from fat, and fat of any kind is simply unobtainable.

Having gotten their soap, the women take their clothes down to the river to wash. Here you don't bring water to the clothes. You take the clothes to the water.

In fact, that's the way most things are done here. If you want to see something in the light, and your mud hut is too dark, you take the item out, look at it, and take it back in. You don't take the light to the object.

Village women in our state have no schooling whatever. This is mostly the fruit of thirty-five years of civil war. The war is over, but there is no way women can catch up in this generation. The only adult education is in the big cities, such as Pemba.

The local women speak Macua and most don't understand Portuguese at all. It is incredibly difficult for them to support their kids. They have no education, no job skills, and no governmental support because the government is nearly as strapped for funds as they are. About the only way they can survive is through agriculture. But the cyclones and flooding two years in a row destroyed even that tiny glimmer of hope.

And so, with no prospects, no resources, and no means they soldier on and raise their children.

Some chop wood. Some make clay pots or grass baskets. Without training, education, or mentors they possess no business acumen whatever and therefore do not earn nearly as much as they ought for the work they do. But they earn. In plots around the house they grow food for the kids and maybe sell a little for a new shirt for the boy.

"New" around here means it is a used piece of clothing from the United States or Europe that is being sold in the local market for the equivalent of fifty cents to a dollar American. This precious purchase must last the whole year until (hopefully!) money comes in again from the next harvest. It is no wonder that children wear their things until they can't retie the pieces of cloth together again.

The lifestyle is very simple. They cook on open fires, and for most, any light they have is the sun or the cooking fire. Some can afford a little diesel or kerosene. They can buy very small amounts for pennies to give them a bit of light beyond sundown. A lamp can be fashioned from a tin can and a cotton cord for a wick. Most of the time, though, they work in the dark.

What about nighttime entertainment? Wood is precious, brought in from a long distance. After so many years of so many people using the bush, burnable wood may be twelve miles away. So it is not wasted by being burned merely for light at night.

Often these women simply sit around in the dark. If they're rich enough to buy batteries, they might listen to a transistor radio.

They talk and tell stories. They sing.

In the evening after a long, long day of hard toil in grueling heat, these women sit around and sing and giggle and laugh. In the near total darkness of the villages after sundown, you hear a lot of laughter.

These are the poorest people in world. A man in this culture makes $1.10 a day if he finds a job. Kids rarely get to school because Mom can't afford the twenty-five or thirty cents for a book and pen. If she has multiple children, she chooses to send one child, if any. Oldest son gets dibs, girls at the bottom.

Nothing here means absolutely nothing. Mud huts, dirt floors, grass roof. Maybe not even an outhouse. They'll put up a grass wall to make their bathing area. But to dig an outhouse takes a lot of effort, so mostly they just pick a spot in the woods. Open latrines lurk everywhere.

They laugh a lot, and they sing.

It blows me away.

When someone asks, "Why do you do what you do over there?" I think this is part of the answer. These people are indomitable. Struck upside the head by cruel fate at every turn, they survive, and they sing. They are not lazy. They care. They try so constantly. And they stay happy. How can you not help them?

So when I talk about water and mothers, the next question from listeners is, but what about your facility? Seventy-two children plus all the mothers and babies that come by, and the clinic, the other programs ... that is a massive amount of water. Surely you don't haul water for all that!

Yeah, we do.

I hire a man to bring my water to my house. He puts two five-gallon containers on his bike for the trip to the well. Until recently we used a well two miles away. But thanks to a gift from a couple in California who wanted to give a memorial gift to poor children for their mother's sake, we were able to drill a good 125-foot-deep well inside the children's center (it is that depth because that's as deep as local drilling rigs can go). It produces 260 gallons a minute. It cost

$5,000–$4,000 from this precious couple and the rest from other supporters. It has an old-timey hand pump like you used to see on *Little House on the Prairie* or in old westerns. It's less than half a mile from my house and much, much easier for the water carrier.

We haul water in quantity with the tractor and trailer. We hope to get some big fiberglass tanks so we can take water to where it is needed, anywhere. And the ultimate dream is a pumping system and maybe even a tower. We could pump water from the tractor trailer up into a roof-high tank and let gravity give us running water for the houses.

Our biggest concern is that running water is too easy, and people will waste it.

In developed countries, a lot of good water goes down the toilets, literally. And there is much discussion among environmentalists about the value of gray water—water that's been used once, such as in a bath or laundry. I've told elsewhere how we reuse all our bath water, pouring it on the garden if nothing else. In the towns, residents might have a toilet seat that flushes with a bucket into a septic system. Grey water is always used for that. Of course, they don't flush every time. Only number two is flushed immediately.

In the center we're building, we plan to have toilet seats with bucket flush in the concrete houses. In the small missionary residences, each about thirty feet long by thirteen feet wide, we'll also build a bathroom in back with a bucket bath and maybe a sink to wash your hands. We're trying to make things as comfortable as we can without encouraging extravagance or wastefulness.

When people with nothing laugh and sing, any extravagance or wastefulness on our part would be the most insulting slap in the face imaginable.

Think about that.

31

A Tractor Tale

Over and over I have been reassuring you, "Be strong and coura-geous, and He'll move mountains."

Or he may tell you to move the mountain. We did it with a gift from God via a wonderful church in Texas. When this one particular ministry-partner church in Texas gives us a present, it's a doozy! You can count on it.

The present in this case was a Massey Ferguson 290 tractor with a front-end loader and four-ton trailer, a $40,000 gift. And don't you ever say a bad word about Texas where I can hear you, hear? A tractor isn't what you'd call a glamour gift, but it was exactly what we needed. Exactly!

So in May of 2000, we ordered it from a factory in England because the front-end loader had to be factory installed. They shipped it in a used container, cutting every cost possible. It went to Durban by ship then by another ship to Pemba. There it was placed in customs.

But the paperwork had an error. It said Maputo (the bottom cor-ner of Moz), not Pemba (the top corner). One word. Therefore all the paper had to be put back through whatever machine handles that sort of thing. So our tractor sat in customs an extra forty-five days before we could get to it.

Finally, it was ours in possession as well as theory.

The real story is about the trailer. We couldn't get the trailer we wanted, so for $1,500 I had a four-ton capacity trailer custom built with dual wheels. I have a friend in RSA who does that. He did great job on it, too. It turned out to be quite a hassle. Patience of Job, that man. He not only had to search out parts, he did the licensing and other paperwork. If he hadn't been persistent and thorough, right down to getting it rated for export, we would have paid heaven knows how much more.

That done, however, we found out he couldn't export it unless I went down to RSA personally to get the trailer papers done. Too, the company wanted a body part to trailer it up to us. There had to be a better way.

Enter a lovely Christian man from Malawi who does import/export. Thanks to the contacts he had, he brought it up to Malawi for us. Compared to Maputo so far away, Malawi is right in our back yard. Still, it sat there another two months because we didn't have all the right paperwork to import it into Moz. It took several trips to Malawi—incidentally, each one takes five days—to get everything straightened out.

At last it was ours. We could bring it home. It turns out the paperwork hassle was nothing compared to the hassle of getting that thing from Malawi to Balama. At the Malawi end, they had no appropriate equipment to put it on a train. The equipment consisted of me hooking it up to my pickup and backing it onto the train car. Then six men shoved and muscled it until they got it positioned where it needed to be. I had to pay them, too!

The train hauled it to Nampula and from thence to a little town named Namialo. A kindly Muslim man had already said he wanted to be of service because we were helping the orphans. He offered to take the trailer on one of his flatbed trucks going to Pemba. He wasn't even going to charge, because he was deadheading in that direction anyway. It was a sweet deal—if we could get the trailer off the train car. Namialo's rail yard does not have an off-loading ramp adequate to handle it.

And besides, the flatbed truck had not arrived yet.

A local man grabbed his own tractor and flatbed trailer and brought it over to the train stop. We were finally able, with ten men to help, to get that four-ton trailer off the narrow train car and onto the narrow flatbed. It was quite an ordeal and took the whole day, complete with pouring rain and assorted other delays. The next day our trailer was finally delivered to Pemba.

A huge forklift used down on the docks for container shipping was able to lift the whole trailer off and set it down like a Tonka toy. There it sat for another four or five days while I wrestled enough paperwork to bury Kilimanjaro. Inspections, licensing...you can't imagine.

Okay, maybe you can.

Anyway, we cleared all the paper, got the trailer onto yet another flatbed truck, and got it hauled out the last leg of its trek to Balama.

Now you may remember I mentioned the tractor was shipped in a used crate. We're talking about a couple of tons inside a box big enough to house hippos.

And of course, now we had to get all that off this latest truck. The only place we could even think about doing it was over at an old house foundation that we used as a makeshift loading dock. They backed the truck up to the foundation, and we put boards between the truck and the masonry. Then we opened up the crate and simply drove the tractor out of it. I considered the tractor navigating down the loose boards to be practice for local bridges.

It worked.

Eventually.

A century or two after the deal was first arranged, we finally had all the parts of our generous gift from Texas on site and in working order.

We also had that humongous box. We had to get that off the truck, too. The box alone weighed almost two tons.

Getting its own container off the flatbed was one of the first jobs our brand new tractor did. We drove the truck down to my place and backed it up to where we wanted the container to sit. We jacked the container up enough to slip logs under it to serve as rollers. Then we attached ropes between the container and our tractor. As the flatbed truck pulled slowly forward, the tractor pulled in the other direction. The container rolled more or less in place on its logs as the truck drove out from under it.

If you want to hear a loud noise, just drop a two-ton crate off a flatbed.

We learned a lot of lessons from that adventure in heavy-equipment transport, patience not the least of them. They are, however, lessons that you who are reading this can profit from as well. No doubt you know some of them already.

We learned that there are always ways to do a thing. It may not always be easy. And you will get lots and lots of advice, very little of it actively solicited. No matter. Sooner or later in all the speculation, someone will figure out how to get it done. Be open to that, for the winning suggestion may well be an unsolicited one!

We learned that what seemed like a monstrous job the first time was no longer scary. We have the confidence now to do it again if we have to. And we see that a lot of life is like that. We accomplished the task simply because we had to. You too can do what you must. You really can! The hardest part is tackling it initially.

And know that once you're out on the field and the ball is in play, faithful people will support what you're doing.

Now we have our equipment on site. That tractor and trailer enabled us to build the church and the kids' center, and this next year we'll do the missions center. I am not exaggerating to say the tractor is now crucial to our success. The mountain site where we get our building rock is four to five miles out of town. The sand for the cement and stonework is three miles away. All of this, every ounce, has to be brought in by tractor or truck (and just imagine what a blessing that front-end loader is when we're loading and hauling construction stone). The vehicle has to have big wheels to get over the trenched roads, too.

In 2000 I had to rent a tractor because the new one wasn't there yet (we bought it in May, and it wasn't there until almost December). The going rental for a tractor was $100 a day. We could not hire a tractor for the time that all our jobs would take us. No way. The rental expense, in fact, is the reason the church gave us the tractor. In 2001, when we again commenced building, we could not have rented a tractor for love or money because there was none at all available in the area. The whole program would have come to a standstill.

The Lord gave us a vision. He then gave us the means to accomplish it. He did not give us an easy way out or a simple job or time to sit by and coast while he did the work. He simply gave us a vision and said, "Go!"

What vision has he given you?

32

Bricks and Stones

You'll often hear a wife complain about dealing with the man in her life. Only one? Puh-leeze! Try dealing with sixty of them!

Among the pictures in our photo section is a shot of the work crew in front of a newly-completed building. This is not an entirely accurate picture because this is only *some* of the crew, the core group if you will. When construction was in full swing, we had forty to sixty men working daily in the facility. By any measure, that's a crowd.

But then you have to have large numbers of workers because all construction is done by hand, without power and usually without running water. To saw a board, you saw it by hand. To saw a hundred boards, you need many hands. Because you can build only in the dry season, May to December, all this handwork must be accomplished quickly. Therefore you employ a lot of workers. And here in rural Africa, workers are almost always cheaper than so-called modern heavy equipment for most tasks.

We started out with a crew of bricklayers and their assistants, water carriers, and carpenters. There were almost no Christians in the area, so the workers were, by and large, Muslims. And as I think about it, the building of our facility and the building of the body of Christ, the believers, run parallel in many regards. Let me show you.

When we began the children's center, the first thing we did was mark out the foundation. Talk about measuring carefully! Here was where obsession with detail was not a bad thing. The walls must be absolutely trued, the corners absolutely squared. If any errors at all are made in the initial measurement, the building will be structurally weak and will come down in the first good storm or high wind.

Similarly, when you start dealing with people, eventually to tell them about Jesus, you must first become a friend. With Muslims or any other unbelievers, friendship evangelism works faster than any other way. First you gain their respect by working alongside them, talking to them, and showing through your actions that you care. This is marking off the foundations.

I always try to be on site when we mark out a building, for that is the most critical part. We almost had a disaster with one of our buildings. The head engineer came out to measure late one afternoon. He was in a hurry; it was getting dark, and he naturally wanted to finish quickly because he had a long way to go to get home. In his haste he made a mistake. One end was narrower than other, off quite slightly over a ten-yard measure. The mistake was so slight you couldn't see it by eye.

That night the Holy Spirit impressed me to recheck the markings before we set our men to digging the foundation. Sure enough, there it was. Two of the walls would not have been parallel. That off-square relationship would have compounded itself as building proceeded, with disaster as the result.

If the foundations of friendship are not well laid, you cannot build successfully on them either. It is critically important for every Christian to lay a good, solid, square, *true* foundation. Get that right, and then you can start laying the bricks in those walls.

One of the things we did when building relationships with these Muslim craftsmen, carpenters, bricklayers, and all was to get in there and work with them and talk with them. As they worked I would go and watch them do it, striking up conversations. Day by day they came to see that I actually knew what I was talking about when it came to erecting solid buildings. I knew what I was talking about when we discussed such esoteric things as the kind of grass that makes the best roof or the proportions of sand and cement to make the best concrete. Respect came first. Then came friendship.

I suggest the first thing you must do when talking to people, any people, is to gain respect. Not until that is accomplished will you truly have their ear. It happened with these men. I watched their job and complimented them on their skills. It was no sham. Some of these workers are absolutely amazing in what they can do with a few boards and a handful of mud. You don't compliment falsely, of course. Strangers quickly see through that sort of thing, and you've lost any chance of winning them. I mean genuine appreciation.

And here is a nice little side benefit of gaining their respect: these folks have been doing things the same way for three hundred years. Sometimes there is a much easier way, even an effective shortcut. Things would go faster and better if they knew about such improvements. How do I express these new ideas without offending them or getting them defensive? Gently, that's how. Very gently. Often I can pose a question to them to make them think along new lines. Hey, maybe there is a simpler way to accomplish such-and-so. Done adequately, that approach really opens their eyes. If I do it in the right way, they accept the new ideas without any problems.

That's what you're facing when you present Jesus to a friend. That person is probably not about to change his or her thinking. You know change is always difficult. "But we've *always* done it this way!" is the bane of anyone seeing a need for change. I have to deal with it among my workers, and you have to deal with it among the unbelieving friends you hope to reach.

Once we've got the measurements down, we dig out the foundation. The foundation must be deep; we learned that in the last flood. We go a full meter now, thirty-nine inches, where the corner posts and middle pillars are to be set. The pillars and posts secure the brickwork. If they are sufficiently deep, the walls will be secure. We set the remainder of the foundation to about a yard deep. The foundation must be formed of strong material. In our case, that is granite rock set into cement mortar. We end up with a firm foundation, a rock-solid foundation.

I know you've heard this before: if you want to raise up a Christian, you build on a solid foundation. You build it on the Rock. The Rock is the Word. The Word is Jesus, and the Word is the Bible. You stick to the basic principles of what the Word of God says. Then the people with whom you are dealing have a firm foundation to build on. When and if they learn to hear God and receive the revelation knowledge that God wants to give them, they themselves, as well as you can build on the foundation laid so carefully. As he trains them up to follow him, they will hear his voice and obey what he says, to their own eternal joy.

In these last days it will be very important that we not hesitate when the Lord tells us to do something. We must keep our ears open and learn to recognize his still, small voice. Jesus sent his Holy Spirit to be counselor, teacher, comforter, and guide. We have to get the people with whom we are working into the Word, that strong foundation, before we can begin building the walls one brick at a time. Once the wall is up, they are ready for the next phase, the roof, for they are really hearing what God is saying to them and walking in the ways of the Lord.

One of the other challenges that befalls these building projects in Balama is that some of the bricklayers are not as sharp to grasp what is told to them as are others. Master bricklayers get the most important jobs. I show them what needs doing and let them go. It's the same with believers. Some will be slower learners than others and need more time to reach the same spiritual level.

We have this one fellow named Nazario, who has a wonderful heart. He is excellent when working with mud brick. He does beautiful work, but is he ever slow! Like a tick crawling down a dog's back. And he never quite got onto mixing cement mortar. So we don't let him do cement work. But when I need mud work done, I give him his time and let him do the job at his own pace, and it always turns out to be a great job.

Baby Christians, too, have to learn at their own pace. I suppose it's true of anything you do. Nazario is a prime example of how you can take each believer at his own pace so he can grasp each brick one at a time and slowly build his wall.

One of other frustrations I find in construction is that none of the workers has more than a ninth-grade education. As I mentioned elsewhere, the education system in rural areas was shut down during the lengthy civil war. A whole generation of these men had no opportunity for education. Also, their ninth grade is not the equivalent of ours. Subtract two years and call it the seventh grade here.

This causes a lot of frustration on my part and probably theirs, too. These people have a strong mindset, but it is not an informed mindset. I remember in 1996 when I told Crispo, the most highly-educated man on staff, about the first man walking on the moon. He refused to believe such a thing until I showed him an article and photos in a magazine. Because of the lack of news, no one in the county had ever heard about it. Once they grasp that Jesus is real, they are on the right path, but they are not ready for it to change anything about their lives. And they cannot easily see the broader view, the longer road.

Isn't it funny how we all will let go and grow in one area of life but not in another. And yet, if you truly want to go with God and be the best that you can be for the Lord, you must be flexible and willing to make changes in your life. It is true of the fledgling believer and just as true for the old veteran. If you don't want to let go of hurts, bitterness, and unforgiveness, he cannot heal you. It puts a brick wall between you and the blessings he wants to give you, and you will never mature into the person he wants you to become.

The men who flex with me have excelled, and I push them to the top of the list. When I need bricklayers, they're the first ones I call. I know they can get the job done well with the improved techniques required by today's building construction codes. Things have changed. New techniques are needed to meet the new challenges and requirements. People who don't accept new ideas are left behind. Jesus is a two-thousand-year-old idea, and yet he is brand new to every beginning believer.

And there is one other thing in construction that parallels raising up a new believer. That is a servant's heart. Every bricklayer has an assistant or servant assigned to him. The servant must be submissive to the bricklayer and do what he's told. He is not to argue, for that just wastes time. The master bricklayer knows what he's talking about, but if he ends up with a servant who decides to do his own program, the work grinds to a halt, dragged down by disunity. Unity is essential in the body of Christ. You have to have a team.

When I pick my bricklayers, I pick six men who work together well and avoid anyone whose work attitude is too independent. I've had this problem in the past. One bricklayer tried to take over and rule the others when that was neither his role nor his disposition. It didn't work.

Because of my back injury, which I will tell you about later (also both rotator cuffs in my shoulders; it all comes from gripping the wheels of bakkies for years while lurching along on these roads), we got a really late start building the malnutrition center in 2002. It's not a huge building, but we had to get it up quickly before the rain stopped everything. We decided to go with six master bricklayers and eight servants. Usually the proportion is six to six, one assistant for each bricklayer. But we were going for speed. Extra assistance given to the masters served speed a lot better than extra masters would have. Too many cooks can indeed spoil the broth, so to speak. That too is a lesson worth knowing. There is great purpose and success in serving.

We see it in missions all the time. When you come into a new ministry, it is wise and necessary to be submissive to the boss. Let me assure you, if you have a bunch of missionaries out in the field, you have a bunch of strong-willed people out there because that's the personality it takes. You can't send wimpy warriors out and expect them to survive, let alone succeed. So you have these bold, take-charge personalities, which is good in itself. Problems arise, though, if one or more of them never learned to submit before they got out into the field.

When I started out in missions, I was taught in mission school that you must go into ministry with a subservient heart. If you want to be a king, be a servant. Jesus himself was the king of kings, but he came as a servant, never exalting himself. It's a hard lesson to learn, this having a servant's heart. And until you learn that, you will never rise to the top in the kingdom of Jesus Christ.

In the mission field, this is the major cause of disunity and discord. It breaks up more good missions team than does anything else. If one or two members of the team decide, "We want to do it our way. From now on we shall, because we think our way is better than yours." Are they improving the system? No, they are rebelling. Those people have to be dismissed if they don't leave on their own. This is the reality.

If I end up with a bricklayer's assistant who doesn't want to mix the mortar right or do whatever he was told to do by the bricklayer, we have to replace him. He's messing up the project. It's a sad thing, especially on the mission field. When someone goes through all that training but, because of his or her attitude, is unable to work with others, particularly the supervisor, that training has been wasted.

I have seen this, and I think you have, too. People with this kind of attitude not only leave one ministry; they bounce from ministry to ministry and may try to start their own where they may be boss. Everything they try falls through. In the end, they just go home. What a waste of a harvester! What a waste of a well-trained life! And all because of an attitude problem.

That is why I say, if you truly want to step out for the Lord, with a servant's attitude you will go far. He will exalt you. He will raise you up and make you into the leader he wants you to be. And it is an ever-growing process. As new team members come in, I too am learning to change my ways. I'm used to being the lone ranger because I was by myself for so many years. It's an adjustment time for everybody as a team starts to grow and as a ministry starts to grow.

All signs indicate that our ministry is about to explode in a great growth spurt, because it's the final days and the final push to get the gospel out. So everyone from the leaders on down must always be growing and changing. Gotta build that firm foundation! Buoy up the new believers and take them under your wing as you would your children. Raise them up one step at a time.

In construction we put one brick on top of the other, slowly and steadily building a wall into a solid mass that will stand for many years, serving the multitudes. This is what we want to accomplish with each and every person we guide into the kingdom. This is what you call discipling.

And that's what it's all about.

One other point: erecting a building is a lot of hard work. Missions is spelled w-o-r-k. People so often go out with wrong ideas, thinking that somehow it is so romantic to walk around all day talking to people about Jesus. They figure that's all that missionaries do.

Sorry. Not so. Missions is very practical, even say pragmatic. Ours is especially unromantic. With the orphanages, we have not only to build but to maintain buildings. Patching a leaky roof in the wet season is not romantic. Buying food, procuring necessities from long distances over rough roads, is tough, especially here. It's hard to find what you need. You also have to know the prices and to organize well, because someone out there is trying to rip you off. That's not just in Africa, of course. It's the same in modern society where you have to be a good shopper and avoid scams.

I work a fourteen-hour day. I try to keep it to six days a week, but sometimes I end up working that seventh day also. Every missions worker has to be willing to put in the time that it will take to get the job done.

There are two reasons that work here is consuming. The first and most important is Jesus. He did not turn people away or work bankers' hours. He was always there, always on the job except for those hours he spent in prayer. Think about it; the children in our care have no one else. Someone must be Momma and Papa to them. That takes time. People come to the door at night with a sick child. We never turn them away.

Time. I beg you, always take the time to minister to people whether you're in missions or in PTA. When the blind man called out to Jesus, He paused on His way and ministered to the guy. That is the role model set before us.

But we are more than just following an example. We are the example. In our worlds, whatever and wherever they may be, we are the example of Jesus that people see, you and me. This is what has touched the people so much in the Balama area.

It is hard for people in the developed countries to grasp that here there is no infrastructure of the kind they're accustomed to. There is no ambulance. There are no police, no pharmacy, no open-all-night facilities of any sort. I will get out of my tent at night to provide medicines. I will get the car out and play ambulance when it's needed. We will go rescue a child in the bush when it's needed. We do what must be done because there is no one else out there who can or will do it.

Incidentally, don't even think about 911 in an emergency. If you want the police, you go get them and provide their transportation to your place. They sort out the problem for you, whatever it is. Then you take them home.

The other reason we work without ceasing is that we are showing the love of Jesus. I mentioned that the men on our construction crews were mostly Muslim when we started. By the end of the first year of building, they had learned to respect us and the pastors working with us. As we talked, our stories were the same; we were all delivering the same message of redemption. Not only did they watch to see that our information was consistent; they watched us.

When we show the love of Jesus by taking care of the women and children, we've done something no other religion out there has done. We put something in their hand instead of just talking. We show in a practical way the love of Jesus and how much He cares. Jesus said that if you have two shirts, give one to one who doesn't have one. If your brother has nothing, you don't say, "Be blessed, brother," and walk away, leaving him empty-handed when he's hungry.

The Bible also says to give a cup of water to someone who asks, and he will greatly bless you. The workers who came had needs like anyone else. Some got sick while working here. We sent medicine and took care of them, treating them like members of our family. This is what witnesses to people; it is not your words, but your actions. Actions speak very loudly.

Some came to know Jesus by the time we finished the building. Then they listened to us. We've been three years in the program, and the majority of the men we hired three years ago, as well as a lot of the men taken on since then, have come to know the Lord.

Many a Mozambican has come to me and said, "I've been watching you for the last three or four months, and I want to come to your church. I want to know more about this person you keep talking about, because you are different from everybody else."

Different from everyone else. A peculiar people, to quote Peter (1 Peter 2:9) in the King James.

It's through your action that people will listen to your words and come to know who your Lord and Savior is. It is through action, consistent, effective action, that a building is erected, that a kingdom is built.

33

E-mail!

Communications today are just amazing.

A friend who lives in tornado alley (Texas, Oklahoma, Kansas—up through there) told me about a guy with a laptop in a tornado shelter. To explain: when the weather gets rummy, citizens either go to hard rooms in their houses or to community shelters until the danger passes. Take, for instance, Moore, Oklahoma, where a tremendous tornado struck several years ago. When the storm began getting ugly, local Oklahoma City television stations immediately cut away from regular programming and went to their weather people. Every person in the area with access to TV could watch the Doppler radar images of the storm and hear the latest up-to-the-second news. Every person could learn exactly where the tornadoes were and what they were doing.

The weather people were so good at tracking the big tornado as it developed that they could say, "It will cross X street just west of Y avenue at 7:10," and at 7:10, by golly, the storm would rip across X street as predicted. Incidentally, during the big one, they also said, "Get out or get down. You won't survive this one aboveground." And they were right. The tornado scrubbed clean a swath over a quarter mile wide.

So here were my friend and his wife in a community shelter deep in a basement. A young man popped open his laptop. It had a cell phone antenna built into it. From that he could pull down the same Doppler radar images that the Severe Weather Center and TV stations were looking at! No wires, no hardlines, no problem. In a lower basement, my friend, that young man and a dozen other people watched the world go by overhead. Amazing!

When I first started working here, radio was it. I've already described that. But now in Africa I am on the crux of a revolution that is just amazing. We don't have cell phones, though that may come someday soon. We don't even have utilities where we are. But I can run the whole ministry from the cab of my pickup.

The method is a strange marriage of ham radio and regular telephone-based e-mail. My laptop uses an unusual e-mail program run out of Pretoria, RSA. You buy a special modem, just a small box, which plugs into my laptop with a regular computer cable. The modem then connects with another cable to the mike port of my ham radio.

That radio is a little giant, too, quite strong. It can literally reach across the world when the airwave patterns are just right. Occasionally I have heard American conversations that were going on in America, especially at night when the air is particularly clear. That doesn't mean they could hear me were I to respond. The signal bounces erratically. I just mention it to point out that my antenna is as strong as a dog's belch.

To use e-mail, I type in a text message, turn on my radio, tune to the right frequency, and turn on the modem. Only one person at a time can sign on e-mail on that frequency—sort of like the old telephone party lines. If no one else is on, I hit send and off it goes. The typed text travels by radio in a beep form a thousand miles across Africa to a computer in Pretoria. There it's converted to a regular telephone internet system and goes out by internet services. Once my radio message connects with that computer, it arrives at its destination anywhere in the world within a hundred seconds.

Awesome system! In less than two years it has revolutionized all the missions bases in Africa, as well as the tourist hotels that are remote. We all use it. It is by far the cheapest method of communication.

"How much?" you ask.

"Eighty-five dollars a month," I reply.

"Oh, that's too expensive!" you might insist.

No, it's not. Not when you consider that the telephone nearest to me is two hours away in Montepuez and completely inaccessible during heavy rains. If it's working, you might be able to make a national or international call. Many times, though, the only place you can call is Pemba. Period. So if you really have to call someone, you drive all the way to Pemba. You have to hope the people you want to talk to are by their phones, of course, and you don't get some answering machine or worse. You usually stay overnight because driving to Pemba is a difficult trip for one day. The cost of the phone call, of course, is additional. A call to the US is six dollars a minute.

So you can see that e-mail is marvelously economical. I can send and receive unlimited messages. And there is phone service of a sort. Sometimes I can call voice to South Africa, and they can patch me in to a person I want to speak to. Twice they have gotten the party I need and then patched me into the line in a special ship-to-shore system. In other words, we can hear and speak in an actual phone call. This costs fifty cents a minute from South Africa to America. What a blessing!

The best part is that I have a mobile unit in my truck. If I need help, quite often I can call out for it. It depends where I am, however. There are some holes in the world that still don't allow radio communication.

Best of all, if I find a high enough spot, my mobile antenna can reach Pretoria's computer. Thus when I travel to Malawi, for example, I don't get behind on messages. The people with whom I'm working can find me, and I can talk to them. True, I have to be in just the right position, but it's workable.

God has really blessed me with this entire system.

September 11

As the United States was waking up on the morning of September 11, 2001, Africa had just gone to bed. After the horrors of thirty-plus years of war, Moz was finally able to appreciate being able to lay its head down in some measure of peace. Our world in Moz, topsy-turvy for so long, had returned to a modicum of order.

When I pulled my e-mail down Friday morning September 12, I had five messages from different people telling me briefly what had happened. The horrors Moz had lived with for over a generation now menaced the fabric of my own home. America was topsy-turvy.

Many times in this book and elsewhere I speak about the awesome changes modern communications have wrought. Less than twelve hours after the bottom fell out of the US, I knew about it in my remote corner. It would have been even sooner had I suffered insomnia and pulled my mail down earlier.

I sat in the cab of my pickup and cried.

Because I was still recovering from the shoulder surgery that I'll tell you about later (it's worth a chapter of its own, believe me), and could not yet drive, a missionary from South Africa, Hedley, was helping out with the driving. He joined me that morning, learned what happened, and sat beside me. We prayed with many tears.

My first thought that moment: *I hope you saved the Christians.* I know that God brings rain on the just as well as the unjust, but my heart went out to his people. I felt an intense sorrow for all those souls who never knew what came bursting through the solid walls to destroy them.

Now it happens that for several weeks I had been witnessing to the dorm leader in the children's center. He was sixteen then, very intelligent, and a communications whiz. He could chat with the kids in Macua and talk with dignity and finesse to people who speak Portuguese. I had been witnessing to him, but I didn't see any effects. I gave him a Bible, and he was even reading it to others, but it obviously was still just a book.

Friday, hours after 9–11, he came to my house. "I want to know more. Tell me more about Jesus."

I explained as best I could—who can explain commandeering an airplane full of people and doing *that* with it?—and answered all his questions. He still was not ready to commit himself.

Sunday he came to church.

That Sunday I was invited to deliver the message in Portuguese. If you are of a denomination that does not give great weight to the anointing of the Holy Spirit, you may not fully grasp what I say when I tell you that on that day, I was anointed. This is not boasting on my part. The Holy Spirit anoints according to the occasion, not the speaker. I was speaking, true, but it was not I who was speaking. My words came from a resource far deeper than can be humanly explained. Too, when the Holy Spirit anoints, he anoints both the speaker and the listeners that the Word might be received in the full power with which it is delivered.

My audience had been hearing about the events of 9–11 on the radio for several days, so all this was not new news to them. Thanks to e-mail from friends in the US, I knew more details than did most of the African radio newsreaders. I could explain what happened, but how could I help these people grasp it? Very few had ever seen a two-story building. How could I describe the fall of a building 108 stories taller than the tallest they'd ever seen? Pemba has a few buildings three stories tall. Stack thirty of those one upon the other and then collapse the pile. See? So hard to explain!

I described how, in less than an hour, thousands died, killed by an unexpected, unimaginable event. They never had a chance.

We showed our audience that there is no guarantee of the next minute, let alone the next hour or the next year. If they want to know where their soul, their spirit man, is going when they die, they need to make the decision now. Right now! Stop playing around.

It was an awesome altar call. Just awesome! A dozen converts came forward that day.

Including the sixteen-year-old from the dorms.

That's not the end of the story. Unknown to us, he went back to the dorms and started talking to the other students. The next Sunday he brought twelve students with him, and by the end of the service, all twelve walked forward to receive Jesus.

That's not the end of the story either. These children came from remote villages all over the area, silent corners of the district that had never heard the name of Jesus. Those kids, you see, were going home for the holidays, and they would tell everyone what they were learning. They are the Lord's evangelistic tools to reach into villages no one else can reach.

Many villages are headed by Muslim leaders who may be against the Jesus Film. If the heads are against it, we're not allowed to show it. So we are praying that these children are not only hearing Jesus in their own right but are opening other doors and other hearts, preparing the way for the Jesus Film and ultimately for Jesus himself!

34

Cabin Fever

I love Balama. I love her people, who are so happy and resourceful in the midst of poverty. I love the way everyone there gets things done, often despite adversity. I love the gentle pace of life and the lively cadence of their language as they tell one another how the day has gone. It is one of God's lovely villages. But frankly God might have situated Balama in a better spot.

In that district several low mountain ridges run parallel, at an angle but roughly east to west. Balama's only road follows a valley between two such low ridges. There is no pass exactly, but the valley narrows down into quite a strait defile less than two miles across. And at nearly the narrowest point, three different rivers come together.

Problems arise when all three rivers are swollen—and that is every rainy season—particularly because several critical bridges cross the meanders, and one of them is right in the defile. Thus the people of Balama district pay even closer-than-usual attention to the weather.

February and March, autumn south of the equator, are Moz's heaviest rain months. They are also the peak cyclone months. In the

United States we would call these storms hurricanes. When they are spawned in the Indian Ocean instead of the Atlantic, they are cyclones. Either way they can be devastatingly costly in lives and property.

I mentioned earlier how, in late February of 2000, a cyclone hit the Mozambique coast well to the south of us. It made landfall at Nacala and churned its way due west inland to Nampula. Abruptly it then turned nearly ninety degrees and swirled north. When it hit Balama with its hurricane-force wind and oceans of rain, the flooding took out most of the farmers' fields, totally destroyed the roads, and dissolved our brand new dorms. The road out of Balama, as well as its bridges, was toast.

In February of 2001, a cyclone again took that exact same path. It touched land at Nacala, roared inland to Nampula, then swung north and sat on top of us in Balama. The only difference was that we had rebuilt our dorms, and this time they withstood the weather just fine. But the fields and crops were destroyed, the bridges again washed out, and the road, our poor road, was ripped up horribly.

Twelve miles of it were totally wiped out. Gone without a whisper. Just within that twelve miles, four bridges collapsed. Flash flooding gouged trenches into the roadway three feet deep. Even the less-damaged sections were left with boulders, debris, and ruts with an attitude.

For six weeks nothing traversed that road except bicycles and motorbikes, and even those had to be carried across some spots.

We were stuck.

Some of the voids where bridges had been were wide enough and deep enough to swallow entire pickups. I kid you not: you could drop a light truck in there and not see the top of it. Other bridges were intact, but the ramps leading up onto them were gone.

I could repair one of them myself and in fact did so. All it needed was an entrance ramp to get up onto it. We could build a makeshift ramp with logs. But the other three bridges in the narrow valley were missing altogether. Their foundations had totally washed away, and they had collapsed into the tumbling, churning rivers. Indeed the area where those three rivers come together was so badly damaged that it took road crews a whole year to get the surface and bridges repaired permanently.

Now as I mentioned, life moves with the rhythm of the season, and part of that rhythm is to always stock up for the rainy months. Then when washouts isolate us, we don't have to go out for anything. We usually have enough of everything on hand. So, in the aftermath of this second cyclone, we were prepared to sit out the months it would take to get the road repaired.

But there was one little kink in the plowline. A young man, Les Reynolds, was coming in from Canada at the end of March. The road would not be ready until April at the earliest. I'm not talking about permanent construction here. The crews had to build temporary bridges and bypasses, as well as get the surface usable again. It was a massive, massive job.

How would we go get Les? He was arriving at the Pemba airport, which is about five hours away under normal conditions. It was eight weeks away under our current washout conditions. Aha! Great idea: an old agricultural road wound sixty miles or so through cotton fields. It had been cut to get workers and machinery into the fields and to haul the crop out. Only really big four-wheel-drive rigs used it, and not many of them had been through lately. We figured it was probably negotiable with our four-wheel drive and a crew of men with shovels, ropes, machetes, and anything else by the kitchen sink. We would have to dig our way out that road and dig our way back in.

Sure it sounds like a lot of work, but I had no choice. So we headed out on March 28, to bring Les Reynolds in.

To put it euphemistically, we encountered challenges. To put it more realistically, the whole cotton-picking road (literally speaking) through those old fields was one big, long, sixty-mile challenge. Every yard presented some new problem. We would make it to a spot, get out, look around, pick out the track to take next, discuss how to manage the next obstacle, get back in, and drive another few hundred yards. We forded streams and squirreled up soggy embankments, the backend whipping and skidding side to side. Mud flew. Fortunately, none of us was wearing a white shirt and tie.

And it was constantly that way. We encountered mud holes seventy-five yards long (that's almost seventy meters for you metric fans). But that was only one dimension. We didn't know how deep they went. The depth doesn't show on the surface. So one of the men would get out with a bamboo pole and probe the length of, testing depth. If it wasn't deep enough to sink us to the axles, we'd pray our way through it. You needed men to dig you out and also to provide raw weight over the wheels for better traction. What am I complaining about? It only took us six hours to get sixty miles.

The worst problem occurred in the last ten miles (sixteen kilometers) of that old farm road. A mud pit stretched out fifty yards long, at least. A couple of other trucks and tractors had gone through and really dug it up, leaving two feet of clay muck that was now deep enough to bury us to the axles. Even the big tractors had trouble getting through that one.

We cut a new bypass, trying to get up onto higher, firmer ground instead of plowing through the deep mud churned up by other larger vehicles. It wasn't pretty. We dug up through a cornfield on the right, laying corn stalks down to improve traction. We made it three fourths of the way before the trunk sank.

So the men got out the shovels, and we dug at the wheels; we used boards; we employed every trick we knew between us, and we were all veterans of mud holes. It only took us about an hour. Fortunately, we had no further trouble with the last ten miles of road leading to civilization.

Les came in about noon. There was no way we would get clear back to Balama anymore that day. I said, "We'll start back immediately and sleep in Montepuez tonight. Then we'll jump off into the bush in the morning. That will give us the day to get through there. It will probably cost us six hours just to get through that [insert unkind word here] mud hole."

Les was, shall we say, amused. Yeah, yeah, yeah. We were just joshing the newcomer. He was sure it couldn't be all that bad.

The next day we took off down the bad stretch. The first ten miles were fine. Then we came to that infamous mud hole. The original lower track was still completely churned up, but someone coming through had churned up our new track also. Now it too was unusable. So again we cleared a new path and laid down as much vegetation as we could, to get as much traction as possible

Now the truck was loaded, because we never come in from the outside empty. The bunch of supplies in the back added up to about eight hundred pounds. That wasn't enough to make us heavy under normal conditions, but it sure was enough to make you sink in the mud. This time we only got halfway before it dropped down to the differential.

This time it cost three hours to free ourselves. We unloaded the truck. We tried getting boards under the tires. No go. There was no way to jack it; the jack had nothing firm to push against. Eventually Les and I and our four helpers and five other men that I hired on the spot simply lifted the vehicle bodily and carried it to firm ground.

Remember that, even though it's late autumn, days get hot on the equator. We were soaked in sweat and covered in mud, all of us.

Welcome to Africa, Les!

The whole incident taught me several important lessons.

One was that Les was one tough cookie. He got broken in the hard way, and he took it well.

Another has to do with the truck. I am no quitter. But by the time we finished that road, I was so shook with the risks to the truck that we had to take, I vowed never to do that again. The truck is our heart and life. Our ministry cannot function without it. It hauls all our supplies and does the million jobs around the facility that only a pickup truck can do. To subject it to possibly irreparable damage or even demolishment is downright foolish.

And the third lesson really surprised me. I didn't realize how stressful being trapped in Balama could be. As I said, I like being there. I will be there for months at a time and not think a thing of it. But when the road was gone, when I could not get out if I wanted, cabin fever set in. It was just like some pioneer in the far north snowed in for a couple months. Even though I could get out on foot or bicycle if need be (and out that agricultural road, though I hadn't thought of it at first), I felt utterly trapped. Claustrophobic. Jailed.

This sense of being helplessly trapped sounds silly when I write about it now, but it was very real then and very stressful. I was not free to go and do what had to be done. The heart and mind do strange things at times.

Praise our Lord for radio-powered e-mail! Had that not been available I would have had no communication at all with the outside. The isolation would have been complete.

Could I have coped? Yes. Isolation is one of hazards we have to deal with. You live with it. But the stress would have exacted its toll, make no mistake. And stress, as you may have noticed, is something we don't need a whole lot extra of at Balama.

Les's Life Lessons

Les, the *cheechako* (newcomer), learned a whole lot in a hurry and not from a book. True, he had read my first book, the one that expanded into this one. But that was just head knowledge.

There was this one early morning when the sun cast its daily gold across the compound and I sat in my truck cab e-mailing.

Here came Les out from his hut.

"Brenda, there's a snake at the foot of my bed."

"You're joking, right?"

"No. There's a snake at the foot of my bed." He was acting so calm about it, but frankly he looked too pale to be in a joking mood. I'm more accustomed to visitors going ballistic when they spot a snake, any snake. His quiet reaction puzzled me.

So we walked back over there, and I took a careful look; it doesn't pay to move quickly with stuff like that around. By cracky there was a foot-and-a-half Black Mamba under the foot of his bed. The April weather was quite cool—in the high sixties or low seventies, maybe—and the snake was pretty sluggish. Snakes, being cold-blooded, are easily affected by temperature.

I hollered to one of the workmen nearby. He brought his machete over and made mincemeat of its head. He was even nice enough to dispose of the remains for us.

I glanced at Les. "Pale" was an understatement.

Now, Les had read the first edition of this book, so he knew that snakes occurred around here. But when you're reading about snakes in a book, the slithery things are just an abstract concept. That morning he suddenly saw that, hey, this stuff is real and snakes actually do get under your bed. It brought home to him the cold reality of danger in Moz.

A few days later Les came around the corner of our kitchen and almost walked into a spitting cobra. Spitting cobras don't stand up and fight unless you corner them. So this one took off like a shot and was out of the yard before we could even tell anyone it was there. Now we knew it was around, though. We just kept our eyes open (Les's were *really* open!), and sure enough, that night around dusk he came back, and this time he came in from behind the food warehouse. My dogs cornered him at the pit where we throw our garbage. He had nowhere to go.

As the four dogs surrounded him, he began spitting rapid fire to blind them. That is a spitting cobra's plan: blind the prey then bite and eat. The plan works so effectively, the snake uses it on attackers as well. One plan fits all.

I was trying to figure out what to do, and Les was standing there wide-eyed, and all four dogs were yelping crazily because they couldn't see. It was a hysterical moment.

I didn't want to approach too closely because it was now too dark to see the snake well. I had no time to run and get a flashlight. So I picked up a four-yard-long bamboo pole and threw it like a lance to break the snake's concentration. The bamboo hit the snake and scared him. The dogs scattered. The snake found a way out and took it, and we never saw him again.

Now we had to chase down the dogs and clean their eyes out. The dogs were too excited and distraught to cooperate cheerfully. That spit really burns your eyes. Finally we wrestled each of them down and got the stuff washed out. All of them came through it just fine.

So what with one thing and another, Les grasped that nothing I had been writing was an exaggeration. I assure you of that as well. The world I describe is the world we live in here, snakes and all.

A short time later, Les and I went down to RSA for supplies. On the way I told Les about the frequent hijackings in Zimbabwe. The pattern is this: as you're going through Harare, three or four men will drive up close behind you. When you stop at a red light (called a robot in Zim; they're quite British in that), one of them hops out and stabs your tire. The tire goes flat within the next hundred yards or so. You stop, and that's when they all jump out to quickly rob you of whatever is portable and quick to sell on the black market. They don't take the vehicle; that's too easy to get caught with. But everything in the vehicle goes bye-bye. If you don't fight or resist, they don't get aggressive. They simply leave you standing there with a sliced tire and nothing else.

Again, Les had a wee bit of problem with finding my veracity credible, so to speak. Big kidder, that Bush Bunny! Right?

Police protection is heavy downtown, so you rarely have trouble there. But on the outskirts of Harare, it's a different story. At one of the last red lights in the city, I noticed a little green car move up close behind me. I think they must have been beginners, because they weren't real smooth at it. I was the first one waiting at the red light. A man stepped out of the green car and moved toward us. Traffic was light, and no one was close (remember, you drive on the left here, also very British). A lane to the left was open.

When the fellow from the green car opened a switchblade, I popped the clutch. Our truck leaped forward. The fellow paused, wide-eyed. Even as the light was changing to green, I hit the accelerator. The guy ran back toward his car as we peeled out. Ever try to peel out in a diesel built for power, not speed? It's like trying to do a wheelie in a Mac truck.

We managed to make it to the expressway ramp and get on the expressway. We thought for a moment that we'd lost them, but they chased us until we were almost out of town. When everyone got stuck in heavy traffic by the big hospital, they couldn't get up close to us. They knew they'd been seen, so they dropped the pursuit.

· When I told Les that most of the missionaries and nearly all the RSA farmers had been attacked and robbed by these hijackers, you know what? He believed me. Eventually he figured out that my wild tales and admonitions are not exaggerated.

As I write this, Zimbabwe is in turmoil, and it's not safe to go through there. Now when I travel between RSA and Balama, I'll seek out other routes that keep me in Moz. The journey will take longer; Zimbabwe's highways are fast and good. But then so are their hijackers.

Speaking of trucks...

35

What Would Jesus Drive?

What is the conductor's job in the orchestra? He stands up on that little box and waves his arms, right? And beautiful music results. But he doesn't make the music. He just makes sure all those who do make music make it together. It's sort of an elite form of traffic control—get everything to stop and go and come in and modulate on cue.

It has always fascinated me the way God orchestrates his stuff in much the same way.

It was July in RSA—the middle of winter—and I was ready to return to Moz after having surgery, getting my right shoulder worked on. I've mentioned elsewhere that both rotator cuffs have been damaged. While I was recuperating, I picked up a couple of books that told about the many miracles that have occurred all over world when Campus Crusade's Jesus Film is shown.

I was excited! The Lord had already laid it on my heart to make the Jesus Film a priority. Now I was beginning to see what it could do. This was a sort of reinforcement and confirmation of what I'd heard. It was a nice thing about the otherwise lousy surgery. I was keyed!

We (Les was with me) had started arrangements in May. We picked up an amplifier, speakers, and a screen from Campus Crusade. I think I bought the last projector in the world, or at least in that part of the world, and it was an expensive little beast—around $3,500. But it was missionary-proof, field tested in Botswana, and I knew it was tough. We were going to need a tough one if we were to take the film to remote villages beyond all those goat tracks I've been describing. We had a generator that would provide the power source. We got everything we'd need except the movie. I couldn't get a copy of the film.

Not only that, when we got home to Balama, we found that they had sold us the wrong plug for the amp. This was not Campus Crusade's fault; it was the sound system people. They were not just around the corner, either; we couldn't just exchange the plug for the right one. Unable to use the equipment, we had to put the project on hold.

When a worker named Darren came down later that year to help out, the Jesus Film was his priority also. He took one look at our stuff and agreed that we could not just jury-rig a sound system. Without that particular plug, we wouldn't have sound.

We also needed a second pickup, a workhorse that could carry the Jesus Film where no movie had gone before. We couldn't spare the one we had; it found daily, even hourly use on site.

Darren was eager to enter the program as a permanent worker, but he was having trouble raising support. For him to come up with a vehicle of his own seemed unlikely. So we prayed.

Now, here are two little lessons in prayer that you've probably already heard: 1) no request is too big or too small, and 2) be specific.

We asked the Lord for another pickup, and Darren knew exactly what he wanted and needed. It was to be a twin cab Mitsubishi Colt. I already operated a Mitz Colt, and it made sense to keep all our trucks the same brand. That would simplify the constant problem of finding repair parts. The truck was to have a canopy so that he could carry the whole team in the cab and all the equipment in back and keep everything secure, both from the weather and from thievery. New Colts go for $30,000 to $35,000, so we'd buy used. Got all that, Lord?

Customs regs had changed recently, so I e-mail-radioed some people in Maputo, the capital. They were a missionary group who had helped before, and they knew about regulations. I asked them what we had to do to import a truck from RSA. I figured delivery would be May of 2002, our next trip south, because we didn't have the money for one at the time.

They e-mailed back three hours later.

"Brenda, I have the exact truck you're looking for, but it's a Toyota."

Now there's only one truck in Africa tougher than a Mitz, and that's Toyota.

Okay!

"An American business man is liquidating, and this is part of the assets. Everything has to be bought right now."

"How much do you want?"

"Seventeen five, and you have to grab it fast. We need cash in hand by Friday."

This was a steal!

Also, it was Monday.

"We don't have 17,500 dollars. How about a down payment, and I'll see if my people in America can scrape together the rest. Thirty days to complete payment?"

He said okay.

So I sent him everything in the bank account and e-mailed America. Remember what I said about the Lord orchestrating His work? This was December. During December one of my supporters had given a large gift and others had given unmarked large gifts, so we had enough one-time gifts to pay off the balance of the truck.

The funds arrived via electronic transfer just before the end of December.

On January 2, I walked into the bank, slapped down the money, and had it sent down to the good folks in Maputo.

The truck was ours.

Peachy, but how would we get our new truck from Maputo up to Balama? I was going to America on February 1. I didn't have time to get down there and fetch the truck as well as get everything organized locally so that I could be gone for ninety days. We ended up with a plan to leave the truck in Maputo. They would then drive it the six hours down to Jo'burg, and I would take possession there, loading it in RSA and driving it home.

Everything always works out. You can always trust the Conductor.

We now had all the equipment, right down to the truck. Darren had just got married, and he and his bride shared the vision to run the Jesus Film team.

The figures pertinent to the Jesus Film are much the same now as they were when we launched the program. They are astounding. Of about 103,000 people in our county, 100,000 have never heard the gospel once. Counties to the north and south of us have no missionaries at all, so there are about 300,000 in the area still untouched. About eighty-five percent of the population is illiterate or nearly so, and many don't even understand Portuguese. No matter. The film is in the local language (in this case, Macua), and the people all understand the spoken word. Many live in back country, ill served by roads, and some have no roads at all.

That is where we went, and we are continuing to go there.

We will send scouts out ahead of time to find good locations, talk to chiefs, and get local permission. Without the blessing of local administrators, nothing can happen. Our work is certainly cut out for us, but the Lord is pushing to get moving quickly. Time is short!

A number of small tribes live along the coast, and most of the missionaries in the state work there. In the interior, though, there is one family in the north-central and me in the westernmost part. That's it. Fewer than thirty work in the whole state, and that number includes ancillary family members. Ten adults, maybe twelve, are serving about one million indigenous people; no one is certain of the population, but one million is a pretty good guess. There are considered to be eighteen million in Moz as a whole. As you can see, we have our work cut out to reach the entire state.

There is a Wycliffe team, a family man with a wife and four children. They are hard at work translating the Bible into Macua Meto (*me-too*), the local dialect.

It will be another tool, but they're nowhere near done, and we won't wait for that. Many local people speak Macua, but very few can read the language, so, frankly, having a Macua translation isn't going to help all that much now. When the literacy rate rises, the Bible will be there. But the Jesus Film is instantaneous, visual, and verbal. The moment the people see it and hear it, they can understand it. That's why the Jesus Film is so important.

The method: we plan to show the film three nights in a row in each village we reach. Stop and think about it. Can you even imagine having never seen a movie in your life? No Bambi, no Arnold Schwarzenegger, no Disney, no nothing. It takes three showings for these people to catch the message. The first time they see it, they're amazed and ecstatic and totally distracted. It's a miracle in living color.

The screen is six feet by six feet. But it is translucent—light goes through it—so that we can set it up in the middle of a crowd and people can watch it from both sides at once. Picture up to five thousand—yes, five thousand—crowding around to see it. Campus Crusade gets that many sometimes.

Normally we set it up in a soccer field, which is the only big, open place most villages have.

The second showing is still pretty gee-whiz.

Campus Crusade says that by the third showing, the people who are interested begin to really grasp it. Then our pastors who speak Macua use the sound system with a mike to explain things to those who are receptive. He asks all who are interested in learning more to come the next day.

During the days, then, we do follow-up meetings. We give out tracts to people who can read. We try to get groups of believers started in small fellowship groups wherever we go. You don't really call it a church. We also try to leave one pastor behind to help guide young believers.

One of biggest problems, obviously, is that there are too few trained pastors to raise up churches in the area. Christianity is brand new here. We have no tradition of people going into the ministry. So we too frequently have no one to guide the sheep when they're born again. It's critically important to get the gospel out there so that these people can know about the Lord. It is also critically important to send out follow-up teams.

To send out the film, to start more teams, to train local pastors, to get the gospel spread, to see churches planted—what a massive, massive work this will be over the next few years! Why do it? Because we know this is what we're mandated to do. In the last chapter of Mark, it's the Great Commission, not the Great Suggestion.

Our Lord is on the conductor's podium, and he is waving his arms.

36

Lost in a Sea of Grass

September 2000

One of the most famous lines in the world is when Stanley the newspaperman set out across Africa to find Livingstone, the explorer. You'll recall that he succeeded, and as he stepped up to the only white man in that part of the world, his words were, "Doctor Livingstone, I presume."

The rest of the world did not hear about those words for months. In those first simple days, there was no communication at all between interior Africa and the rest of the planet. Finally the wireless came in, and people could radio from place to place, so long as those places were not too far apart. As I described earlier, my early days in Moz were closer to that era than to this new one. Now the great new revolution I described is changing the way anyone on Earth can communicate directly with anyone else on Earth, and I am reaping the benefit.

I explained how my radio and laptop now work together. I can communicate in writing with anyone in the world instantly instead of having to rely on the vagaries of surface postal service. In fact, anyone in the world can e-mail me in Moz for the price of a local phone call. That still amazes me, and I've been using the system for a while. Here I am in remote Balama with no phone and no electricity, and I can run the whole ministry from the cab of my pickup.

It is not seamlessly smooth, of course. I need strong batteries to send e-mail. I can deplete two eleven-amp batteries quickly if I'm sending out a lot of messages. I have to start the motor in the pickup or they die even faster.

And, as is true everywhere else in the world, now and then the equipment quits doing what it's being paid to do. And therein lies adventure. For example, in September 2000 my transmitter started fouling up. It wouldn't send e-mail. I managed to get in touch with Pretoria, South Africa, a thousand miles away, by radio. The radio could be repaired, but that would take several months. I needed it before then, of course. The folks down in RSA radioed a game reserve about ten hours north of us. Yes, the people at the reserve had an extra radio, and they were willing to loan it to me until I could get mine fixed.

It was already 8:00 a.m. I had no time to lose. I hastily arranged for Duplo, the head pastor, to come along and packed the truck with food and sleeping gear. They said it would probably take me about eight hours to drive up there on the rough road. Plopped down in the middle of a vast game reserve, they themselves didn't bother with the road; they flew in and out in a Cessna.

Oh well, we can get there. We headed out and found good road for the first three-fourths of the way. Then it sort of drizzled down to a narrow dirt path, more like a bicycle path than a road, full of elephant tracks.

A word here about elephants: in areas of dense forest, they like to walk roads. Roads provide nice wide avenues for those huge, wide bodies. Dry ground supports elephants just fine, but during the rainy season, it's a different story. The African elephant is the world's largest, so we're looking at six or seven tons of weight. And elephant feet are the size of serving platters. Everywhere during the muddy season, those massive feet punch craters into the rain-softened roads. The tracks vary in depth from a couple of inches up to half a foot. On this particular road, the tracks where the elephants walked were about two inches deep.

The truck's wheels sort of tumbled clumsily from one cake-pan-sized track into the next. Needless to say, progress was very bumpy and very, very slow because there was a lot of wooded area, and the roads were therefore most inviting to the elephantine migrants.

But the way wouldn't get much worse, would it?

You won't hear me complain about the bridges out there either. There were none. We would slam our vehicle down into four-wheel drive granny gear and lumber down steep sloping ramps into the streambeds, waddle across, and grind up the other side. Most were dry, but the loose sand could bog you down in a heartbeat.

Just before dark we passed the last village, then a camp for visiting hunters. This was not the camp we were looking for. We were told that the camp we wanted was about nine miles away through tall grass out in the middle of the reserve. There would be no clear road as such. I might also mention that this was Africa's version of tall grass, eight or nine feet high!

Thanks to our late start and those wandering elephants, it was getting dark. The men at the remote camp knew we were on the way, so they had come through earlier with a Land Rover dragging a log. It mashed the grass down to show us the way.

We found where that trail started and took off. This was okay. We were making progress. As we wound through the bush, we could see where the log had been dragged. No problem.

Then we moved out of the sparse woodland into the sea of grass. It grew quite dark. Our headlight beams penetrated the wall of grass a good couple of feet and bounced back into our eyes. Even worse, the grass that had been bent down by the dragged log earlier in the day had by now bent itself back up. The flattened track disappeared.

The way couldn't get much worse.

A couple of miles deep into this and we were stymied. We got out and searched with flashlights, but we could see no sign of a way to go. We honked the horn and listened for an answer. Nothing chirped but crickets.

We were lost, surrounded by a sea of grass higher than the truck. We had no choice but to stop for the night and hope to pick up clues in the morning when visibility returned. We dined on beans eaten directly from the can.

I have mentioned that this was a game park. That meant grazers that bound about in the impossibly thick grass and carnivores that eat the grazers. People pay a lot of money to go out on safari and see exotic animals in their native habitat. Frankly, I'd consider paying a lot of money to avoid that.

Lions, leopards, and hyenas are scary and, in a way, romantic—or at least dramatic—but the most vexing of the reserve's animals are the mosquitoes, horrendous clouds of mosquitoes whining at our faces and ears. I almost could claim that the mosquitoes outweighed the elephants, but that would be exaggerating a little.

Duplo settled into the back, and I tried to get comfortable in the cab. If I opened the windows I became instant skeeter bait, so I could barely crack them. Too, in dense, high grass there is almost no breeze. It was warm and humid and stuffy and one of the worst nights I had spent in a long, long time

Almost daylight. We were up! Nothing had bothered us in that long, dreary night, although leopard tracks circled the truck, and we could hear elephants at their morning meal no farther than a hundred yards away. I climbed up on the truck's roof rack, looking around; the pastor examined the ground. We eventually found a beaten-down trail and followed it. Breakfast was a pitifully light snack from the stash of canned goods. We didn't want to waste time sitting around eating. We wanted to get there. After all, the way couldn't get much worse, could it?

Within another mile or so we hung up in a ravine. It happened so smoothly, too. As we went over the side, dirt collapsed under one front wheel, and it sank into an old termite hole. The truck bottomed out. There it sat, the frame firmly pressed into the dirt, and no matter what we tried, it could not pull itself out. It took us thirty minutes to dig the frame free and back the truck out of that hole.

We covered seven miles more. We were almost there! We waddled out into a big, sandy riverbed. We managed to cross through the loose sand without bogging, but getting out of the streambed was another cup of tea. On the far side, the track climbed out up an eight-foot ramp onto solid land. Ahead lay firm ground supporting open woodland. It wouldn't get any worse, right?

Incidentally, did I mention the red ants? They skittled over and started stinging us whenever we set a foot on the ground. They stung like fire, too.

Unfortunately, an elephant had broken a tree down across the path; I've mentioned elsewhere how they'll ride a tree down and break it off to get to the tender greenery in its top. Now we had no room to get around, and the tree was too big for us to cut through. We were stuck once more.

Enough. We locked up and walked the final few miles.

This was about our only choice, but it was not a good choice. A lot of leopard tracks followed the same ragged road that we did. We prayed a lot as we moved briskly along!

This was the beginning of the hard, dry season. The trees were dropping their leaves, leaving them light, open, and lacy overhead. Leopards prefer to hang out on a limb and pounce from above, but the lost foliage left the limbs nearly bare with nowhere for cats to hide. That weighed greatly in our favor.

The threat of death aside, it was a lovely walk. Antelope of various sorts drifted in and out through the open scrub. Gazelles, sweet and graceful, watched us momentarily then sponged away or simply trotted daintily off beyond sight. Even a family of boars appeared beautiful in its own delightfully grotesque way as they shuffled off into the bush.

When we stumbled out onto an airstrip, we knew we were there. But there was no plane!

Had we come all this way only to miss them?

We slogged on into the camp, and you should have seen the wide eyes and gaping mouths of the Mozambiquan cook and helpers. It isn't every day that strangers pop out of the bush on foot.

With much gesture and exclamation, we explained in Portuguese about the fallen tree that blocked our way.

"We have to wait till the bosses get back," they said. The three white men who managed the camp were out in the plane counting elephants and buffalo, we learned; they would soon return.

And then in true bush hospitality, our hosts offered us tea, cookies, and a hot shower with genuine running water! What a joyous luxury.

The surroundings were just as sumptuous. The camp sits on the Lugenda River as it winds its way north, eventually to form part of the boundary between Moz and Tanzania. In the tale about the elephant's child in his *Just so Stories,* Rudyard Kipling describes the "great, gray-green, greasy Limpopo River, all set about with fever trees." I think that Kipling wanted to impart an exotic, somewhat sinister quality to one of Africa's great rivers, the better to emphasize the vivid danger into which the elephant's child walked. The Lugenda, also one of Africa's great rivers, is exotic and great (about a hundred yards across) and, in fact, gray-green. But there's nothing sinister to mar the pleasant, relaxed feeling of that place. There is a massive beauty to it and to the rolling land around it. Waving grass and open savannah, the kind of classic scenery that says "Africa!" shimmered in the brilliant sunlight.

The three managers returned betimes, most relieved. They had decided that if we hadn't yet made it in by the time they got back, they would go out looking for us. They loaded men and axes into their Land Rover, took us back to our truck, cleared the tree, and we drove up the ramp onto high ground, following them back. Incidentally, that tree came as quite a surprise to them; they had just driven that track the day before. Elephants work fast.

My original plan had been to get the radio and start right home. But between the elephants, mosquitoes, sand, ants, and downed trees, not to mention my poor old weary body, I was about finished. It was now 9:00 or 10:00 a.m. We would never make it the whole way before dark. And frankly, my traveling partner wasn't any bucket of cheer and enthusiasm either. The trek had been horribly draining. Reluctantly, we decided to rest there for the day and start back early tomorrow.

God had work for us, unbeknownst.

The Moz men at the reserve had never heard of Jesus. Duplo hung out with them a good six hours and, in the course of that time, was able to bring the conversation around to Jesus. The men listened attentively, for we had earned the right to be heard. They were just plain shocked that we had survived the night out on the reserve.

"No one would ever sleep out there!" they insisted. "It's very dangerous, and many who try end up killed! This protection of Jesus is an amazing thing!"

The tracks had shown us that the leopard prowled, yet nothing had bothered us during the night or on the walk in. This weighed mightily in the eyes of those men. One of them could read, so the pastor left printed information and promised to bring them the Jesus Film one day.

While all this was going on, I was witnessing to the three white men in English. We swapped war stories, which is always fun. They told crazy tales that had happened to them, and neither they nor I dared inflate or exaggerate, for we were all bushwise. Lies and excesses would be revealed instantly, discrediting the speaker.

But then they hardly had to exaggerate. These folks dealt with everything from lions jumping onto their trucks and trying to come through the windows to sixteen-foot pythons. One of the men had grabbed the tail of said python just to see what it would do. Okay, that's not something I would think to do right off. The fellow almost lost an arm when the snake whipped back with most of its body to chase him off. Another man lost his little finger when a lion charged their open Land Rover, swatting his hand and sending his rifle flying into the bush. Another hunter managed to shoot it before it took more than a finger.

And I told them what God had done for me. One of the three was, so to speak, open to recognizing the temporal and spiritual protection of Jesus. The other two were closed.

This was neither defeat nor victory on my part. Reception of the Word is the business of the Holy Spirit. My business is to deliver it.

You will remember that when Jonah preached to Nineveh, they all repented, much to Jonah's chagrin. When Nahum came to the same city a generation later, they closed their ears and refused the message. Both Jonah and Nahum were in God's will. Both were equally successful therefore, for both obeyed God. Obedience is the name of the game, not numbers on a scoreboard.

Were we wasting our time because our audience that day was so few in number? Of course not! In fact, Luke, in his fourth chapter, points out that God himself does not work purely on numbers. For instance, even though a great many people were afflicted by famine, Elijah came only to the widow in Zarephath.

No life is immaterial, not theirs and not yours. There are never "too few to bother with." Every life is precious. Every life is worth saving. And he will send whomever he can get to go.

What amazes me is that there were needs, those men's and ours, that God met. He met our need by keeping us under his protection, and we could take the message of love and eternal life into the deepest bush. And I do mean deepest. No one lived beyond that camp where we spent the day resting. The village we had passed through as we jumped off into the bush was the village the cook and helpers belonged to, and that was the end of civilization.

What a privilege to spread his message there! We promised we'd be back, and we will, despite the awful road. This was the mission the Lord gave us in 2002 and 2003. He loves those few men, you see, just as much as he loves whole nations.

There is a postscript. Two, actually. We slept in real beds in bungalows of grass and bamboo on concrete slabs. There were bathrooms with bucket-flush toilets (these have the normal toilet seat like yours, but they're flushed by tossing a bucket of water into the commode). What unexpected pleasure in so distant an outpost!

We were reaping the benefit of visiting a hunting camp. People come in with special permits and big bucks to hunt game. Bush camps therefore pamper the hunters as much as they can, courting return trips and good recommendations. Accommodations are understandably rugged, but by the norm of the area, they can be called extravagant.

And so we showered, slept well, and took off by daylight with the loaned radio tucked into our load. We managed to get back through all that and arrived home by dark. In daylight, those nine miles through tall grass are a lot easier to get through.

The other postscript was a genuine treat. We were just leaving the grass and getting back onto the narrow, one-lane path that is the highway, headed for civilization. As we came around a blind curve in the woods, we encountered a huge male leopard walking in the road (This, we learned later, was an excellent sign. When the leopard moves abroad by day, he is not concerned about poachers).

That sleek and golden angel of death broke into a casual gallop, loping easily along in front of the truck. We clocked him at about fifteen miles an hour, and he wasn't even trying. Suddenly the cat leapt aside into the bush. The brush was particularly dense at that spot, unyielding. There was nowhere he could have gone, and we were right behind him. And yet he instantly disappeared.

Gone. Not a leaf moved. Not a blade of grass rustled. There was no sign of him, no hint that a killer prowled so close at hand.

The angel of death had simply evaporated.

A Word about Game Reserves

The Great White Hunter in his pith helmet strides through tall grass, following his simple native guides, with picturesque acacia trees posing on the horizon behind him. The black guides, invariably dressed in a loincloth or something, freeze and point. Game! The Great White Hunter raises his very expensive rifle and aims. Bang. A big-game animal falls.

What nonsense!

Well into the '30s and '40s, people in the northern countries still had no real idea of what Africa was truly like. Their notions mostly came from *National Geographic* articles, nearly every one of which would have a black and white photo from a small airplane looking down on running wildebeest (that's gnus) or elephants.

They remembered that President Teddy Roosevelt liked to shoot elephants and things somewhere in Africa. When her father died, Elizabeth II ascended to the throne of England as she slept at Tree Tops, a unique African hotel built up in a tree, literally. You looked down on a waterhole from the elevated verandah, and they turned on floodlights at night when the elephants came in. And people everywhere just loved a rather aloof gentleman named Martin Johnson and his cute, perky, energetic wife, Osa. The Johnsons wrote articles and took movies of their escapades in Darkest Africa. They were internationally popular. All these adventures were pretty much manufactured for profit, and their hokey hubris bore very little resemblance to the real Africa.

Finally, reality began to take hold. Television series such as *Zoo Parade* with Marlon Perkins started to paint a better picture. Walt Disney Studios made *The African Lion,* one of their True Life adventures. And now there's the Discovery channel and similar venues where people can see a close-to-accurate depiction of the continent. Attitudes have changed from everything-is-dangerous-and-out-to-get-you to wow-this-is-so-neat!

The real gee-whiz of Africa, at least for Americans, is still the animals. Although their numbers and habitat are woefully depleted, the African animals are still out there, and there is nothing else like them in all the world. Not everything is dangerous, but a surprising lot of it is. And yes, it is all so very neat and gee-whiz unless you live right next to it. Then it loses a bit of its glamour.

Many of Africa's wild animals now live on reserves. Some rich game areas, in fact, have become household names. Many Americans recognize Tsavo and Serengeti or simply Kenya. What lives there? Who knows? Game managers do counts of the big stuff, usually by airplane or helicopter, but I don't think the birds and reptiles and all the little species have ever been censused. We don't know how many animals are out in the game reserves or even exactly what they are.

To add to the confusion, animals are called by many names. There is the Latin name, of course, bestowed by taxonomists. Each African dialect has its own glossary of animals. The Boers and other European cultural groups have theirs. For example, we speak of various kinds of bucks and often call them deer, but they're antelope. Even field guides have to provide half a dozen names for each kind.

The game reserve where we traversed the sea of grass in order to borrow the radio is one such, and a very nice one. But many places in northern Moz are similarly graced with lion, leopard, elephant, a large variety of antelope, baboons, crocodiles, hippo, snakes (oh, my goodness, snakes!), a lot of wild boar, the most amazing birds, and wild dogs.

Interestingly the things that the old movies and travelogues described as most dangerous are usually not the things most likely to be dangerous. For example, in the old Hanna-Barbera *Yogi Bear* cartoons, Yogi was constantly trying to thwart the park ranger and steal picnic goodies. And in some of America's national parks, bears can indeed present a problem for campers and picnickers. The bears can become quite sophisticated about stealing edibles. There is no such bear problem in the game park just west of Johannesburg, but designated picnic areas are fenced anyway. A friend, Thelma, and I found out why.

We toured the park on a Saturday afternoon, and I loved it. We saw a lot of animals and enjoyed pleasant vistas. We yakked and laughed, alternately solving the world's problems and catching up on the past. Then we turned aside into a picnic area for lunch. It looked like picnic areas the world over with gorgeous shade trees and those weather-proof cement tables. We parked under a particularly lovely tree and chatted away as we set out fruit and built our sandwiches. Neither of us took note of the fact that our backs were to the gate.

Thelma suddenly leapt back a step, open-mouthed and speechless, staring behind me in horror. A gray flash darted past my shoulder and grabbed a peach.

"What in the world ... ?"

I wheeled around and waved my arms wildly at—an ostrich!

The greedy ratite had slipped in through the gate when no one was looking. There it stood, a feathered thief nearly six feet tall, eyeing our food for another quick grab. Thelma told me later that she spotted the bird running right for us with neck outstretched moments before it seized the peach. She said her voice wouldn't come, she was so shocked.

That's understandable. An ostrich?

It stepped back a moment, hesitating, its black eyes darting from the food to us to the food ... Then a campground attendant came running and shooed the bird back out the gate.

We stood there laughing until our rattled nerves settled down a little. You see, an ostrich is not cute like a mischievous little gray jay stealing potato chips in a Canadian picnic site. Ostriches kick. A blow from those powerful legs can crush ribs or break your back. And of course that's not to mention the murderously fast, sharp beak right up there at eye level. We could easily have lost a fight over our picnic supplies.

My immediate lesson in that one was a simple one; never turn your back on a gate, particularly one that is obviously there for a reason. Derive whatever spiritual message from that that you wish.

You may not have expected an ostrich to be dangerous, which it is, but you are certain, I'm sure, that the African lion is king of the jungle, right? Really bad news for anything that crosses its path, right?

Well, I have a missionary friend who tells of an incident that occurred in her district in December of 2001. An old lady was sitting in her hut on the edge of her village, stretched out in a hammock sort of bed slung in a wood frame. Suddenly a lion came charging out of the bush and ran straight at her! It came galumphing right up to her—and dived down under her hammock. There it crouched, trying its best to hide!

She started screaming, of course. Who wouldn't? Her relatives came running. They grabbed her and pulled her into the house next door. They slammed the door just in time, for here came a pack of wild dogs, chasing after the lion. The dogs found it instantly, of course, and shredded the king of beasts on the spot.

The villagers were shocked. They knew that if it's a fight between wild dogs and anything, including lions, you put your money on the dogs. But they had never before seen dogs get brave enough to enter the village like that.

The locals near game reserves know a lot about the animals around them. They understand their habits and their ways. Most are highly competent in the bush.

Unfortunately, the locals also think that anything that moves is free game, and they'll kill it if possible. The animals ostensibly protected by the reserve have no idea where the property line is and wander outside the boundaries, as the dogs and their lion prey did. The locals know where the line is and violate it anyway. They poach the big ones, poachers from Tanzania with guns.

Game departments send patrols out, but here you're talking about a very large area. Just in our neck of the woods, two normal counties stretch 200 miles (320 kilometers) across each direction. There are no easy trails back in there, so enforcement personnel prefer to use an airplane for patrols. Poachers prefer that also. Airplanes are very easy to hide from when you're out in the bush.

While we're on the subject of reality versus glamour, I might mention that the African people are neither more nor less exotic than Texans. If we did a travelogue of Texas to show to an audience of rural Africans, the way they make travelogues of Africa to show to Texans, the good folks in Dallas and San Angelo would look pretty weird to the audience. African viewers would have just as much trouble grasping the concept of shopping at Nieman-Marcus as Texans do grasping the African ways of life.

Despite poaching and all, though, the north of Moz is an untapped treasure. If that treasure is exploited wisely, everyone wins. Once the rest of the world catches on that the area is beautiful and blessed with game, it will beat a path to our door, bringing money with it.

And yes, I see a spiritual lesson even here. Within every faith-filled person there is a huge, untapped resource just waiting to be exploited. It can be exploited wisely or foolishly, thoroughly or not at all. But it's there.

It is inside you right now. But it is up to you to tap it through prayer, listening, and obedience. Oh, the things Jesus could do if only his followers could realize their full potential in him!

37

The Kids We Serve

Triplets

Things were not going well for this lady. Her husband, a known thief, had escaped from police and was currently on the run. No one had seen him lately. She had a three-year-old girl and a seven-year-old boy and one basket of manioc root to feed them all on. Remember, manioc is an empty carbohydrate containing no nutrients.

And then she gave birth.

To triplets.

Starvation was drying up her breasts. She could not sustain one baby let alone three, and her two older children were slowly starving. Buy some formula? A can of formula costs a week's wages if it's available, and in this area it was not.

I was eating lunch at my house that Friday in December 2001 when a social worker came by with a letter. Triplets had been born, and they weren't going to make it without intervention. The woman's local government official had sent a man on a bike to ask us to come get them. They might be dead already.

We dropped everything and took off in the truck. We were fifteen miles from the main village, and the woman's village lay beyond that. There was no road to it. We drove through shortgrass along a bike path, praying for our poor, put-upon tires the whole way. It took awhile to find her place; we finally located it by asking directions of chiefs and everyone else.

There she sat in her hut with three babies that weighed about three pounds each. She had been to her local clinic after the births, and her birth cards were in order. From them we knew the date of birth and the infants' weights. They had neither gained nor lost anything in three weeks.

She spoke only Macua. We explained to her, with a social worker interpreting, that we had a house for her and that we would be pleased to take her and her children. She agreed to come with us.

We helped her pack up all her belongings, which consisted of a pot and that basket of manioc. It took us less than five minutes.

We arrived back at Balama just as it was getting dark. We settled them into a little house with beds and blankets and some food for the night with the promise that we would outfit them the next morning.

The family's complete wardrobe consisted of what they were wearing. Beginning the next morning, we gave them clothes and started feeding them three times a day. The kids especially were amazed. It was beautiful—they had just walked into another world.

But this idyllic turn of events could not last forever. The woman needed more long-term help than we could give her. Fortunately, we managed to find the grandmother. She came down from her village to help the mother with her three new babies.

The mother arrived in our care in such bad condition we were afraid we were going to lose her. Malnutrition, stress, and the birth each drained her—a triple whammy. But she was strong-willed. She began to recuperate.

Grandmother was the real powerhouse in the family, though. She grasped hold of Jesus and told everyone Jesus was the one doing this. She insisted that they all needed to go to church and learn more about Jesus. As a result the whole family never missed a Sunday. The kids were there because Grandmother said so, the mother came because she had to, and the grandmother eagerly blotted up the Word with a spiritual hunger even greater than the kids' need for physical food. What a joy!

How about you? Like these children, are you going to church because the rest of the family does? Or maybe you're like the mother, who has no real choice. I hope that you're like the grandmother. She realized immediately where real strength and protection lay. She grasped the immediate, easy-to-see help of Jesus, which led her to the ultimate help, salvation. Salvation is not immediate; it's impossible to see, and we've no clear idea what lies beyond the grave.

But that lady is marching stalwartly down the right road, as I hope you are. And the rest of her family, whom she loves so dearly, are being pulled along with her.

We gave them a field, a piece of acreage. We also gave them seed and helped them plant and hoe. There is a purpose in this, and it is not charity. This woman and her brood had nothing. Zip. She had not a single resource upon which to survive let alone build a life. We gave her the resources to get started.

It is essentially the same objective that we serve with the malnutrition program and baby clinic. The objective is to see the mother and children on their feet and thriving. The idea is to get them independent when they have no other way to get there. It's not a dole.

The triplets, though, threw another marble into the blender. How many women can tend two young children *and* three babies *and* a plot farmed with nothing but hand tools? So far, this mom has been Superwoman and has been able to handle the load pretty much by herself. She's taking it a day at a time.

When I left for the States a few months later, the triplets had doubled their weight and all concerned were doing fine. It looks like they will all make it.

The husband still hasn't shown up.

And the police will be waiting.

Pasheko

Pasheko's mother died when he was a few weeks old. His grandmother tried to find a wet nurse, but in her area women are very superstitious about feeding someone else's baby. Then she heard that maybe someone in that school place in Balama had milk for him. She brought Pasheko to us.

Before she died, the little guy's mom never did produce enough milk to feed a baby, so he got a very rough start in life. He was nearly starved to death when he arrived. I was going to the States in two days, but I was able to quickly set up a feeding/milk program for him. I left instructions with the healthcare workers and departed on a three-month speaking and fund-raising tour. Frankly, I pretty much assumed that little Pashenko would not be there when I returned.

He survived. He improved. The folks at our facility put him on formula. At three months they gave him the baby food we make from local corn flour.

Incidentally the recipe is pretty simple. We boil corn flour into a soupy breakfast cereal sort of mush and add sugar. We also stir in crushed beans and peanuts if the infant's tummy can take it. Neither beans nor corn nor peanuts provide complete protein by themselves (no vegetable protein source does). But when eaten together, corn, beans, rice, and peanuts provide all the amino acids that growing babies require (and it's cheap, too!).

Pasheko was one of those babies whose stomach couldn't handle beans, so he got peanuts and a few other local foods. He did well on that. When I got back I was amazed to see him not only surviving but looking good.

And he laughed.

You cannot imagine the feel-good vibes you get when a tiny baby, sickly yesterday and healthy today, laughs for you.

In the States Pasheko would be identified with the generalized tag, "Failure to thrive." He had a lot of respiratory problems, true. Usually antibiotics took care of them. A couple of times, his weak lungs landed him in the hospital for more intensive treatment. But for an orphaned baby who started life starved, he was holding his own and doing all right.

His little tum never did develop the ability to handle beans. This presented the problem of how to get enough protein into him.

Normally we wean babies off formula at age three months because formula and milk are so scarce and hard to get. But we kept Pasheko on supplemental formula a lot longer than three months, trying to build him up.

At ten months of age, he weighed almost ten pounds. You may gasp, aghast, but believe me; by the standards of the situation, this wasn't bad.

Then he started losing weight. On the chance that the foster mother taking care of him wasn't doing something right, we put him with a different foster mom. I *knew* she was doing it right, feeding him six times daily. She lived right next to me!

At age two years, he weighed eight pounds. We were pumping malnutrition formula into him and trying everything else we could think of, to no avail.

"Tuberculosis is very common in this area, and his lungs aren't doing well," the doctor suggested. "Let's treat for TB and see how he does. It can't hurt."

Pasheko's failure to thrive sure wasn't for lack of appetite. Every time his elbow bent, his mouth flew open. He was eating everything in sight. So he was a good candidate for TB treatment. He sailed through the first two weeks of the TB regimen. If it was going to work, and the problem was just TB, he'd perk up and start to respond.

He didn't.

The doctor said, "I strongly suspect he has AIDS."

We were all devastated. All of us. We prayed, of course, but there was nothing to be done for him. There is no treatment, and in that area not even tests, for AIDS. His little body was terribly depleted, and it just kept deteriorating.

I had to go on a supply run south to Nampula. I left early Friday morning after checking in on him Thursday night. His skin seemed loose, but he was holding his own. When I got back Sunday, he was gone. He had died on Saturday.

We all knew it was coming, and yet it was a shock to everybody. We really thought that just possibly it wasn't AIDS and that we had him on the road to recovery.

Pasheko was textbook typical, as AIDS babies go. They usually do not live more than two and a half years. He was two years, three months. They often suffer from tuberculosis and other infections that healthier people resist. They do not develop well. They keep getting problem after problem without bouncing back from any of them. That was Pasheko.

He was the first orphan given into our direct care that was lost, and his passing hit us all surprisingly hard. We try not to get too attached, but every time I see his picture or watch the video that we take around to the churches, I lose it. I think about his beautiful spirit, that laugh he always had, and it's like losing my own son. In fact, I am in tears right now as I tell you about him.

Certainly we will see him again in heaven. God promises me that, and I am claiming his promise. But to be honest, that's cold comfort when I think about Pasheko's goofy little smile. No matter how theological and heavenly I try to be, *now* affects me so much more intensely than does *someday*. The best I can say is that we did all we could for him. He had more prayer going than anyone else.

And he died loved.

The AIDS Problem

When I am Stateside, the question I get asked most, and the topic that invariably comes up when I speak is, "What about AIDS?"

It seems everyone has heard about the havoc AIDS is causing in sub-Saharan Africa. I see the concern everywhere I turn. What *is* the situation, and what is being done?

An important ministry that gets very little press outside Africa is what I might call simple comfort. For example, there is a home in Blantyre, Malawi, that was founded by American doctors. There is nothing they can do to cure or even prevent AIDS. Their ministry is to give AIDS-stricken children the best life they can have for the few years they have. This home is for nothing but AIDS babies, a place where they can spend their few days in as much comfort as is possible.

We do something of the same sort at Balama. We employ prayer constantly, of course. We reach out to other children like Pasheko, trying to show them we love them and through our example that God loves them. We try to maximize what little temporal life that they have and prepare them for eternity.

What Americans hear is largely true: AIDS is rampant in Africa. Last year, out of Mozambique's population of about fifteen million, we lost a hundred thousand. The AIDS problem has not peaked yet either. It's growing, and the orphan problem is growing.

Under conditions and times like these, the Gospel takes on a dual role. It leads to eternal life, which is its most important function. Absolutely! But it is also the key to a better temporal life. The Christian is called to curb promiscuity, and AIDS is a sexually transmitted disease. Our goal therefore is not only to lead all whom God has called to eternal life but to secure here on earth a better temporal life, minimizing the curse of AIDS.

The AIDS stats I mentioned above, 100,000 gone out of 15 to 18 million, were posted for the year 2000, and they are probably low. Tests for the AIDS virus are not given in Moz or in most of the rest of Africa. Testing is just too expensive and therefore not done. Many who die of AIDS are recorded as having succumbed to something else more immediate. They may have contracted tuberculosis, another respiratory disease, or another disease altogether. But their general health had already been greatly impaired by the HIV, and the disease of which they die is simply the last straw loaded onto the camel.

How many are affected? God only knows.

No one else does.

Death Diverted

There are a lot of words to describe our facility at Balama, but *sleepy* isn't one of them. Each day, all day there's this low background hum of activity. You realize, I trust, that in the USA and other such regions, all the cooking, kitchen cleanup, laundry, and so forth are done in private, behind closed doors. Even barbecues and family get-togethers usually happen in backyards and patios away from public view. As you drive down streets, the neighborhood may look deserted when actually people are busy doing lots of things.

At Balama many of the buildings are quite open. Cooking is done on open fires. Everything pretty much happens right out in plain sight. With people constantly moving around out in the open, visiting and doing household things as well as outdoor things—hauling wood and water, for instance—it's quite an active place. That's what I call the background hum.

Every now and again, though, the place bursts into wild busy-ness.

In late July the joint was jumping in one of those spurts of activity in addition to the usual stuff. Our work crew was preparing our year's supply of food for storage. They were putting beans and corn into easy-to-manage sacks and stowing them in the storehouse. Remember, we're talking tons here, a huge, huge job.

One person was not taking part in this frenzy of action.

Me.

I doddered like a ninety-year-old in a three-legged race. True, I was steadily gaining strength, but I had not yet fully recovered. It was my back. I'll tell you about it in greater detail later. The Lord had miraculously corrected an out-of-line vertebra jarred askew by that constant driving on our terrible rural roads. I felt better—so much better—but I couldn't bend over yet or kneel easily, and running was out of the question. Pick up a heavy sack? It is to laugh.

Suddenly a woman screamed and everything froze! The workers stopped cold to listen. The whole facility went dead silent.

It was a mother close by, and she was screaming that her child was dead!

I waddled as fast as I could around the bamboo fences to her house. Everyone else had heard the yell. They all dropped what they were doing and came running. Quite a crowd surrounded the child when I finally got there a minute later.

A seven-year-old boy had suffered a massive seizure and ceased breathing. His body lay totally limp, like wet dish towels. His eyes were fixed open, the pupils dilated. Stinking vomit covered his mouth and clothes.

My years of ICU training took hold automatically. Rescue breathing, followed by CPR if necessary.

But my back wouldn't let me bend over enough to deliver mouth-to-mouth! So I knelt by his side, praying, "Lord, give him breath! Bring him back!"

There are other rescue moves you can do. I cleared his airway. I gave him a hard slap on the back and a firm sternal rub on his breastbone. All the while I was yelling, "Breathe, kid! Breathe!"

He coughed and took a breath. I continued to stimulate him, calling his name and commanding him to breathe. He sluggishly sucked in more air and coughed again.

His eyes rolled and lost that death stare. He was back.

The onlookers started murmuring. The murmur became noise.

As I was praising and thanking Jesus, here came the child's father pushing his way through the crowd. I knew the fellow, a stalwart and upright man and a devoted Muslim.

The distraught look on his face told the world that he was a loving father, too.

I told him, "Jesus has just saved your son. May I have your permission to pray for his full recovery?"

You see, the child had aspirated; that is, he had sucked some of the vomit into his lungs. Aspiration causes a septic pneumonia that invariably kills in three days or less. Invariably. That is why ambulance crews work so hard to prevent any vomit from getting into air passages.

The distraught man nodded.

"Yes, pray. I want my son to live."

The bubbling crowd fell silent. Many who were members of our church prayed with me.

"Where two or three are gathered, there I am among you," Jesus said in Matthew 18:20, and we always took him at his word. When a whole horde of praying people is gathered, miracles happen!

Within minutes the little boy was on his feet. His color looked good, his balance was restored, his eyes were bright; in a word, he was normal.

Normal!

Karen Sterzer, who was helping us at the time, drove him to the hospital. There he received medicine for febrile seizures caused by malaria. Half an hour later they were back, and Karen delivered him to his house.

He was smiling happily as he jumped out of the car. Know why? It was his first car ride. Kids have their own priorities in life.

His parents were beaming, too, and a car ride had nothing to do with it.

Postscript

For the next two days I kept a close check on his lungs and found no sign whatever of aspiration pneumonia.

He has been completely cured.

A Big Pig Problem

Her mother died in childbirth, so this little baby went home with her grandma. Under Grandma's wise care, and with our formula and food supplements, the infant did well. The child was about six months old when this story took place.

One day, like any other day, Grandma left the baby inside her grass hut near their small cooking fire. Grandma then went off to fetch water from a nearby well. The baby began screaming loudly enough that Grandma could hear her from down the trail a way. She returned, running.

An uncle nearby also came roaring up to see what was wrong. As they approached, a pig came trotting out of the hut with the baby in its mouth! The pig had picked up the child by the back of her left thigh. Now it was hauling the noisy, tender morsel away toward the bush.

Uncle and Grandma pounded on the pig's head until it dropped the baby. The pig beat a hasty retreat. The baby's leg was horribly mauled, with massive bruises and deep rips up the back of her thigh.

A word here about pigs: for starters, forget about the movie pig Babe. Babe was cute and had sound moral principles. Feral pigs in Third World countries are neither cute nor moralistic. The animals themselves are big, lean, and powerful, like the mean old razorbacks in your Southeast United States. They have huge, nasty teeth and massive jaws. They will eat anything they can find, and they are downright vicious. If you have to fight either an attacking dog or an attacking pig, choose the dog; your chances are better.

Grandma and Uncle stopped the baby's bleeding and bound the leg as best they could then took her to a local clinic several miles away. The nurse there would not treat the baby further. They could not afford treatment, you see; a penicillin shot cost five cents American, and Grandma didn't have that much. Frustrated, the uncle walked the eight miles to my house and asked for five cents, explaining the situation.

Now think about this. If a stranger came to your door saying a pig tried to eat his niece, would you give him money? You would give him points for imagination and consider him loony to expect you to believe such a tale. In our part of the world—indeed, throughout the Third World—his tale was not the least far-fetched. Nearly all pigs are free-range, and their diet consists of whatever they can find. Stories of seized children are not all that rare, though I had not up until then seen it personally.

We gave him the money for treatment, begged him to take good care of his niece, and asked him to bring her when she was well enough to make the trip. They came in about ten days later, Uncle and Grandma, to pick up their regular food supply for the baby. They allowed me to photograph the child's leg; that picture is in the center section. It is a true miracle that there are not any complications. The muscles were severely damaged, and probably some nerves as well. We are hoping she will walk without a limp, but her physical health is just fine.

Since then I've heard more than one story of pigs eating babies.

You don't find it in places where pigs are well fed, naturally. But missionaries I've talked to in other emerging countries say it is a problem. This is just another of the plain old gross things we have to deal with. The challenges we meet are abnormal, to say the least.

But pigs are not nearly as bad as the diseases.

Problems

An acquaintance in Texas waved her hand across the front page of the *Dallas Morning News* with its daily litany of death and crime.

"Look at all this! This is America," she said. "Aren't you glad you don't live here?"

I didn't bother explaining anything. But her assumption that in Africa you don't have all these drug- and alcohol-related problems is false. People who are more aware of the realities in Third World countries, however, ask legitimate questions about the problems faced both by missionaries and by the indigenous people. I try to answer their questions carefully and fully, for problems abound in Moz as they abound everywhere else.

In fact, many of the problems in Moz are very much like the problems in the States or Europe or in other industrially advanced countries. The details vary, but the root causes are the same.

Drugs, Alcohol, and Addiction

Drugs and alcohol cause as many problems in Moz as they do anywhere else. The big difference is that incomes are so low—minimum wage is $1.10 for an eight-hour day—that the folks can't afford anything fancy. You don't see the heroin-based drugs or fancy designer drugs cooked with chemicals. Not much hard stuff is used. The local people make their own. This is very easy. I will tell later how a fellow wanted to kill me. He was high on marijuana at the time. Marijuana is basically a semitropical plant that doesn't do well in cold. It grows just fine in Moz and is a cheap, even say free, drug of choice.

All the men grow their own tobacco because commercially made cigarettes are prohibitively expensive. Need I mention that the quality of these do-it-yourself products varies wildly.

They also make their own beer and corn liquor. Again, they cannot afford to buy fermented beverages, so they ferment some of their food crop. This is a double whammy. It takes corn out of the mouths of people whose diet is borderline anyway. And of course it gives rise to the problems associated with drunkenness the world over.

Disease

Disease is the major reason for the extraordinarily high death rate in developing countries, Moz among them. This is true for children and adults as well.

The fastest killers in Moz, flat out, are malaria and dysentery. If the malarial organisms attach to the brain, you're dead. Period. And because medical resources are so scanty, we lose people who might have been saved with more intensive treatment in a major medical facility.

AIDS? Who knows? It is undoubtedly the most underdetected disease in sub-Saharan Africa. Medical personnel in most parts of Moz lack the testing facilities to diagnose it. There are no drugs available to combat it or even to alleviate the suffering. Because their immune systems take a dive, people usually succumb to some other disease fairly rapidly. It is that disease that shows up in the records as the cause of death when actually, if the victim's immune system were up to snuff, he or she wouldn't have gotten it in the first place. The majority of diseases that take people down untimely are malaria, pneumonia, cholera, and dysentery. How many of these deaths are of AIDS masked by some secondary infection, no one knows. The only thing you can be certain of when you read statistics on AIDS in Moz is that they are guesses. How good as guesses? No one has any idea.

Children such as Pacheco succumb to AIDS in their first two years or so, but to the best of my knowledge, AIDS is not common in the children of Moz. We don't see a lot of it in babies.

Even without AIDS, malaria and cholera wreak havoc and always

have. Malaria is mosquito-born, as you no doubt know, and mosquitoes abound. Quinine and other drugs can control it to some degree.

Cholera and dysentery come from impure water, and sad to say,
that abounds also. Cholera is most common near the end of the dry
season. October and November, maybe December, are the prime
cholera months. The wells have dried up, and what little water there
is left has become polluted.

When one says "well," most people think of a deep hole in the
ground, usually drilled, with the water piped up. Wells in the USA's
arid Southwest can go down more than 1,500 feet. Now that's a well!
Here wells are hand dug in some swampy area where the groundwater
rises near the surface. They're maybe two or three feet across and five
feet deep. Toward the end of the dry season, they are nothing more
than slow seeps.

The people, usually the women, let water seep into these holes,
dip it out, and that's the household water used for food and drink. It
will be contaminated because these waterholes are pathetically dirty,
teeming with fecal bacteria. I think every animal in the district tries
to find a water source to defecate in. Okay, maybe I'm exaggerating,
but you get the idea. At the close of the dry season, as the more shallow waterholes sink away, people have fewer sources. So they con-
centrate around the few that remain, and the polluted wells get even
more so.

Cholera and dysentery abound.

Combating All This

We may not have AIDS drugs or diagnostic tools, but the Lord
has blessed us with a remarkable assortment of medications. Drug
costs in America are super high, but we are able to buy medicine
in bulk from drug companies in another country. Fifteen dollars
American purchases a thousand tablets of the simple, basic antibiotics. At pennies per dose for a child, usually less than a dollar a day
for adults, we can stop some diseases or at least blunt the misery they
cause. We can obtain drugs for malaria and cholera. We have a large

pharmacy compared even to some hospitals, so we have access to a variety of medicines, and we usually have enough in stock.

I emphasize that this is *only* because the Lord provides the money for us to do this. And the money comes from caring people a world away who will never in their lives see a case of cholera.

We approach each case with prayer anyway, drugs or no. And believe me, the prayers get really specific when the drugs don't work or are unavailable!

When I don't know what is wrong with someone, I ask and the Lord shows me what to do for him or her. I take to heart James 4:2, "You have not because you ask not." I ask. He reveals.

We don't have the regular diagnostic aids, so the Lord fills in for our lack. No joke. His Word says we must ask, and he will do it if we believe. He keeps his Word.

I am constantly in awe of what the Lord does to help those in need. Faith is meant to be simple and uncomplicated. Many times it is our own head (especially so for medical and other highly educated people) that gets in the way, stopping an answer from flowing through. I assure you, the Holy Spirit is available twenty-four hours a day, seven days a week to answer prayer.

When your brain scoffs, "No way!" spiritual hearing is blocked. Faith is believing in what you ask for even when you cannot see it!

Keep it simple. Whether you're in Mozambique or in your living room, faith like a child's is all we need. Say it, believe it, and receive it!

In the end I find that we are working as a team with our Lord as the hub of information. We don't have the knowledge and expertise to do the job. The Great Physician does.

Eva and Assimuno

Little Eva and her mother lived in Nyassa, the state to the west of Cabo Delgado. One day they came to Balama to visit Eva's grandma, Elisa. While they were in the district, Eva's mother died of cholera, and as a consequence Eva remained nearby with her grandma.

Now Eva had serious problems. Ever since she was three or four months old she suffered seizures. She was four and seizing up to six times a day when her momma brought her to Balama. She did not walk. She did not talk. She never crawled. Adults had to carry her everywhere. Understandably she was a nervous wreck, so agitated that she constantly ate the skin off the backs of her hands, leaving open, infected sores. In our picture section is a photo of her getting her hand treated. She became instantly hysterical whenever she was ousted from the security of her Grandma Elisa's arms. Speaking quite frankly, she was almost impossible to handle, especially because of her irritability. Why, this child could not even play. That is no life for a child, and our hearts went out to her.

Elisa, understandably, was desperate to find help.

They came to us, and as we treated Eva's open sores, Elisa begged us to do anything we could. Anything! We managed a medical consult with the only doctor in the area some thirty miles away. He gave her a ten-day supply of phenobarbitol, a standard medication to help calm the seizures. The barbiturate didn't stop anything, but it did slow them down a little. More importantly it showed that medication would indeed help, but neither the doctor nor we had a long-term supply.

Often it's not what you have but whom you know. I emailed some doctor friends in Tulsa. One of them, Doctor Regina, discussed the case with a pediatric neurologist who recommended an effective prescription. The doctors were coming over to Africa shortly to see us, so they brought the medicine with them.

As soon as they arrived at Balama, we plumped Eva down in front of them, and they did a detailed medical analysis. We started the child on a good medical regime. It took three or four weeks to get her adequately regulated, but the seizures came under control. Grandma Elisa was in awe.

While we were adjusting the dosage, we realized that witchcraft was also involved. It wasn't just a physical problem. There was a spiritual dimension as well. As we learned, her mother had indeed taken her to a witch doctor many times, desperate to get her cured of seizures. This opened the door to unclean spirits.

The first step is always prayer. In prayer, under the cover of Jesus, we commanded the demonic powers to leave. Eva calmed down considerably, and her seizures further diminished. Because she was much less nervous, she stopped chewing skin off the backs of her hands. She was still quite irritable, but Elisa and we could all see that prayer and pills were working together to ease her misery.

The doctors had come in September of 2000. In March of 2001, we realized the year's supply of medicine wouldn't last much longer. So we asked a gentleman from Canada to bring along more. He did so, and we were able to keep Eva going, doling the medicine out in measured amounts to Elisa to give to Eva.

In May of 2001, Elisa failed to bring Eva in from her village to get her medicine. She was due to come in. Then she was overdue. We didn't know where she lived or what village she belonged to. We were stymied.

A fortnight later Elisa showed up at the house.

"I hurt my foot," she explained, "and I haven't been able to travel. Very sorry."

"What about Eva? She's been out of medicine for two weeks!"

"Oh, she doesn't have seizures anymore."

"Not *any?*"

"No, none at all."

We laughed for joy. Since Elisa had come in all that way, I gave her a few pills in case Eva seized, rather assuming she wouldn't need them.

"If she suffers a seizure, give her these, but if she doesn't, don't."

We had been petitioning Jesus to heal Eva fully, and it became obvious that he had done exactly that!

What is most beautiful is the progress Eva has made since then. In addition to establishing the right prescription and dosage, we put her on a high protein, high fat diet. She responded well, gaining weight and strength. But she had an awful lot of catching up to do!

The first sign of improvement was that she started trying to stand. She had a terrible problem with balance; her brain had never had to make all those little wiring connections that help most people balance without thinking about it. Then with assistance she began taking a step or two. At first her legs wouldn't hold her weight. But slowly, slowly, the improvement came.

In church she started clapping to the music. Then she'd try to mouth the words. Everyone else in the world talks; she wanted to, too! When eventually she was walking up and down the aisles, sometimes even at inappropriate times, no one said, "Tsk tsk!" or hindered her. The Lord was rehabilitating her, and there was no other explanation. We rejoiced in a genuine miracle of love.

But what about her medicine? You will remember that the Canadian had brought along a new supply of medicine for Eva and it was no longer needed. We left it sitting on a shelf.

Seven months later, in September of 2001, Darren Clevenger came in to give us a hand. One fine day he and I were beside a little house with a brick-lined veranda, loading roofing grass into a trailer. Now when heavy equipment is out, or even semi-heavy equipment like our tractor, a bunch of kids soon gathers around to watch. I guess a fascination for loud things with wheels is pretty much universal. Among the kids this day was an emaciated little girl with a deformed hand.

Darren asked around, "Who is that?"

He was answered with shrugs. "I dunno. She's new here. Her parents just walked in from Tanzania."

Suddenly the child hit the ground in a full-blown grand mal seizure.

The other children ran off screaming. Darren instantly commenced praying.

I held her head to keep her from hurting herself on the veranda bricks until the seizure passed. As I was holding her, I too was praying against demonic influence.

She was breathing well when her mom and dad came hastening up. Her father snatched her away, obviously embarrassed, and trundled her off to a hut.

Before the mother left, I told her, "If you want help, please come to my house, that one right over there." I pointed it out.

The father was not the least receptive to any foreigner's help, and especially not some white woman's. I let it go at that. I could do nothing without permission.

The next morning, though, praise God, the mother came calling at my house with the little girl in hand. The child walked with a strange gait, the right leg swinging out oddly. Almost certainly some retardation or brain damage was affecting her right side. The seizures were frequent and terribly draining, the mother told me. The child could barely function.

Her name was Assimuno.

I asked permission to get the child a medical consult because, I told the mother, we knew of some medicine that might help.

You're right! I was referring to the medicine that had been brought for Eva and was not needed now.

Momma said yes.

Sure enough, the doctor—who had been Eva's doctor—helped get the right dosage figured out, and we gave Assimuno the medicine that had been brought for another. The seizures stopped in three weeks. Simultaneously we were able to put her on our high-protein, high-fat diet. Within a week or so of getting her regulated, we watched her play in my front yard with the other kids. That in itself was a miracle.

From the beginning Assimuno had such a wonderful personality. She seemed totally content, and she always gave me her beautiful, shy smile. I'd hug her and tell her I was her friend. She spoke only Macua, but that's what interpreters are for. Many a day she would come by my front gate. I might be busy, but she'd always wave, and I'd wave.

She comes to the Sunday school. Even though she has been seizure free for months, in one Sunday school class she manifested a small seizure, frightening the other children. I laid hands on her and rebuked the demonic spirit. The seizure stopped instantly.

Aha! Now I knew the mother needed more education in the power of spiritual forces. She'd been opening the door to demonic powers, and they need only a tiny crack of an opening to do their evil work.

Doors. Doors are so important in the spiritual world.

Here in Africa drums open doors. It is with drumming that the local shaman, or witch doctors, call down spirits. Incidentally, or perhaps not so incidentally, the rhythms are basically rock beats.

Assimuno, we learned from her mother, continues to have episodes because she is fascinated by the drums she hears. So we keep a close eye on her progress and rebuke the demons when necessary. She is unable to understand why she must not go to the drums.

It's a good thing to remember about life in the suburbs of America or Europe just as much as in Africa. Doors are opened whether you see them or not. People who think séances or Ouija boards are harmless fun open doors to demonic forces. Most people do not believe in witches and magic, and even fewer accept the notion of a real devil, Satan. They consider forays into that dark world to be cute or harmless mental exercises based in myth. Why, shucks. Don't the Harry Potter books help children develop an interest in reading? That's good, right? Would that every child were as hungry to read as are the Harry Potter fans, right?

Hardly! Where dark forces are glamorized, no matter how "cute" the medium, doors are opened. It is one thing to teach children about dark forces, and I believe every older child should know about them so that the child can be armed against them. But every child should also know that these forces are dangerous, not cute or desirable.

Doors. So important, doors.

In many parts of the world, including my corner of Africa, the local people fully accept the spiritual nature of their world. They accept, too, that those spiritual forces can influence their lives heavily. What they don't realize is the source of malign spiritual powers.

As you can see, it takes both physical and spiritual healing to handle many of the problems here in my world, and it takes both realms to gain wholeness in your part of the world, too.

Now we're praying that somehow the doors Assimuno finds so attractive can be closed to her. Then our Lord can complete his work in Assimuno as he did Eva.

Evil Spirits

What can you say when some belligerent agnostic or unbeliever confronts you and demands, "How can you *know* with such certainty that there is a God?"

The only thing I can say is, "I know he exists because I have met him."

I know that there is a Satan for much the same reason—I have personally encountered his power. It is no theological theory or abstract philosophy. Whether you choose to believe it or not, this is true: there is a Satan, and he and his minions are able to enter the physical realm.

Twice in the last eleven years I have experienced serious demonic attacks that are physical. This is not his usual attack mode, which is to plant doubts, wrong thoughts, and fears. Putting fear into you is one of his biggies because it disables you. Rather, these were attacks on my person.

On both occasions I was sound asleep in the middle of the night. I was awakened with a crushing feeling on all of my body except for the head and neck. My whole body was being pressed beneath an immense weight. Both times that it happened I awakened immediately, because I could not breathe. My chest was compressed so tightly that I certainly could not draw in enough air to make a sound or say anything.

The only way to combat the attacks of Satan is to invoke the name of Jesus. I couldn't say it out loud; the pressure was too intense. I thought the name, *Jesus! Jesus!* and just kept thinking it.

The great weight went *woof* and was gone. Then and only then was I able to speak aloud. The presence totally disappeared when it heard that name. Evil cannot stand against the name of Jesus.

Silly? I'm deluding myself? Stop and think. Would I describe something like this to you just to provoke a debate, knowing I might lose credibility? Hardly.

It's a terrifying thing to happen! Afterwards I sat up and thanked Jesus. I just kept on thanking him, praying and praising. On neither occasion did the presence return. That was a good confirmation that this was demonic power; demonic forces cannot remain in the presence of the name of Jesus.

Although those two attacks were unusual, they were not the only encounters I have had with evil forces. In fact, such encounters occur very frequently. I am absolutely at loggerheads with the area's witch doctors, and it was true of VOL as well. Indeed wherever the people of Jesus Christ enter realms held in Satan's sway, confrontation results.

Not to put too fine a point on it, but the witch doctors hate my guts. Many a night they drum nearby. The beat of the drum is a proven way to call down demonic powers. They dance and sing all night and call in evil spirits to descend on me and do evil to me.

Why do they consider me their worst enemy? Because I am. The most important reason is that I am fully the servant, and nothing less, of the one true God through his Son, Jesus. That puts me opposite Satan immediately. But in a more practical context, I cut their profits.

When women bring their sick children in, those children will almost certainly have juju sacks tied around their necks. Juju bags are protections against illness. The fact that mothers are bringing their sickly children to us tells more eloquently than words how well the juju works.

The children will probably also be wearing health strings. These are plain old cotton string that has been blessed by a witch doctor for a fee. I need not mention, I'm sure, that he does not work for free.

The very first thing we tell mothers who enter our system is, "This is a program of Jesus Christ, and he is more powerful than any witch doctor. He is the most powerful doctor on earth. If you want us to help you, you must remove all these strings and never take your child back to the witch doctor. We will pray for your child's protection, and we'll give you the medicine that will help your child."

It's almost unanimous. They dump the shaman. Once in a while a mother falters, of course. We're dealing with extremely powerful forces, superstitions, and cultural habits here. She says okay, and probably she really means it at the time. She cuts off the juju sacks and the health strings and tries to put them in her pocket. Naturally, when she gets home, they would go back on. She bought them, after all, and it never hurts to play all the cards you have.

We don't buy into that. When we cut them off, we burn them. So I am hitting witch doctors and shaman where it hurts most—in their income.

There is a lot we do out there in the physical, natural world to combat the spiritual. It's all about opening doors. Juju sacks and health strings are huge, wide, barn-sized doors.

I feel that it is important for you to know that this is spiritual business never ever to be taken lightly. Anyone who would work in the mission field, foreign or domestic, exotic locale or right in the neighborhood, must be spiritually covered. *Must!* We pray for the blood of Jesus over our body because the blood of Jesus does indeed protect. We have from God three spiritual weapons: the name of Jesus, prayer, and the blood of Jesus. You use them all to be fully armed against demons.

When demons come, you know that you're not under the spiritual cover of prayer as deep as you should be. Those two spiritual attacks taught me that the hard way. Darren, the Jesus Film guy, in July of 2002, also had such an experience. I had forgotten to warn him. One night at about midnight or one, the witch doctors were doing their thing, drumming out there in the darkness. Darren started screaming.

My guard came roaring out of his sleeping quarters. I was scrambling to get my shoes on, grab the flashlight, get over to Darren's quarters, and find out what was wrong. I yelled his name, but he kept screaming. I stuck my head in his door; he was sleeping in a bed with mosquito netting tented over it. A grown man shrieking full-voice in terror really rattles you!

"Darren! What's the matter?"

That woke him up. He yanked himself to sitting.

"Did you see it? Did you see it?"

"No, what?"

"It was eating my feet! This grossly horrible creature was here in my bed, eating my feet,

and I couldn't get it off me!"

So I explained how the demonic powers get after the enemies of Satan. I told him that what he experienced was not a normal nightmare. It was not a dream at all. It was an evil spirit coming against him.

There is a difference between demonic action and a normal nightmare, no matter how ugly or terrifying the nightmare might be, and I don't know how to explain it. But the difference does exist. I know that Darren visualized the demonic power, and only when we came close and awakened him did it disappear. We prayed with him and pled the blood of Jesus over him. The next morning I explained to him in more detail about the influence of evil spirits.

Africa is full of them! In that regard, the Dark Continent truly is dark. There are tons of witch doctors. They have a witch doctor society in the same way Americans have the American Medical Association. They even attend conferences to encourage one another and to share ideas.

Darren had never experienced a problem like this before. For the balance of his stay, he kept himself covered with the blood of Jesus and had no further difficulties.

You have to use the power that God gives you. When you are doing something for God, know that the powers will come against you. In Africa the powers of darkness are right there in your face, working blatantly against God's people. In most developed countries such as the United States, people simply refuse to believe that demons exist, and that should take care of it, right? Yeah, sure. You've just given Satan *carte blanche* to do as he wishes undisturbed. And he does operate in suburban America.

Over here in Moz, we can tell that we're moving in the right direction when spiritual and physical attacks come. We know we have the enemy on the run. What kind of attacks? Sickness is a biggie. Even more so are false powers. Let me describe an incident involving false powers.

It occurred when I was in the USA on the 2002 trip. Now, a year before I had tried to go to North Carolina to join good friends who have shared the ministry with me since the beginning. I was down on my back, and the visit fell through. This year I was determined to go!

So at the Nashville airport, I boarded a plane for North Carolina. As I stepped onto the plane, I started shivering. Within minutes I exhibited all the old, familiar symptoms of malaria—fever, aching all over, a howling headache.

Lord, this can't be malaria! But frankly, it certainly could be. I knew I had been bitten by mosquitoes, and the timing was right, just about three weeks into the trip.

I began to rebuke it, commanding it to die and leave my body. *Go!* When I got to Charlotte to change planes, I was so sick I almost passed out. I bought a bottle of orange juice and sipped on that. I seemed to improve during the layover, and I felt better when I got to Raleigh. The headache was hanging on, but the fever had diminished.

And then my friends, my wonderful Christian friends, surrounded me. We prayed and continued to rebuke it. Immediately I was whisked away to a barbecue done up as only these people can do. What a feast! I ended up speaking and answering millions of questions. All that takes a startling lot of energy. But by ten o'clock that night, all symptoms except a mild headache had gone. I was bushed, but the disease was over.

The next morning my health was back to normal.

Of course it wasn't malaria. A malarial attack is caused by a population explosion of tiny organisms in the host's blood. Malaria therefore runs a particular course as the organisms develop then die. It cannot be shortened, and it usually does not lengthen. A malarial attack simply does not last half a day, especially when no drugs are given. It was a spiritual attack to make me think I had malaria.

And let me warn you, this applies to you, too. You, my friend, are not immune to spiritual attacks. The trick is learning to recognize them.

For one thing, the attack will seem plausible. It will be some bad thing that you could reasonably expect. For example, I could certainly be coming down with malaria. Satan would not come against you by making you think you have malaria, because it's not something expected in your life. Rather, he would use a familiar problem or health concern or series of circumstances very normal to your life.

The appropriate response is to rebuke it. I chose not to receive it. So can you. If the event or disease or situation is not real, it will go. It has to. Oh, how Satan loves to make you think you're sick! False power. You might call it a bluff. If you buy into the bluff and accept that mentally, you will get sick.

I had to learn that the hard way. The lesson comes of experience, and I'm passing that experience on to you.

The Program Expands

The baby was a year old. He weighed maybe six pounds. His mother, anguished, thrust this tiny human being at me. I didn't have to speak her language. I could read in her hollow eyes that she was begging me, could I save it? Her son looked like a spider, so weak and emaciated was he. His arms and legs were the diameter of clothesline rope. His abdomen bulged, distended. Starving babies' abdomens do that. And he was cold. Mid-summer, the ambient temperature hovering uncomfortably near a hundred, and he was clammy cold. "Cold as death" is so apt a phrase.

No. I could not save him. He died in my arms.

I am constantly awed by the sheer power of mother love. More than a few times, mothers will walk twenty or thirty kilometers to get their babies to us in a desperate attempt to save them. These babies are not neglected. Their mothers' own nutrition is so poor that what little milk they can give their child does not contain the necessary nutrients to keep the child alive. Infants in that area rely entirely upon breast milk. Formula is far too costly to buy, and if the mother does indeed obtain some, she reconstitutes it with local water. Local water is rife with bacteria and parasites that disable or kill a baby.

If the mother dies before her infant is weaned, the child is virtually doomed. A grandmother or aunt may take the child from door to door, seeking a lactating mother to nurse the child. Each time the baby gets hungry, a different stranger feeds it.

Or not. Nursing a child not your own is considered taboo in many areas.

Here are a few statistics for you. There are maybe 103,000 people in Balama, give or take. Sixty percent of that population is under the age of fifteen. The cyclone in 2000 that took out our first dorms caused severe food shortages because it hit during growing season. The second cyclone hard on its heels the next year exacerbated the shortages into famine. When corn and bean fields lay under water awhile, they don't produce corn or beans.

Many of the people whose fields were wiped out were abandoned or widowed women with a house full of kids. They depended on their farm crops for survival. Suddenly the harvest was limited or, in some cases, completely destroyed. Mothers had no food. They were living off cassava, a carbohydrate root that's empty of vitamins, minerals, or protein. It's a stomach filler. Nothing more. An adult can survive on it for a couple of months because the adult body can get by with little or no protein for a while. Children die after thirty to forty-five days on a cassava diet, no matter how much cassava they eat, because they get none of the essential nutrients that an ordinary diet provides.

Thus we see malnutrition and all the deficiency diseases that come with it. These children's needs are massive, and no one else is helping. Some may step in this next year, but up to now the children have had no place to go to and no one to turn to if the parents die.

Our success with the dorm facility opened a number of doors. First and most important, I think, was the way social attitudes toward us changed. The local people were understandably leery at first as this crazy white woman came storming in with grandiose plans. Now we enjoy a measure of credibility. This credibility is allowing me to house orphans and build and enlarge a comprehensive nutrition program. In turn this program has opened the doors to work with orphans and malnourished children throughout the area.

I have had many babies thrust into my hands as they gasped their last breaths, their little bodies so cold. Too often there is nothing we can do for them. And yet, praise God, we manage to save many. We never turn any away, of course. They just keep coming, adding up sterile numbers that hide the terrible emotional price these destitute mothers pay.

But God has proven himself faithful. We have been able to provide for everyone who comes to our door. Just in the year 2001, our numbers went from thirty orphans to 350-plus children in the nutrition program.

Our new goal now is to build a mission station to expand the infant care and nutrition program. We have just been given forty acres on which to establish a nutrition center with an eight-bed intensive care unit for babies.

Until that happens we do what we can, and that's quite a bit, praise God. They almost always come in severely malnourished, and most are under three. We teach the mothers basic nutrition and disease hygiene. "This is what causes this malady. This is how you avoid sickness." We keep the child a month or so to get his or her strength built up and to make sure the mother is secure in what she must do. When they leave our care, both are stronger for it.

And in all this we have a wonderful secret weapon that you can employ in your neighborhood as well: prayer and spiritual counsel. These are the two key factors that promote our success.

All five of our Mozambican pastors are trained in how to give wise counsel for everyday problems, both temporal and spiritual. They know far more intimately than I do just what the local superstitions and pitfalls are. They do a wonderful job, and we have reaped many new souls for Jesus because of their work.

That is what causes the life-changing attitudes in these women; we work from the inside out. It is an effective method whether you are in rural Africa or in an Internet-saturated suburb.

Heart knowledge combined with head knowledge—but of most lasting importance is the heart knowledge.

Our Kids' Futures

Babies are such miracles! They are 100% hope! You cradle this newborn on your arm and think about a world without limits into which that tiny child will enter. If it weren't for stark reality, each little one could be politically successful, heroic, wealthy, admired—you name it.

But then stark reality does set in and the limitless potential narrows rapidly. What are the realistic expectations of the children who come into our care? People ask me that all the time.

Our children's expectations are, in fact, quite good.

We try our best to get our children as far advanced in education as we can because there certainly is a future for them, a bright one. But they have to get the grounding. We therefore give them the broadest grounding available.

So what exactly are the prospects?

Before the war Moz was a fabulous tourist attraction, and we certainly can be again, and not just at the top end. Our variety of birds, animals, and habitats are quite inviting to eco-tourists, bird watchers, and other such visitors. Miles of wonderful white ocean beaches appeal to jaded city folks. Several of Africa's great and storied rivers, most notably the Zambesi and the Limpopo, are at their picturesque best as they flow through Moz. The country enjoys a wonderful potential for growth in what is pretty much a profitable and eco-friendly industry—tourism.

To handle visitors as well as day-to-day transactions, banks, hotels, and other businesses use the same computer-based accounting, reservations, etc., that the rest of the world uses. Too, new industries are coming into Moz attracted by the inexpensive labor and potential for growth.

In all this there is a drastic need for interpreters and for people who speak English. Everyone needs interpreters, and they're not being trained quickly enough. The lack of good interpreters is a big problem in Moz. Yes, but English? A friend of mine told of laying over in the airport at Copenhagen, Denmark. At the help desk, a man of Middle-Eastern appearance and dress was explaining his problem to the young Danish woman behind the counter. They were using English, the second language that they both knew. This is increasingly becoming the norm wherever tourism is prominent. The visitors either speak English or at least know some English.

The need, then, is for languages and computer proficiency. However, English classes and computer classes are usually missing or inadequate in Moz schools, particularly rural schools in places such as Balama. In schools that teach these courses, the Mozambican teachers do not speak English as a first language or sometimes even as a second. Some have not seen a computer before getting the teaching job. It's not the fault of the system. It's a stark reality of the country's recent history.

Village schools were all shut down during the war. They're up and going again, but they only go to grade five, and this is the level where most students stop. The average "decent" education is seventh grade. A few have attended up to ninth or twelfth grade. This lack of schooling is usually not by choice. It was exceedingly difficult to get any kind of education during the war (which lasted over a generation, remember), and those who did go on had to do so in big cities. Rural students could not afford that.

Moz, then, has a lot of catching up to do, and the nation is beginning that catch-up as we speak. We are helping as best we can.

Several of our workers, such as Darren, are computer-savvy. We want to train our older kids in the use of what we have, which is two laptops. Good jobs are waiting for them if they master the basics.

Kids who don't want to mess with computers as such may instead wish to get into technical schools. We can enable them to do that. There is an excellent technical school in Montepuez that teaches carpentry, basic auto mechanics, building supervision and other similar skills. Moz urgently needs trained young people in all these fields right now, and jobs are waiting for capable people to fill them. We're preparing our kids to enter the school and learn the technical trades.

In short, we're aiming our education at what the job needs are right now in Moz and are preparing our kids to step into those jobs. Our investment in education is certainly not for nothing. These kids face a good future.

And this is only at the secular level. At the spiritual level, there is a dire need for pastors and other Christian workers in Moz. We must raise up workers in the Christian community. You cannot imagine the lack of pastors here.

When I pick up a newborn baby, I have no idea what God plans for the child. But I do know that there are opportunities for this little bundle of hope and that this baby, as well as our other children, can seize them.

38

Dealing with People

Quiz: quick now; name an enterprise or project that sank because the people involved in it couldn't get along.

Answer: it's not a trick question, because everyone can cite a project, sometimes a potentially very profitable or spiritual project, that got bombed by personality conflicts.

Oh, my, is that danger ever latent in Balama!

It goes without saying that I and the local people of Balama and the people who come in to minister from outside and the people over in Pemba and the folks down in the capital of Maputo and our supporters away off in South Africa are all terribly, horribly, wonderfully different. Besides the cultural conflicts, you have the tensions of city versus country, of "high born" versus "humble," etc. etc. etc., ad infinitum. The miracle is that Balama and other projects of this sort flow along as smoothly as they do.

Still, I get so frustrated sometimes, and I know others get just as frustrated with me. We all bend until we think we'll break. But we don't break, and the work goes on. I never stop being amazed at God's grace in this matter of people getting along.

So when I talk about the frustrations I feel, please keep in mind that you are only hearing my side of it. There is that whole other side! Please don't forget that.

A friend in the States tells of visiting one of those park-type living history pioneer farms. The visitors come out to see how farming used to be done 150 years ago. They may try a hand at churning butter or even milking a cow. They then return home to their modern conveniences and think they had a taste of pioneer life.

As my friend was talking to the director, a team of Percheron horses—you know, the huge plow horses with massive feet—came cantering around the end of the barn. They were harnessed to a simple sledge, and the driver, standing on the sledge, was doing his best to drag them to a stop. They weren't stopping.

"What is going on?" my friend asked.

The team and sledge disappeared beyond a shed.

"He's breaking a new team in."

"The horses are winning. Has that fellow ever done anything like this before?"

The director shrugged. "No, but it can't be too difficult. I mean, simple farmers used to do it all the time." That was the attitude, you see. Because farming did not require a PhD, it was considered uneducated. Simple. What could be so hard about it? Any "smart" person could do it instinctively.

And nothing could be further from the truth. A good farmer, even a farmer whose formal education ended in sixth grade, is practicing a highly-specialized skill that takes a lifetime to learn well. The director was fooled into thinking that just because farmers as a rule don't do "sophisticated" things, they're dumb, or what they do is simple.

That mindset is very easy to fall into here in rural Moz because the farming methods are in no way sophisticated. *But*! We will give a woman a handful of seeds and a little plot of ground. Equipped with a bit of weather luck and sometimes only with a stick, she will raise a year's supply of food. That's pretty darned sophisticated, if you ask me.

Still, there is room to learn. And that is where my frustration surfaces. Farming in this rural area has remained the same for centuries. "Stagnated" is not too strong a word. A few changes in agricultural practices, changes as simple as rotating crops, for example, could improve yields so much. But that's not the way it's always been done. We find resistance to the simplest improvements. I have an agricultural background and agricultural training, and this whole matter is a constant source of frustration to me.

We recognize that rural Africans need opportunity most of all. We provide training as best we can to the people who work for us. We help them learn more about whatever fields they seem to have a bent for. Many are highly intelligent. There is no brains problem in the area. The problem is lack of opportunity.

We deal with a lot of superstitions, too. Some are silly, some are deadly. On the silly side, I was sternly warned that if you eat duck eggs, your hair will fall out. On the deadly side, some chiefs tell the mothers, "Don't feed your child solid food," for whatever reason. I don't know. But the village chiefs are powerful. The mother has such fear of these people that she obeys. Her child then gets into trouble because she is so protein-starved that her mother's breast milk is inadequate. So a lot of cultural obstacles create difficult mindsets that exacerbate local problems.

The climate itself is both a blessing and a frustration. We see three seasons. December to April is warm and wet, with rain almost daily. This is the growing time. You plant in November and December for harvest in April and May. From May into August is our winter, cool and dry. Temperatures dip to the fifties at night, climbing to balmy seventies by day. Great weather! This is our pleasant time, when malaria is at its lowest incidence.

Spring comes in September and with it the heat. This, our third season, is hot and dry, with temperatures to a hundred degrees Fahrenheit. The hot, dry time lasts until the summer rains begin again in December.

In other words, you're either working and slogging through a lot of mud, or you're choking in a lot of dust. There is no middle ground, excuse the pun.

The unspoken dress code is another thing to deal with. In Africa's westernized cities, women wear just about anything, although missionaries avoid shorts. As a rule of thumb, if you're showing your kneecaps, you're a prostitute (display of kneecaps is quite okay for men).

Women wear skirts to below the knee. Culottes are popular. Some wear long skirts with sweat pants underneath, an Indian cultural thing that is generally acceptable. In the villages women wear wraparound skirts. That's all you see. You are therefore considered strange and non-Christian if you wear anything other than a long skirt.

You have to be ever vigilant and sensitive to those things. It is so very easy to destroy your witness simply by wearing the wrong clothes.

But when you think about it, that's true in American churches, as well.

Some things are the same the world over.

So just how many people are we talking about here? And where do I fit in?

For starters, I'm the construction supervisor. As I describe elsewhere, it's a massive and goofy job, usually just a plain old massive headache. Just settling the blueprints and gathering all the government documents, permits, licenses, etc., can give you a migraine moment. Buying supplies and then arranging their transport is another duty I pretty much have to either do myself or supervise closely. Problems come with construction, and I get to find them, figure them out, and usually solve them. The trick is to spot them before they get too far along.

I have Moz workers and leaders helping with all this every step of the way, and they're very good, but the buck still stops here. When they make mistakes or fail to notice problems in time, I get the fallout. So I still inspect every day, making sure it's all going in the right direction. And I do praise God for the wonderful helpers he has given me.

Four pastors help with the evangelistic program. Without these guys we flat out couldn't do it. Women and kids and some men don't speak Portuguese, and I don't speak Macua adequately. I am only fluent in Portuguese. They organize outreaches, church building construction, services for Sunday and for special occasions, and fill Jesus Film needs. But the technical end is still up to me because they are uncertain how to make modern technology work. This is, I'm sure, no surprise. And indeed, it boggles my mind, too. Fortunately, more missionaries are coming who can help with technical equipment.

Taking on new staff members and training up leaders is my responsibility. Whether others assist or not, training is ultimately my bailiwick.

So in essence I wear seven different hats, and the job description for any one of them calls for a full-time position. That's why I praise the Lord without ceasing for all that he's done for me over the last eleven years. He has sent so many people to lend a hand.

For example, several couples will be working here more than just sporadically, as was in the past. And from Georgia come Ken and Patty Sanders. Eliminating their indebtedness, which often requires liquidating homes and encumbered property, is the one thing I require of missionaries coming onto the field. There is no way they can pay off outstanding debts a half a world away while they try to support themselves in the field.

This, you see, is why we are eager to complete the three houses that will be used by missionary couples coming to work here. It is so hard to get backers to provide you with housing money when the total income of any one worker in the field is five hundred dollars or less (sometimes much less) per month. When brand new first-time missionaries come onto the field, it's very hard for them to function because nobody wants to stand behind them until they're proven. How can you prove yourself if you don't have the money to do it?

The answer is to trust God to raise up the support. And right here I appeal to you who are reading this. If you know of someone going out for the first time, and God lays it on your heart, please support that worker. It is as essential to get the new ones started as it is to support the seasoned workers.

One of the most pressing needs is laborers, and it's getting harder and harder to get people to come out. The failure rate is tremendous because they don't have the finances. I have seen that if new people are adequately trained and prepared and have the money, they'll make it. Often I will tell my missionary, if you don't quite have the support, come on anyway. Trust God. He will provide.

I am confident that essential needs will be met because I know how badly God needs laborers in the field. And that, coming full circle, is why the faithful supporters are so critical to success.

Some of the biggest partners in the world are the thousands of people who give a little each month to save our children. They help through faithful prayer. They give into the general fund, which supports the nutrition program. They become monthly sponsors with whatever God puts on their hearts.

Every donor is an unsung hero. It is fairly easy to see a disaster or tragedy—the World Trade Center, for example, or the aftermath of a severe tornado—and give to relieve that crisis. It is extremely difficult to give faithfully to a cause you never see in person, never taste at close range, never hear about on the six o'clock news. That takes supreme discipline and a servant's heart. We have many, many supporters who take that difficult course willingly. They are making the program work, and many of them I will never even know.

God is so mysterious in his ways!

Attempted Murder—Mine!

Not always do I succeed in interpersonal relationships. I alluded earlier to a madman with a machete. Let me tell you about that.

You have probably heard the phrase "the tyranny of the urgent," a bitter reflection on the way important things that ought to be done are scuttled by less important things that just happen to need immediate attention. In Moz we fall victim to the tyranny of the urgent just as does everyone else, but beyond that is the over-arching tyranny of the seasons.

You plan your life around wet and dry months, and you know exactly when they are coming. Fortunes ride on getting the timing right. You raise neither crop nor building without allowing for the seasons.

For example, we could do exterior construction only in the dry season. But you can't pour cement without water, and getting water in the dry season is hard work. When we brought in water for the construction work, people found it a lot easier to dip into our supply than to go long distances to wells and seeps. As a result I had to keep a twelve-hour-per-day guard on the construction water. We weren't being selfish; it's just that a few hundred people dipping into it depletes it in a hurry, and we'd have nothing with which to make cement, as well as to meet other building needs.

Come the end of December 2000, with the rains hard upon us, we completed the first phase of our project. I paid off the construction workers, including the water guard. Work would resume when the rains left off in May. We also threw a big thank-you party for the workers, a happy feast full of goats and rice, to end the construction year.

This was on a Saturday night. At the feast, I later learned, the water guard sat around smoking pot and telling everyone I never should have laid him off because he needed the work. He insisted he would get his revenge for so savage a slight.

The other workers laughed and just sort of blew him off. People say dumb stuff when they're high, and this fellow was far too old and wasted to be taken seriously regarding such a threat. No one bothered to mention it to me. It was gas. That's all.

That night at about 8:00 p.m., I retired as usual to my bed. At that time I had no night guard. Why? I'm a light sleeper, and four guard dogs stand between me and the world. We always chained and padlocked the compound gate to prevent our tractor and pickup from "accidentally" wandering off on their own, and the gate was also secured with a slide bolt. In short, if you planned to enter, you had to go over the fence, and the dogs would be waiting for you on the other side.

Thus I was not concerned when I heard someone at the gate. Hey, it was Saturday night. It wouldn't be the first drunk to get a little disoriented, singing and yelling. But the rattling had awakened me, so I shined my flashlight on the gate. Here was this arm and hand groping around inside the gate, trying to somehow unlock it. The racket set off the dogs. Buck, our best dog, lunged up and bit the trespassing arm. The arm's owner screamed, pulled his arm out, and took off. Fortunately, the dog let go.

I still wasn't concerned. Things happen.

The next morning at 4:30 a.m., a ten-ton truck arrived with lumber and bamboo for our fencing. This was Sunday morning, mind you. But the area is mostly non-Christians who don't care if it's a day of rest.

"I got your bamboo," he announced. "Where do we unload it?"

Five o'clock a.m. Sunday. Heavy sigh. I arranged a work crew and someone to watch the house, got on my bike, and pedaled down to the dorms to show him where to unload.

So here we were at the crack of dawn, the big truck parked smack dab behind the dorms, our work crew unloading lumber and bamboo. The general mood was, "Let's get this over with." Even our permanent guard laid his machete aside and temporarily left his post to help schlep fencing.

From behind the other side of the dorms, a howling maniac came running. It was our erstwhile water guard. He had moved stealthily in behind the dorms and stolen the guard's machete. Now he was swinging it wildly, chasing the workers.

But we still didn't take him seriously. In Portuguese I yelled at him to stop that.

Then the situation turned deadly. He threw the machete at the guard, catching the man across the back. The machete did a half turn in the air, though, so that the flat blade slapped against the potential victim and fell away. It knocked him forward, almost off his feet, but it didn't cut him.

It occurred to me that I had forgotten to say, "In the name of Jesus." No wonder there was no power in my silly little "stop." The deranged man snatched up the fallen knife and came after me next.

I had a twelve-foot head start, and I used to be pretty good sprinter when I ran track at A&M. I took off, majorly motivated!

I wanted to get out of his way, of course. But he and I were on the same side of the truck. I had to get around it, to put it between him and me. That would give the workers time to jump him. As I reached the front of truck, I'm sure he realized he wasn't going to outrun me. He threw the machete again.

Again the knife turned in the air. It caught me flat across the left shoulder blade. The blow knocked me to my hands and knees into a mud hole, for the rainy season was starting. The knife bounced off me and fell about three feet to my left.

I knew well enough what I had to do—get to that knife—but my body didn't respond. It was as if I were caught in a slow-motion sequence in a dream. My breath was coming in gasps, and I was scared—what an ignominious way to go! *Okay, Lord, this is it.*

The guy kept yelling, "I'm gonna cut your head off!" as he came running toward me. I made a lunge for the knife, but I missed by three inches. Just as his hand closed on the hilt, my work supervisor, Tosquino, jumped him from behind. Tosquino bulldogged him, grabbing him by the chin, and wrenching his neck around in best rodeo style. Emboldened, four others piled on him.

He had dropped the knife when Tosquino grabbed him, giving me the chance to get it. He was so high that it took those five men several minutes to subdue him and get him tied up firmly. When the truck was empty, they threw him up onto the bed and hauled him in to the police department.

He stayed crazy for a couple of days. When he finally came down, he didn't remember a thing. He had no idea what he'd done. He was transferred to the regional jail and held there for a couple of months. As the final disposition of the case, he was banished from Balama district. They told him to find some other place to live. I guess they didn't want him near me if he started smoking pot again.

The blow from that machete left a welt three inches wide across my back. I couldn't sit back in a chair for almost a week. If the blade hadn't turned, it would have sushied me. But it healed up quickly. Life went on.

The incident shook up the whole town. Now, as then, I am just about the only one out there really helping, and the last thing they want is someone hurting me, killing me, or scaring me off. But missionaries and others, myself included, know we're taking big risks. There are always people who will come against us, as the witch doctors did earlier. Every missionary makes sacrifices to do what he or she is doing, because the sacrifices are temporal, but the fruits are God's. You always know you may have to die. And it's a daily walk. The important thing is getting the message out.

Satan, of course, will use whatever means he can to prevent getting that message of salvation out. Satan used this old man. There was no rational reason for the man to act as he did. He had not been singled out or otherwise mistreated. Most of the rest of the crew had been dismissed as well when work ran out.

So this is not just a matter of a pot-high guy; it's spiritual warfare of a very dangerous and deadly sort. I'm glad I'm on the side I'm on.

Needless to say, the whole incident was a wake-up call. It reminded me to keep both my physical and my spiritual guard up better. A whole lot better. Most important, though, I can't let my spiritual guard down. I don't know what's around the corner, but I can rest assured that spiritual warfare is involved.

The incident also taught my workmen a valuable lesson—to take idle threats seriously!

I subsequently hired a guard to sleep near the house so that a man would be available close at hand should some other wacko come along. The first year at Balama, I never thought about posting a guard, especially someone to guard *me*. We guard construction water, sure. We guard the site itself so that small, easily-transported items don't walk away. But not me, surely. I slept outside in a tent, and I'm a fairly light sleeper. I could hear any weird stuff going on, and of course, there are those four guard dogs who like to worry mambas. Besides, as I have been saying this whole book, I depend upon the strength of the Lord for protection.

Then someone started a rumor that I didn't want a guard because I was sending out secret messages on my radio at night. Where that came from I have no idea. Secret messages?

Too, there are the guests. I had quite a parade of male visitors this year—Les from March to May, Hedley from July to September, Darren from September to November. And here I sat, a single lady and obviously in charge. I could indulge in any kind of—you get my drift. Rumors about secret messages is one thing, but rumors of that other sort would be quite another, and such rumors are impossible to stop once started. They never die. They would completely undercut my credibility in ministry. Local people think nothing of promiscuity, but the lady preaching clean living (to prevent AIDS if not godless immorality) had better be toeing the mark herself. The attempted murder proved the last straw.

To prevent all kinds of rumors, therefore, I set up a guard program. A full-time male guard, usually a trusted church member, serves both as guard and as chaperone. He sleeps close by in the warehouse, coming in around seven at night (about dark), and returning home at 5:00 a.m. or so.

Now I'm safe, right? Right, and I was safe before. The things I've said throughout this book about depending on the Lord still hold. And then there's the queen.

A friend told me about a little article she read in her (American) paper about the Queen of England, Elizabeth II. Apparently an intruder got past a monitored electronic security system, several human guards, and some domestic help to visit the queen clandestinely. A maid came in to the queen's chamber, saw the intruder perched on the edge of the queen's bed conversing with Her Highness, and ran to fetch the guards. Had the maid not entered just then, the intruder would have had time for several hands of whist, or whatever card game he preferred.

See? The arm of man is no protection. To quote a friend who doesn't like the gated communities springing up in the States, "The gate keeps out only people who want to be kept out." The palace undoubtedly boasts one of the world's best security systems, and this guy crashed it. I have a very simple system, and someone could crash it were my divine protection withdrawn.

But my friends claim they sleep easier knowing I have protection that they can see. Perhaps the guard is God's means of protecting me from those who would do me harm. He certainly uses human agency to do his work, or I wouldn't be in Africa.

And the guard/chaperone does minimize rumors.

… Secret messages about *what?*

Snake in the Grass Roof

Now you may assume that if Satan had to send pot smokers after me, he has relented in his use of snakes. Not so. They are still just as woefully attracted to me.

Our old church was not quite St Paul's Cathedral. It had mud-brick benches, but we put a cement cap on them so that people didn't get dirty sitting on them. The ceiling on the inside was the other side of the grass roof on the outside. If you looked up, you could count the bamboo cross-supports. Outside the grass roof provided excellent shelter from sun and rain. It also provided nesting space for a variety of small rodents. They would simply nibble themselves a cozy chamber in which to raise their plentiful young.

But as more and more sheep came into the fold, this old grass church got smaller and smaller. They shoved the pulpit back against the far wall to make room for more benches. Then they built an extension to the side. It didn't have the normal dihedral roof with gables. It was a simple lean-to with a sloping shed roof. It wasn't exactly square either. It came down behind us in a sort of oval. When I assisted with the children's service and Sunday school, I would tuck back into that extension with the ceiling slanting down behind my head. Eventually I was jammed so far back in there that I could touch the bamboo cross-supports if I wished. They were only about six feet above.

One Sunday morning we were doing an action song with all the lusty good cheer these children could muster, and they can muster plenty. I was waving my hands and going through all these motions.

The children's pastor started walking toward me. He pointed silently at a motion he had seen right beside my head.

Once he caught my attention, I turned and looked up where he indicated.

Staring back at me, virtually nose to nose, was a small head with a sinister little face and black, beady eyes. Snakes have no eyelids, so there was no way I would win a stare-down here.

The slim tongue flicked.

Mamba!

It did not like arm-waving and other excited motions. It was clearly becoming very defensive and getting into position to strike. Fortunately, it's hard for a mamba to assume a strike pose when it's hanging down like a rope from the rafters.

Instantly my knees buckled, and I scooted out of the overhang. I plunged in amongst the children. I mean, I can move really fast under extraordinary circumstances!

The kids cracked up laughing. Boy, was I funny!

Then they saw the snake.

The commotion attracted some of the men who had arrived for church, and they came in to investigate. Now *these* guys started laughing at me, too! "Oh it's just a little baby snake, it's no big deal. What are you afraid of?"

They helped us knock him to the floor.

The thing turned out to be three feet long and therefore possessed very good potential for striking some distance. What was I afraid of indeed.

They dispatched the snake forthwith, but the incident disrupted the church service for the rest of the day. Everyone was restless, glancing about nervously, wondering where the next one might be coming from. They even carefully checked the roof.

This was just one more incident of divine protection, because I was basically sticking my hand right in front of the serpent's face. He was so close I could have grabbed him around the neck!

Believe me, it never occurred to me.

Culture Shock

I get a lot of questions more or less along this line: "If I went to Africa to work as a missionary, what kind of culture shock would I feel?" The person usually goes on to assure me it would not happen to her or him because she or he understands about all that, and therefore there wouldn't be a problem.

Oh, I wish the situation were as simple as that! For one thing, culture shock is unavoidable. I don't care how well prepared you or I might be; it hits us anyway in ways we don't expect. Yes, me too. Also, once you come to terms with Africa, culture shock nails you all over again when you return to your original home.

I will not get into how you are affected when first you arrive in Africa, because every person's experiences are different. I will, however, describe how culture shock hits me when I return stateside. I think it says something about life in the United States.

Travel and Simply Getting around the Area

The developed countries have good roads going just about anywhere. Even in outback Australia where traffic on some roads consists of two semis a week (albeit huge, three-trailer road trains), at least part of the road is sealed. Africa has good sealed roads also, including freeways. But they don't go everywhere. You are either driving along on a good paved surface or wallowing in muck down a dirt track. There's not a lot of in-between.

If you live in, say, Phoenix, and a friend or relative gets sick in Atlanta, requiring your immediate presence, you get on a plane in Phoenix and fly to Atlanta. You may have to wait awhile for a seat if you buy the ticket without a reservation, but within a day you'll get there.

Flights from Pemba, our nearest airport, to Jo'burg do not happen every day. Too, schedules are terribly convoluted. You have to plan carefully well in advance if you want to go the full distance of Pemba to RSA in a day, because that combination of flights only occurs twice a week. Otherwise you end up staying over a while in Maputo.

Many flights in Africa fly at night for reasons of fuel economy. It has to do with meteorology and physics—for the most part, the prevailing winds are more favorable, and the cooler air is heavier, providing better lift, and therefore less fuel is required

The flight from Jo'burg to Atlanta is uphill all the way, as it were.

The jet stream is against us, and grinding against the prevailing high-altitude winds burns a lot of fuel. For that reason the plane stops off at the Cape Verde Islands to refuel. Flying from Atlanta to Jo'burg, though, follows the air currents, so no stops are needed. Flight time? Fifteen or sixteen hours.

Time Changes

I'll bet most of my readers know about jet lag. You start out all bright-eyed and bushy-tailed in one time zone, fly east-to-west or west-to-east, and the bright disappears from your eyes, the bushy from your tail. Your brain decides to go on vacation, sometimes for as long as a couple of days. In some ways a complete reversal of night and day is easier to work past than is a three- to eight-hour change. It's eight hours' difference between Moz and Texas's Central Standard Time.

Impressions, having just arrived ...

Busy-ness

The first thing I notice as I clear customs in Atlanta and step out onto the streets of my former world is sensory overload. I stand there like a stunned mullet, overwhelmed. Comparatively it's awfully quiet in the bush, with few people around. Suddenly I'm drowning in the midst of a zillion lights burning at various intensities from exit signs to floodlights. Thousands of people churn around me. The noise of traffic, airplanes, talking, yelling, etc., assails the ears.

And the ads! There was the Stone Age, the Iron Age, the Industrial Age—now we have the Advertising Age. There is no advertising in the bush, and it is not well plied in most developing nations. In the USA you cannot look in a direction where there is not an ad. I'm just not used to that.

Material differences

Elsewhere I describe shopping in northern Moz. There, one-room general stores are it. And there is not as much in that whole store as I see in one aisle of a US grocery store. I am not exaggerating. In short, it is physically very difficult to come from an area with nothing into an area with everything. The contrasts and extremes are too stark.

Non-material differences

The first thing you see as you view today's developed world is the self-centredness, the materialism, the comparative selfishness. It's all what's in it for me. In general you don't see people helping and supporting one another. In Moz you certainly see some of this, but the scale is so different. The great majority are very poor. If one person suffers, the whole village jumps in and helps out.

In the United States and other developed countries, when a member of the church, whatever church it is, suffers setback, the other members of the body rally round. They do that in Moz also; the big difference in Moz is that people with extremely different religion and cultural backgrounds act like family much more so than here.

For example: elsewhere I told how we went out to pick up a set of triplets in the bush. The only reason they survived their first three weeks when the mother had no protein and no good milk is that a couple of other friends came and suckled her babies for her.

This seems mild to American ears, but to African ears it's an immense sacrifice. A great gift. Many women would not do that because of local superstitions, especially Muslim women. It's a terrible omen to suckle another's child. I mean, it's *bad*. I was amazed at how many chipped in to help this lady as much as they could.

I find another thing strange and weird and very disturbing to me when I come back. I cannot believe the things that anyone can watch in movies and on TV. I remember what it was like a decade or so ago when I left. Now when I come back, here is all this vulgarity. The change from then to now is vivid, yes, but I can see change for the worse in that respect from year to year.

It's like when you befriend your neighbor's small children. The family moves away, or you do, and when you reunite some years later, you instinctively expect the three-year-old to still be three. But now he's taller than you are and working on his first beard! It shakes me up because I remember not many years ago when they didn't allow violence and sex on television, and here it is in my face.

People tell me, "Well, yeah, that's the way it is now. I just tune it out." Or, "I don't even notice it anymore."

There is a phrase in Scripture for that: it's called "hardening the heart."

The person who is bombarded by something constantly, be it noise or an attitude, eventually ceases to consciously notice it. But the subconscious is still registering it! That's why James (1:27) warned us to guard our hearts from the world. You can depend on this: what has gone in will come out, and at the most inopportune time.

Homogeneity

This last item is not culture shock as such, but it's culturally related. When I come in for the ninety-day speaking tour to make more people aware of our program, I stay in various people's homes.

There are excellent reasons for doing so.

First, I enjoy getting to know the people who love and pray for us. The family atmosphere is something I really miss in Moz, being single and alone so much of the time.

Second, it is good stewardship, of course, a much wiser use of travel funds than hotel accommodations would be. And if I may speak bluntly, people who know you, your goals, and your program form stronger links with your ministry. It becomes up-close and personal and not just some program they send a check to each month. In missionary lingo we call this "friend raising." It's nothing new. Jesus taught it to his disciples and led by example as he stayed with those who welcomed him in the towns he visited.

Too, I see the wisdom of moving a guest from family to family every few days. No one household is burdened with the whole visit, and many people in the congregation can get to know the visitor well. But the downside is the greatly increased stress this places upon the visitor.

These are gracious homes, wonderful homes, and comfortable. But America is not nearly as homogenized as Americans like to think it is. Every home, especially from region to region, has different rules and a different setup, and different things are expected of you as a visitor. When meeting a lot of new people, I sometimes am not sure how to react to different situations. Cultures in the southern United States are much different from those of the North, for example.

Then there are the individual personality differences of the hosts themselves. Some people can take a joke; others cannot, so you have to be very careful when being a guest. This constant need for caution—for diplomacy, you might say—takes a heavy toll, as does any situation where you are constantly on watch and on your guard. I don't want to offend anyone or be a burden, and that can happen even when you don't realize you're doing so. It's a severe stress at times.

Because this billeting can be so hard on the visitor, and because visitors to a church or area are commonly hosted in private homes by families, I would like to offer some suggestions from the missionary's point of view, as it were. No congregation wants to lay an unnecessary stress burden on visitors.

Here's how to minimize the stress and maximize the visitor's effectiveness:

1. Travel, sensory overload, public meetings, and accommodations with families are all heavy stress factors. You can help reduce this stress by placing your guest in a home that is quiet and makes few demands on visitors, allowing them the freedom to rest and prepare for meetings in the area. Being moved from house to house every few nights within a church body is very stressful.

2. Sharing a missionary among church members is best done by having them over for a meal but not to stay the night. Giving them a home base within a town is the most restful option.

3. Rapid, well-organized travel is a must when doing a nationwide speaking tour. Having transportation organized to and from airports, as well as to and from each speaking engagement is a great help. So is an occasional quick stop at a store where personal items can be obtained or restocked. To missionaries on a lim-

ited budget, being dependent on others can be embarrassing and therefore stressful.

4. It helps me most when I have one organizer for each town. These persons allow me to release their home phone number via my newsletter so that interested groups know whom to contact if they want me to speak to their church.

Incidentally organizers take requests for my speaking schedule in that town but make no promises until the date is discussed with me and written in my book. In short, if you are the designated organizer for an area, *always* confirm the requested schedule with your missionary before arranging such things as times and transportation. Long-time supporters usually contact me directly, bypassing the organizer to arrange a meeting. Coordination is essential, as this one simple rule can avoid all sorts of embarrassing conflicts. Once the final schedule is organized then, transportation problems can be resolved.

Please know I am not complaining! Absolutely not! My purpose in writing this is to pass on my experiences and observations and to help new hosts understand the behind-the-scenes needs of any missionary.

It is the way things are; that's all. And I extend a warm and heartfelt thank you to all those who host me and try to understand my point of view. In the thirteen years I've traveled around the world, the great majority of homes in which I've stayed have been extremely friendly and loving and the experience very positive. I really appreciate all the love and kindness shown me during those stays. It's the warm fuzzy that missionaries need.

And yes, I appreciate the cultural differences, too. After all, flexibility is a missionary's middle name no matter where he or she may be.

Stress

I suspect this section will sound like one long whine tasting, a non-stop litany of complaint. Actually, I promise you, I am *not* complaining. Really! I'll even try to keep it fairly light-hearted. But most written works that talk about service projects and mission efforts such as ours conveniently gloss over the high prices workers pay. Perhaps the writers want the calling to sound so glamorous that people will flock to it. Perhaps they just don't realize the toll. But I think the subject should be addressed, and it should not be sugar-coated.

Many of the sources of stress are pretty obvious. Clubbing a lethal snake to death lest it kill you does tend to get the old blood racing. So does being pursued by a maniac with a machete. True life-and-death situations exact a far greater penalty than does the temporary thrill of a simulated life-and-death experience such as a loop-dee-loop ride at an amusement park.

I need not dwell on these obvious stress sources because you can see them as well as I. You know without being told that these pressures are emotional and psychological. I mentioned, for example, the feeling of being trapped when the roads washed out. It may have been all in my head; however, it was genuine stress.

But there is also tension. And that tension very often causes physical problems.

One of the biggest tensions in the lives of workers such as I is off-road driving. It affects everyone who does it in two ways.

Primary, of course, is the physical punishment. For hours at a time, you muscle a big vehicle over roads that would give a goat pause, bumping and jolting, gripping the wheel lest a pothole or trench rip it out of your grasp and dump you. And the physical tension destroys your body.

But with that tension also comes a very heavy sense of responsibility, in itself an important source of stress. If you accidentally damage your vehicle, whether from weariness, distraction, or inattention, you're dead in the water. You could be stuck there for weeks, and I'm not exaggerating. There are no tow trucks, usually no repair parts, and mechanics are scarcer than mice in a cattery. Most areas are remote and quite often dangerous. So there is that constant nagging fear of making any little careless mistake, because you pay dearly for the slightest slip.

Does that mean that because I am constantly on the alert for trouble that I don't have accidents? Don't I wish!

My first accident occurred when I was driving my old yellow Isuzu up from RSA. It was a little 2.2 diesel pickup loaded with more supplies than it really wanted to carry, coming through the mountain pass from Lichinga out to VOL. The rainy season was nearing its end, and it had not rained for nearly a week. The mud was starting to dry out, but mud it still was. People climbing up through the pass had been laying big sticks and poles across the road to improve traction and buoy up their wheels a little. Not much traffic would pass before those sticks and branches would end up all a-tangle, some squashed down into the mud, and some pushed up at odd angles.

One of the angled-up ones shafted into the tie rod of my front left wheel. It jammed the wheel, jerking it all the way to the left. I was gripping the steering wheel tightly, as one must always do. The steering wheel jammed my arm into my side and tore the rotator cuff in my left shoulder. The loaded pickup slid backwards into a deep ditch. It wasn't my choice; I couldn't hold it, and the tires couldn't bite into the mud-slick surface. The brakes might as well have stayed in RSA for all the good they could do.

So there I sat, stuck deep. A lovely man on a bicycle happened by and helped me dig out. We worked two hours, and I with the messed-up shoulder. I figured at the time that I had merely strained some muscles. Digging was definitely not a good idea. I drove on.

I was less than twenty miles from home when the same thing happened and I was back in a ditch. But it was raining now, and I had to wait for that to pass. It took ten men to shove my humble little yellow bakkie back up onto the road.

Not content with tearing my left shoulder up, I've also messed up my right shoulder. In May of 2001, I drove south, and Les accompanied me. Yes, the same Les who got introduced to African mud the hard way. Fifteen miles took us more than an hour, so miserable was the road. Then the wheel caught a hole wrong, and the steering wheel jerked as the tires twisted opposite the direction I was trying to send them. That took out the right rotator cuff. There are only two rotator cuffs per shoulder girdle, and I have successfully scotched both.

I have had both hands ruined and carpal tunnel done on them both—in fact, one had to be done a second time—all from the constant, heavy gripping needed to maintain control. It's like trying to ride a bucking bronco for a whole day while you're simultaneously wrestling an alligator. My back required surgery in 2002, and the doctors tell me it all comes directly from the years of off-road and might-as-well-be-off-road driving.

So, yes, in a sense I'm complaining. But not about me. I feel a strong need to make people aware of the sacrifices involved, including the physical. To be forewarned, they say, is to be forearmed. What a waste and a pity it would be to hear God's call, spend all the time and resources needed to prepare for a ministry like this, and then decide to disobey because there is such a price to pay.

The Price of Service

"Count the cost," Jesus said, as for example in Luke 14:28. Then he told a young man to sell everything he had and give the proceeds to the poor, which apparently would have come to quite a tidy sum. He told me to do the same thing, as I relate elsewhere. So what about the cost?

In dollars and cents, this is about what it takes here in Moz:

We ask missionaries coming in to have $500 a month available. Actual living costs, though, are maybe $250 a month. The rest covers extras like travel and medical.

Travel expenses often as not come as a surprise; suddenly you have to go here or want to go there. They also come in irregular chunks, not spread evenly across the months. So I put aside a travel fund for just such exigencies.

Medical is the biggie. Hospitals will not accept insurance vouchers from foreign carriers. They want their cash up front. So you pay and then try to get it back from your insurer later. International policies are available but prohibitively expensive, around $200 a month with a $5,000 deductible (yes, I got the decimal in the right spot.

That's five thousand deductible). Medical care is perhaps a third of what it is in the USA and other developed countries, so we consider international policies to be a poor use of funds.

My personal living allowance is $400 a month. I make my own insurance fund by putting aside a portion for medical and other emergencies and live very comfortably.

And heaven knows emergencies do crop up.

When I had the extensive back surgery in RSA last year, I couldn't drive, I couldn't lift, I couldn't even sit up well. So God provided me with a personal nurse. Literally. When I was speaking to Karen Sterzer's church in Ohio, God told her to come over and help me for thirty days. She has worked in a nursing home for retarded children and is no stranger to the arcane world of rendering practical assistance to people. The union folks she worked with at Ford Motor Company even financed most of her airfare. So for my first month back in Balama, she was there, too, taking care of what I couldn't handle. She went back home the last of July. The next day God's replacement, Andries Van Zyl of South Africa, flew in to be my driver and helper for August.

Andries started out as a professional accountant, so he knows how to add a column. He was trained by Youth with a Mission (YWAM) and has accumulated six years of experience in the mission field. The reason I'm talking about him in the chapter discussing costs is that his whole life and mission is summed in the phrase, *living by faith*. This man has been working in the field for six years with no pledged support at all. *Nada*.

Do I recommend just taking off without any backing? Not really. On the other hand, yes I do. Andries simply goes out and does what God asks. God in his turn always supplies all that his servant needs. It is an arrangement the two of them have made together.

And that is the key. Every person must respond individually to whatever call that person receives. The person opens himself or herself to God's direction. No two people will receive exactly the same direction. What works for Andries or anyone else may or may not work for you.

There is no one-rule-fits-all. I take that back. There is one.
Surrender your whole being to God.
He'll handle the rest.

39

The Daily Grind

There are certain activities that seem to be sacrosanct to the
American way. No need, I'm sure, for me to mention that they don't
operate the same in Moz. People often ask what my usual day is like.
Let me describe it to you in terms of "American" activities.

1. Shopping

There are two kinds of shopping: the kind where you get necessities (I'll use toilet paper as an example of that) and the kind where
you prowl quaint shops actively looking for unique purchases. I don't
do a whole lot of that second kind, but I'm always shopping for necessities just as you do.

The small town of Balama has a couple of little stores. They do
their best to keep their stock up, and considering the depressed nature
of the whole area, they are wondrously successful. They sometimes
carry our flagship item for this chapter, toilet paper. Tinned fish and a
few packets of cheap, locally made stale cookies often show up on the
shelves. The availability of soft drinks depends upon when they last
went out for merchandise. Cold soft drinks? Maybe, if the local bar's
generator is working and fuel is available for it.

Whoa! The local bar? Yep. They serve more than alcohol. Only at
bars can you get anything to drink. So even we missionaries breeze in
and out of them when necessary.

Balama, in other words, poses a few problems. Sometimes stores
have what you need, and sometimes they've run out. You never
know.

Thirty miles away—that's a two-hour drive—is Montepuez,
where you can get

a fair amount of stuff. I can usually find the basic construction supplies we need. Toilet paper and some canned goods are available. The stores stock what most people buy often, but there is not a large variety.

Pemba offers much more in the way of items, and stores run out of stock far less often there. One little hitch: it takes five hours to drive the 165 miles. The good news: they're putting in a new asphalt road that will cut the driving time to three-and-a-half hours. Pemba, the state capital of Cabo Delgado, is the only other large city besides Montepuez. Several stores there carry imported South African goods, such as canned green beans at a dollar per can. Yes, prices are pretty high, and a can of tuna may also run a dollar or so. Again, it all depends on what stores find available to stock their shelves with.

So, you see, our problem is basically one of uncertainty. The shopper seeking necessities can never be quite sure whether that favorite store will have what is needed or when they can get it, anywhere from six weeks to three months. One thing for sure: when you find something you will need in the next four to six months, you buy it immediately. Right then. Waiting until you need it can mean doing without.

Lack of variety would also come as a disappointment to Americans accustomed to not only every kind of food imaginable but several difference brands at various prices. We're limited to certain kinds of canned goods, usually available in one brand only. Take it or leave it.

"Yes," you say, "but what about that second kind of shopping? You know, where you go seeking the perfect gift or souvenir in some cute little shop not yet overrun by tourists?"

I don't know. I never have time for that.

2. Food storage

Most folks in the USA don't think of food storage as a particularly American thing to do, but that is because you don't really have to think about it at all. Nearly every American home has a refrigerator of some sort, even if (as for example at a remote cabin) there is no electricity. There are kerosene-powered refrigerators in the States, and you can get ice just about anywhere in the country for icing down a cooler or ice chest.

Not in Moz.

Here foods are packaged and marketed on the assumption that no refrigeration is available. Almost always, especially out in the country, the assumption is valid. Nearly every food product is a little different from that which you find in the States.

For example, take margarine. Ours is sold in a can or squeeze packet and does not spoil at room temperature. There is no dairy in it.

When guests come over from Europe or the States, the first thing we teach them is to avoid sticking a dirty knife or other utensil into anything. Any contamination whatever will cause the food to start spoiling within twenty-four hours. We have to be excruciatingly careful. In the US, if you accidentally get a little jelly in your peanut butter jar as you build your classic sandwich, so what? Next time you can scoop out the offending contaminant, no problem. Over here, heat and humidity keep bacterial counts high all the time, and any bit of contamination causes foods to go rancid.

A far more insidious problem of food storage is posed by rats. I mentioned that because of the wet and dry seasons, crops are grown only half the year. Enough food must be put away then to keep everyone going for the other half of the year. Stored corn attracts rats. Period. Can't get away from it.

Thousands of rats follow the corn in out of the fields. They get into warehouses, they invade my house, they can climb a slick pole or a vertical wall. You can't keep them out. And they destroy so many things. We keep important stuff in metal containers or very heavy plastic crates such as you get at Wal-Mart. The rats can eat through the plastic, given enough time, but at least it forces them to work at it. They go after the food like a dog chasing chickens, the corn especially, and they do love rice. They don't mess with the beans too much, and I don't know why not. Maybe it's the texture.

Although the food is the main draw, they also do a number on our token necessity, toilet paper. They don't eat it, but they love to line their nests with it. So soft. So cushy. Just think of all those baby rats snuggling into the luxury of our ruined rear-end savers.

What feeds on rats? Snakes.

The rats invade, and the snakes follow the rats. This is a major reason why so many snakes show up at our door. If we fail to control the rats, the snakes become an immense problem. Last year just before we brought in the year's corn, we decided to clean out the warehouse. I mean, we did a complete cleaning. We even pulled up the tin floor to clean out underneath it. We found three different snakes living under there!

I have no idea how long those snakes had been there. But I do know that visitors had been sleeping not ten feet from the corn bins. Please don't tell them.

We frown on using snakes to control rats, since most of the snakes around the area are poisonous. Mostly we put out poisoned baits for the rats. Warfarin based, the poison is fast acting. In essence it dries the rat up. The rat gets excessively thirsty but it cannot drink enough. Internal bleeding hastens the fatal dehydration. We can buy it from the Department of Agriculture, which well knows how much damage rats can do to a food supply.

3. Daily bread

My breakfast is usually a large bread roll. Don't expect a loaf of the soft white nothing that American supermarkets call bread. We call ours lead bread. It is made from imported flour, but the flour is not self-rising, and local bakers don't use much in the way of leavening. The bread is very heavy. Eat one large roll, and you know you've really eaten something!

I usually have a little margarine and peanut butter on it.

Lunch is always rice and beans. We have three kinds of beans available locally, a black-eyed pea sort, a pinto sort, and a small white bean that looks just like a soybean. That latter type is the dandy. You can make it either sweet or savory, depending on the sauce you serve with it, and it tastes good both ways. It makes a great soup, thick and nutritious, like pea soup. It's my favorite. Visitors love it. America doesn't have anything like it, and I don't know of any other name for it.

Supper is some kind of food that I cook myself. We have a cook who gets the breakfast bread each day at a local bakery in Balama. Several people around about have those old-fashioned bread ovens that in the Southwest US would be called hornos. They're heated with a wood fire. In them are baked the fresh buns, sold at a nickel apiece.

Supper is spaghetti or bread unless I can lay hands on some potatoes, but potatoes can be hard to get. Potatoes can be fixed so many ways—mashed, fried, boiled... I like to scramble eggs with them.

Speaking of eggs: in most of the world, pullets are very young hens that have just begun to lay. Pullet eggs are very small. In Moz those dinky eggs would be giants. Badly inbred and certainly not improved, the local chickens put out eggs so small that they look like an oversized wild bird egg. And they're expensive to boot! A nickel gets you one tiny, worthless chicken egg.

So I buy duck eggs. If you've tried duck eggs, you know they're huge. They are perhaps one and a half times as large as a US hen egg. They taste very nice with a full, rich flavor better than that of chicken eggs. Scrambled or fried, they're a treat. In the afternoon the cook will go out to find five or six eggs. Don't expect a full dozen—it's hard to find eggs of any sort in quantity. The mark of a good cook is not just cooking but successful scrounging.

Fortunately, I've developed a reputation for buying food. Now when people bring food in to market, they often fetch it by my place first. For instance, in watermelon season I've gotten juicy red melons every week, even when you can't find them in the local markets. I never know what will show up at my door, but it is almost always something interesting. This is how I get a lot of my local food supplies. The surrounding farmers hear that I am in the market for something and bring it in for a sure sale. It gives me a little variety, and lack of variety in our diet is a continual problem.

Stopping at the Corner Gas Station

The corner gas station closest to us is in Montepuez. When I'm going into town for another reason, I never go without maximizing the load and therefore minimizing the cost of the trip, because fuel is so costly. We make every trip count. For the return run we load up empty containers to stock up on whatever fuel we're short on.

We use three types of fuel. Gasoline goes into the generators, so when we show the Jesus Film, we have to have gas. That can be a big problem; it's expensive, and not everyone uses it. Just about everything else runs off diesel.

There is also kerosene, called paraffin in Europe and southern Africa. The big use for kerosene is in old miner's lanterns. All the mothers' houses have them, so each week they get an allotment of kerosene. I use it too.

Again, availability is a challenge. We always stockpile fuel because we never know when the dealers may run out. It's happened any number of times. In Montepuez gasoline especially is in short supply. However, nobody buys kerosene in large quantities, so that's available most of the time. I can think of more than one occasion when we doddered along eight weeks without diesel.

Our other fuel is firewood. All the cooking gets done on firewood. They use twenty or thirty sticks of stovewood a day in the dorms just for cooking. That's not surprising; we cook for seventy-two kids.

A stick of firewood is a yard long and grip size. We either contract someone to go cut it, or we buy it from the local market. Wood purchased in the market is expensive, and they sell only small amounts because they never have a lot in stock. To encourage local people to make money for themselves, we tell them we want so many bundles of wood, each bundle having twenty pieces. They cut it and send a messenger to us that it's ready. We then take the tractor out and get it. We pay them for however many bundles are brought in. We also reward good quality—that is, sound wood that's dried out enough to deliver a hot fire and good coals. The system has worked extremely well so far, and we can therefore stockpile enough that we don't run out.

And church on Sunday

At last, here's an easily identified aspect of my life that is the same the world over where Christians congregate. Our facility is a Christian community, and every week I can formally and corporately worship God. The next time you are in church, I hope you will take special thought of your brothers and sisters a world away in Moz. We're doing the same thing you are.

Isn't God good?

And Then There are the Flies

At a picnic or barbecue, flies can be a nuisance, right? They settle on the food, maybe alight on your face, and some of them bite painfully. They are known to all. What could be more mundane?

Let me tell you about the flies.

While I was in Vilanculos, I got a painful boil on the outer part of my thigh. Tropical sores such as boils almost always become infected and therefore usually heal only with difficulty. Especially before the age of antibiotics, stubborn, open sores were at the top of explorers' gripe lists in hot, wet climates. So with a heavy sigh, and upon the advice of my African doctor, I sat back to wait for it to come to a head. Then the doctor would lance it and it would, ideally, heal up.

Boils, however, are not normally accompanied by intense pain. This one was. Every time I moved the least bit, pain shot down my leg, top to bottom. Even when I slept, the smallest movement was excruciating.

Finally, I could see a little white dot in its centre. Aha! At last it was coming to a head. Soon we would be able to lance it and it—it moved! *The head of my boil just moved!*

The outer part of one's thigh is not the easiest place to work on. It's not as bad as, say, an elbow, but I really had to twist and crank my body around. I employed the only appropriate surgical tool at hand, a straight pin, and began poking at the boil. I shafted the minute head and carefully, slowly, pulled out a worm three eighths of an inch long!

The pain abated instantly.

I was fascinated and aghast. This maggot was not even bothering to wait until I was dead to start feasting. It was eating me alive. Worried about those nasty flies alighting on your food? I *was* the food!

The fly involved here has an ovipositor—a piercing tool on its abdomen—with which to insert its egg deep within the flesh of the host (*host:* such a detached, abstract word for a living creature being eaten from the inside out). The egg hatches, and the larva, a true maggot, begins eating the flesh and slurping the juices in which it finds itself. Basically, it starts down deep where the egg was deposited and eats its way to the surface. Every time the muscle in which it lives flexes, it bites in annoyance. Thus the pain. It pupates, and an adult fly emerges to go off, mate, and deposit more eggs within hapless victims.

It's not the only worm out there that can do you wrong. North of Mozambique live worms that drill into the ball of your foot if you go barefoot. You have to pop them out with needles. And of course there's the well-known tsetse fly, which carries sleeping sickness germs that don't much bother it but devastate human beings infected by fly bites.

But my personal fly maggot was dead and gone and would not reproduce its kind. I figured the ordeal ended with the demise of the maggot. Silly me. I made the mistake of showing it to my doctor. She looked at it and declared that I might not have gotten it all out. So with cotton swabs the size of floor mops and antiseptic made out of liquid flame (but no anesthetic; oh, heavens no), she went in looking for more.

Then, and not until then, did I scream.

The Not-So-Daily Grind

Okay, I admit I have a really weird lifestyle. It's even weird compared with urban Africans. But I have something most of them do not have: big plans. There is vast work to be done here, and the program is growing commensurately.

In the USA and Europe, a builder makes sure the title to the land is clear then builds on it. In Moz you don't have to worry about title; the government owns it all. You obtain permission to use it for fifty years at a time.

Thus it is that the first thing I do going into an area is to sit down with the local governing people, whoever they may be. It is from them that we obtain official permission to establish our facility, build, etc.

At Balama we contracted forty acres and could commence building immediately, as I had mentioned. I have also described our immediate plans elsewhere in this book. The church and maize mill went in quickly. The three houses, warehouse, outdoor kitchen, and screened-in dining/meeting room will come soon, possibly even as you are reading this.

"But fifty years is not a very long time!" you might say. "You just get a ministry going, and your time is up."

In a sense that's true. Some Bible schools, for example, such as Moody Bible Institute, see nearly 150 years into their past. But I am amazed how rapidly the world is changing. Communication, for instance. The industrially advanced countries developed the telegraph, radio, television. First we learned to stretch wires across whole continents and lay cable across whole oceans. Now we launch satellites. The Third World countries do not have to take those baby steps, laying cable and stringing wires. They leapfrog ahead, directly to the radio and satellite communication. Who would have guessed?

Likewise we have no idea what the ministry is going to be like in fifty years. We cannot begin to see what the needs will be then. I am pretty well certain that it will differ radically from whatever we envision it to be, because that is how the change we see now is performing. Change occurs more and more rapidly, and new developments bounce around in directions we cannot predict. What will ministry needs be in fifty years, particularly as regards land use? We haven't the foggiest.

What I do know is that at this moment, in our time, we have been graced with a good piece of land that serves our needs as they exist today.

Of course our ministry will change! Jesus does not, but the shape of the ministry does. In fact, the ministry itself is changing as we speak. With our nutrition program, we originally intended to help the little guys get a better start—that is, the babies three and under whose moms cannot produce enough wholesome milk. And we still emphasize that. How can we not? We are getting infants six months old that weigh twelve pounds, babies fourteen months old weighing eight pounds.

But we had to expand it this year because everybody is suffering, older kids as well as little ones. Now the rehabilitation aspect is more prominent. That is, we try to get the older children back on their feet and growing again.

Because our resources are limited but the need is not, we serve only the most destitute. We help those who cannot in any way afford on their own the things we offer free.

The mother usually comes to us by signing up through social services with whom we have an excellent working relationship. Some mothers come to my house directly, and we do not turn them away. They do have to bring a letter from the chief of their village saying that they truly are destitute.

What we give them depends on what they have. We usually give them corn flour, dried beans, cooking oil, and salt. If their baby is under three months, they receive a supplement of formula. Mothers of older babies, who can handle solid foods, get baby food.

We show the mothers how to make their own nutritious baby food and also how to boil water to mix baby food and formula. It sounds a little odd to say we teach mothers how to boil water. But dysentery is the biggest problem here, and the disease agents live in the local water.

Dysentery is an intestinal irritation that gives a baby severe diarrhea. This in turn causes massive and rapid dehydration. A baby nailed by a good case of dysentery can die in twelve to twenty-four hours. Several different agents can be a source of irritation, an amoeba being the commonest. Boiling all water that a baby consumes is the safest, surest way of preventing the deadly illness.

Mothers give their children our milk or formula from a medicine cup. Yes, it is hard for baby, who intuitively wants to suck. Drinking from a cup does not come easily to an infant so tiny. However, baby bottles are not only expensive, they create far worse problems. Unless the woman is right under our nose where we can supervise, she'll not boil the water well enough, and germs will survive. Or she'll mix a little too much milk, and it goes rancid. Remember, I've mentioned elsewhere how quickly things spoil without refrigeration here. She may fail just once to clean the bottle thoroughly, and bang! Her baby is sick.

If the mother lives very far away, and many do, her baby can die simply because she cannot get it to us in time.

At first we devoted one day a week solely to educating mothers and meeting their needs. But we have so many women in the program that to serve them adequately we had to split that into two days. Each woman comes in on either a Thursday or a Friday by assignment. She receives what she's going to need for the next week. Also, we give her corn and bean seed.

Most Moz farmers grow tomatoes and onions, along with their corn and beans. We provide onion and tomato seed also, and we encourage our women to plant additional vegetables such as lettuce and pumpkins. We're trying to get them to expand their options and diet. Tomatoes and onions are good sources of vitamin C, but tomatoes especially do not store well. A wide variety of vegetables would be a good buffer against crop failure and nutritional shortages.

Recently, for example, we've been limited on peanuts. So many peanut crops in a row have failed that we could only get enough for the nutrition program. So we couldn't give out any peanut seed this year. We're hoping enough farmers were able to plant peanuts this year that the crop will be restored.

We also do a lot of teaching. We even have a classroom, an open-air roofed ramada with bench seats. The mothers listen to a short lecture in Macua, very simplified, about some aspect of health or nutrition.

We have a rule that the mothers must bring their babies in every week in order to get their week's food. There's a reason for this. We want to see that the baby is doing all right and judge whether adjustments should be made. As babies grow we increase the food allotment. But also, we want to see that the baby is alive. Now and then a mother tells of her baby back home when in truth her own child has died and she's reaping a food allotment for other children or, heaven forbid, the black market.

On those two days a nurse comes in to serve as medic and interpreter. He works closely with us and decides what medicines to give, if any. He knows his work well. Based on the success of this aspect of the program, we hope to expand the nutrition center this year to provide baby exams and consultations. The nurse will eventually help me set up classroom facilities.

The classrooms, we hope, will serve more than just the health and nutrition program. As we get more and better equipment, we will, for instance, set up sewing classes with pedal swing machines. Remember, there is no dependable power in the area, and everything is done manually, including sewing. This and other crafts we can come up with will produce items to sell and thereby bring in money for these families on the edge.

Naturally a few try to take unfair advantage of the freebies. That's human nature, unfortunately. We ended up with a couple of families who didn't really need our services. But they had great stories. What they didn't know was that we check out as many as we can, so as to provide follow-up later. If they have lied to us, we expel them from the program. To date we have served hundreds of women. Know how often we've found fraud?

Only twice.

40

Epiphanies

Flipping for Jesus

I have mentioned before about the road from Marrupa to Balama. It's the back way, essentially ninety miles of wildness. The first and last thirty-mile sections are desolate and the middle thirty totally uninhabited by any human being. We're talking elephant, baboon, lion, and leopard here. It's a single-lane dirt track through lots of forest, and not one tractor a week ventures along there. You absolutely have to have four-wheel drive to negotiate the trenches and bad bridges. Most of the time, you have to repair the bridge before crossing it.

It may come as no surprise that one of my rules of life is *always* to bring a man along with me when I have to drive that particular stretch. Another rule is always to carry a machete, shovel, and hoe, as well as a rope in case my vehicle needs to be pulled out of some ditch.

This was May of 2000, when I was returning from the United States. As always, I loaded up on supplies in Jo'burg. It was a load, too—about three quarters of a ton in a half-ton pickup. But what the hey, my truck was equipped with heavy-duty shocks and springs for just this sort of occasion. There was no question of maybe lightening the load; we really needed the stuff I was bringing up.

I had to make the trip north without a companion simply because I could find no one to accompany me. When I spent the night at the last mission outpost, everyone there was worried. I wasn't. God had always provided my needs. He knew my rule, and I expected him to provide a rider before I jumped off into the bush beyond the last town, Marrupa

So when I reached Marrupa, I asked around in the market. No one needed or wanted to go to Balama. I was getting concerned. You might even say I was growing a little upset with the Lord. I mean— after all, he knew my rule for the bush. Why wasn't he providing a rider? I tried and tried, but eventually I had to bite the bullet and get going. I put it in four-wheel drive and headed out into the wilderness, angry that I was taking off alone.

I soon started maneuvering through the trenches and holes. This is not your piddly little back road through a national forest in the States. These trenches are indescribable, with some up to eight feet deep, yawning wide enough to swallow the entire pickup. No joking. To fall into one means an upside-down truck and a badly-injured driver. You always hope someone has cut a bypass to get around the problem, but that doesn't always happen. Sometimes it is not even possible.

The only vehicles that normally use this road are tractors and logging trucks—and me, of course. I was the only missionary living in that area, so no one else had reason to use this stretch of insanity.

The road monsters that come through are very big and very heavy, with huge tires to help them cross the trenches and soft sand-pits with their cargo (compare that with my midget-sized 2.5 turbo diesel, half-ton pickup). The big guys cut ruts you wouldn't believe, deep, difficult, and soft. Then the rains come along, and runoff turns the ruts into chasms.

And the bridges! After repairing a bridge enough to maybe make it all the way across, you have to pray that nothing moves. The bridge is no more than loose logs on stringers, and the logs shift as you cross them. If they move enough or buck when your tire hits them, your truck can fall through. Too often a loose log will get jammed up into the undercarriage and hang you up.

There is one saving grace: all the bridges occur in the first ten miles of road. Once I got past that last nasty little bridge, all I had to worry about were huge ruts and soft sandpits. No sweat, right? Well?

It had rained the night before, and the ground was damp, but it wasn't slick or goopy. I didn't think anything about it.

At about the twenty-five-mile mark, I came around a curve to find the road trenched out to a canyon-like depth. I'm exaggerating but not much. Forget about shoulders. The left edge of the road-way was a vertical clay embankment that went straight up nearly a foot and a half. No way could I get my left two wheels to crawl up onto that. The right edge of the road dropped away into a rut sixteen inches deep. I couldn't simply drive around the problem spot because forest trees crowded right up to the edge on both sides.

I climbed out and measured. If I put my left wheels hard up against the embankment, my right wheels would stay on the road with three inches to spare before the surface dropped away into the trench. That was not a lot of space to play with, but the dirt felt solid.

On the other hand, if I bogged down or a wheel slipped off into the ditch, I had no one to help me dig out.

My alternative was to turn around, cross those seven shaky bridges again, and take another road that would get me to Balama three days later. So you can see why I was determined to get past this sixty-foot hole if at all possible.

I shivered at the absolute, intense silence surrounding me as I prayed for the solution. Imagination in a tense moment can be your worst enemy. What golden cat-eyes in the silence were watching me from out there, unseen? I dismissed the thought and tried to focus on the challenge. You don't see the animals that see you until perhaps it is too late.

I decided to go for it. I kept it in four-wheel drive, of course, and started easing my way along. So far, so good. The trouble spot only extended about sixty feet before the trench grew shallow and disappeared. Sixty feet. I could do that.

I had failed to allow for that three-quarters of a ton of supplies in the back.

When the back wheels rolled out onto the road beside the trench, the surface began to crumble under the weight of the load. My three precious inches and the rain-softened dirt beneath the back wheel collapsed into the rut. As the back wheel slid off into trench, the whole truck wallowed and began to roll over. Out the right side I could see the ground coming up to meet me. My right shoulder hit the driver's door and I clung to the wheel to avoid falling out the open window.

I couldn't think fast enough to avert disaster. I screamed, "Jesus, help me!" as my hands moved. I swung the wheel to the left, hit the accelerator, and spun the wheel to the right. Why? I have no idea. That's what I did. I did know one thing: my heavily loaded truck was now tipping more than forty-five degrees, and when a vehicle rolls that far, it's going to go over. The laws of physics guarantee it.

The truck's nose swung left and gouged into the steep clay bank as both back tires skidded down into the trench. Cranking the steering wheel to the right got the front wheels aimed in the right direction.

I ground across that whole sixty feet of trenched-out road sideways with both front wheels up on the road surface and both back wheels down in the ditch. Then the trench got shallower and shallower, and the ordeal ended. Bucking and pitching, the truck lurched onto level roadway, all four wheels on fair ground, and I braked to a stop.

I was shaking so badly I didn't move for fifteen minutes.

Part of that shaking was fury, pure and simple. I was so angry with God I couldn't see straight. My spirit screamed at him, *You sent me out here alone! And look what almost happened! All that stuff stacked on the seat to my left? I would have had it on top of me! And as the truck was rolling, I saw all those rocks and boulders sticking up in the trench. My truck was tipped so far over I was looking straight at them! There was no way to avoid them if they decided to come in through the window. I could have been dead now!* And on and on I ranted.

He let me spout off a while. Then, when his small, unhurried voice broke through into my spirit, all it said was, *I am sufficient for you.*

I heard it as clearly as if someone beside me had spoken it.

It was like throwing a gallon of cold water on a burning match. The tirade ended just that quickly. I wanted to crawl into a hole, I felt so ashamed. He had shown time again that he is always with me. I was scolding him for being sent out alone when I was never alone. That simple sentence—*I am sufficient for you*—was not only so very true, it was all I ever needed, all the time. I was relying on man for safety when all along I had angels waiting to hold that truck to keep it on its feet. A little while later I got out and studied the tracks where I'd come through sideways without tipping. I guarantee you, God's angels were involved in my escape from disaster.

That moment was what philosophers call an epiphany. I have been tutored in many faith lessons about God's grace and presence, but this was graduate school. This incident impacted me more than anything else that has ever happened. I find him so awesome in the miracles he's pulled to save my life. Awhile ago some friends and I counted up at least ten times that I should have been dead already. This was one of those times. If the truck had rolled, I would have been alone there for days in the company of carnivores. Injury, death, even hypothermia—it was May, I was dressed in very lightweight clothing, and temperatures dipped into the 50s at night—were all averted because God was with me.

Ever since then, if he says climb a mountain or jump off a cliff, I don't worry about it anymore. In the future he will send me into even more remote areas than I'm in now, and that lack of fear, obtained from grad school, is going to be so necessary. I'm going to need every bit of faith and strength to do the work he has for me.

Every person has the potential to experience an epiphany, a moment when the clouds part, the curtain rises, and you see in a whole new dimension. You don't have to be bouncing sideways down a rutted track with your vehicle about to roll. You might be in your own kitchen or out in the garage. Something happens—and for every person in the world, that something will be uniquely different from anyone else's—and you see God's grace and beauty in a whole new light.

Whether you pioneer in the mission field or teach a Sunday school class, the epiphany can turn your life around. No matter what you do for God, the times to come are going to be perilous. Be bold! Be strong! For the Lord your God is with you!

Listen up!

Be advised also that one epiphany won't do it. We all need many, and they come in the most unexpected places.

Everybody knows Branson, Missouri, is the new entertainment capital of the world. It has lots of people, lots of shows, lots of glitzy things to do. I'm not real into shows and glitz, thank you anyway. But Branson also has wonderful wooded areas surrounding it.

I was there in 2002 to get a break from the constant speaking engagements throughout the States. And while I was there I found a chance to get out of town. Beside the nearly-deserted RV park where we camped, a gentle woodland stretched up the hillside, pleasant, quiet, and gloomy in a cheerful sort of way (if you've ever spent a peaceful hour in such a place, you understand what I mean).

And what kept going through my mind over and over was, "This is awesome! This is so awesome."

I had not realized how very much I missed being out. I had spent the last six or seven weeks in cities. Everything I did, I did inside buildings, all cooped up. Now here I was in the woods among genuine trees out in God's world. I watched a humongous hawk circling, on the lookout for breakfast. I listened to a dozen kinds of birds I could not recognize by song because Texas birds and Missouri birds differ. They were sorting out territories and whistling up mates in eager anticipation of the upcoming nesting season. And that results in lots of chirps and singing!

Awesome!

Once you've gotten used to living and working in what might be called raw nature, being confined to cities, especially in all those environmentally correct buildings, will drive you nuts. And that little datum got me thinking about the profound changes that occur in every person who chooses a particular lifestyle.

I am not talking only about missionaries in equatorial Africa. I mean every person. If you are a person of city high-rises, working downtown and living in an Nth floor apartment, sitting in the woods like I was doing would drive you nuts. The heavy silence except for all those incessantly twittering birds, the close and grasping vegetation would wear on you quickly. A farmer would never feel at home in San Francisco, etc. You get my meaning.

What are your ordinary life circumstances? Not equatorial Africa, probably. Maybe not even a large town. Whatever it is, that is your comfort zone. But why? Why is it your place? It may not be anything like where you were raised. For example, this here little ol' Texas girl had never even heard of Mozambique when she was growing up on the rangeland. And yet the Lord has quietly and efficiently re-shaped me to fit comfortably into the new circumstance where he wants me. I have been changed profoundly.

But that does not mean that now I enjoy a perfect fit with my circumstance. Some aspects of my circumstance still weigh very, very heavily.

One—perhaps the biggest—is loneliness. For a moment picture yourself in my circumstance. Eventually each night the work ends. It may not be finished, but it ends because it is dark. So you go to your quarters and fix yourself a simple supper over the open campfire. You have no one with whom to share conversation, your dinner, the evening, or anything. Then it's just you and your time with the Lord. Time with the Lord is wonderful, don't misunderstand me. But.

You read your Bible. You read a book. There is nothing else to do.

I still haven't been able to teach the dogs to play Scrabble. Their spelling is pathetic, especially when it's more than three letters long.

There are, of course, others nearby, although the workers all go home to their families. But they can't fill the void. You know, Jesus spent lonely time even when he was surrounded by people. You can be alone in a crowd. There's people all over, but it's not the same when you can't all appreciate the same cultural and educational level. It's not a snob thing and certainly not a racial thing. It's just—different. They can't understand things in my context, and I can't function well in theirs. The only way to find socialization is to drive clear out to Pemba where I can find companionship with some other missionaries.

The loneliness is massive. I admit that sometimes I just lie in bed at night and cry. It gets to you.

My heart is screaming, *Bring me team members! Please! If you won't bring me a husband, I can handle that, but at least bring me some friends. Help me break up the lonely times.*

I often think how lonely Paul must have been when he was imprisoned so much. His people visited him and all, but he spent a lot of time in loneliness. His last words to his protégé in 2 Timothy 4:21 are so wrenching to me, so plaintive: "Do your best to get here before winter."

Another need in anyone who does what we're doing here is to learn to be extremely flexible. It's extremely difficult to "go with the flow" because the flow keeps shifting. Something that's perfectly fine one day is all boogered up the next. True, every person in every culture experiences that, but out in the bush, little difficulties and inconveniences seem to loom larger than life. I need a lot of self-control, and I admit I don't always have it. Anger, especially, is a big problem for me.

There are times I get extremely angry, and I really shouldn't. Most of my male co-workers have a fifth-grade education, and most of the women have had none at all. I cannot talk to many of the women because they don't speak Portuguese, and, as I mentioned, I can't handle Macua well. The work we do is difficult and requires good, rapid communication. That communication too often sputters and dies at the very moment it is most needed.

So I do lose my temper sometimes, and that's not of the Lord. I know it. But I thank the Lord for letting me be human, and I ask his forgiveness. Then of course I also have to ask for forgiveness from the people I've wronged.

The work takes a lot of patience, and things will try your patience that you can't imagine.

The temper problem is exacerbated by malaria. Malaria is my middle name or might as well be. I've had sixty cases in the eleven years I've been in Africa. That's an average of six to eight cases a year. The day when I'm coming down with another bout of it is the day you don't want to get in my face with any minuscule problems. When I am coming out of malaria, I am also extremely irritable. I find my temper snaps over something I normally wouldn't think twice about.

But just as I start writing out the invitations to my pity party, the Lord pulls me up short with a clear, *Listen up!* My circumstance is not perfect, but it certainly is acceptable.

Malaria? I believe the Lord has increasingly given me a divine protection. I notice that over the last few years I haven't had to go to bed with the severe headache and sluggishness, the intense malaise. I get tired and very irritable, but I can still function.

The Lord has strengthened me in this and kept me safe in many other ways as well. The disease and the medicines to combat it usually do a number on your liver. What amazes me is that when they did a workup on my liver enzymes, they found no liver damage in any of this. Things are working very well. Three times I've had malaria try to go cerebral—that is, the responsible microbes lodge directly in the brain—and that can kill you. Within a matter of hours, your temperature rises to 1060F and fries all those little nerve endings. In a sense, it cooks your brain.

Each time that particular complication has threatened, the Lord has either allowed me to get out ahead of time or provided what I needed to take care of me. In one case he said, *Get out and get cleaned out.* Now that sounds really asinine to anyone who does not understand that the Lord does indeed communicate directly if you are properly attuned to him.

I got out instantly. Left the facility straightway. And the day after I left, it rained for a solid three weeks. Had I not been attuned to him and obedient to him; had I not responded immediately; I would have been trapped. By the time I got to RSA, I had come down with the most severe case of malaria I ever had.

And as I just mentioned, the Lord also has provided what I needed to recover. When I showed up on the doorstep of RSA with my raging malaria, my doctor was upset because the hospital was going to charge me double; you see, I was so sick I needed intensive care. So the doctor made up an ICU in his bedroom and had an off-duty nurse come in to care for me and see me through it. I convalesced in his home for over two weeks. That was one of the times it tried to kill me, but God got me to the right place at the right time.

Why didn't he just stop the malaria? I don't know. I do know Jesus reminded us that his rain falls on the just and the unjust. Everyone starts out being treated alike. But in the midst of pain and difficulty, he takes care of his own.

So when the Lord tells you, *Listen up!* how will he do it? Will it be a roar or a whisper, a lightning bolt or a still, small voice? That is between you and him. Everyone is different. He honors that difference. Work it out between you. He's ready to do that.

Then, even when you come down with illness, the Lord is there. And as long as you hold onto your faith and stand firm, he'll see you through.

Listening. Trust. Obedience. I say them over and over, but they are the foundation of all.

Trust and obey.

There is no other way.

Airlift

Several times now I have mentioned my back problems. Many of my friends and supporters know some of the details, for I have told about my back in my newsletters. It is a genuine miracle and a lot of agony all mixed together. And it is indicative of how the Lord sometimes works.

You have no doubt heard the old adage, "Never pray for patience." The result, of course, is that God will answer your prayer by so severely testing your patience that it is greatly strengthened. I do not recommend this way of gaining patience, although it is certainly effective. Boy, is it!

From February to April of 2002, I completed fifty-five speaking engagements in seven US states and Canada. I was pooped. Immediately thereafter I headed back to Moz. Twenty hours in planes and airports pretty much finished me off. I was tired when I left the United States and very, *very* tired when I reached RSA.

But we were all eager to see construction get started on our new station. In RSA a gentleman named Peter helped me pack and load supplies. We were doing each other a favor, as he needed a ride, and I needed help and a second driver. What normally takes me two weeks to accomplish, the two of us completed in eight days. Now I really was exhausted. I don't like starting out so tired on a long drive to Moz, but what are you going to do when the clock is ticking? We only had a six-month window to build in. So off we went.

In the first four days, we passed through all of the various borders you cross—from RSA into Zimbabwe, through there into Tete province in Moz, across Tete and into Malawi. Lastly, we crossed from Malawi back into Moz. That's eight border stations, which can get very unpleasant if they decide you might be carrying contraband. Finally, without undo complications from customs, we stopped for night number four at an Operation Mobilization mission base camp in Mocuba. There we would pause.

They had a tent for Peter but not for me. Oh well. We were driving the Toyota, our brand new Jesus Film truck, and it had on its cab a brand new rooftop tent. This was the perfect time to try it out.

Almost perfect. The tent is also an excellent storage bay. We had it loaded to the max with supplies we were hauling. So I crawled up on the roof and opened up the tent. I knelt on the aluminum tent floor and handed supplies down to Peter. Grab a box or bundle, rotate on my knees, pass it down to Peter, over and over. But it was ninety-six degrees out, at least—and much hotter in that stuffy tent. Wet with sweat, my left knee slipped out from under me. Searing, paralyzing pain shot up my back and down my left leg.

When the initial jolt subsided a bit, I managed to finish the task and climb down, but it was immediately obvious that I wasn't going to be able to climb back up. They fixed me a makeshift bed in an unused storage room.

Sleep did wonders. The next morning I felt better, so we drove on to Nampula. It's the largest town in the north end of Moz and therefore the best place for Missions Aviation Fellowship to base. Being the largest city also makes it the best supply post. So we shopped there, stocking up on baby formula (which our station badly needed) and other last-minute supplies. We spent the night with the MAF pilot, David L., and his family.

Sleep did not do wonders. The next day I was unable to put any weight at all on my left leg. Nurse that I am, I suspected disk damage. I could barely hobble.

As I sat on their sofa weeping with the excruciating pain, the pilot's wife said, "Shall we fly you out of here?"

"I don't have any choice."

David fueled up, and we were on our way to Blantyre in two hours.

Peter packed up and continued on to Balama with the load of supplies for the orphans. By giving him a ride, I was doing him a great favor. He was able to return the favor by blessing my kids with what they needed.

Now one of the greatest blessings in the world—and I do mean the whole world—is Missions Aviation Fellowship (MAF). Their personnel and planes fly everything from passenger runs to mercy missions just about anywhere on earth. My need was on the mercy side of the spectrum.

The Christie family met us at the Blantyre airport and whisked me away to a hospital for meds. The next day I flew to RSA via commercial jet. We had just spent days crossing border checkpoints. I breezed back over them in a matter of hours.

In RSA I called the orthopedic surgeon who had done such an excellent job on the torn rotator cuff in my shoulder. What with all my various injuries courtesy of off-road driving, I was getting to know doctors on a first-name basis. An MRI showed that a disk had ruptured. The surgeons removed the damaged disk and relieved the pressure on my leg nerve. The operation was declared a success. I was released to go convalesce and do exercises to strengthen the muscles in that area.

I started this section talking about patience. Since I had not prayed for patience, there was no reason to think this surgery would go any differently from my previous ones. I assumed I would soon be on my way back to work.

Eight days post-op, increasing pain in my left side told me that all was not well. Exercises made it worse. By the next morning, I could not stand up or bear weight. My back rebelled and went into total spasm.

The doctor readmitted me, gave me pain medication, and redid X-rays. Nothing appeared amiss. But things were not improving. The doctor patted me on the head and said, "Your nerves are inflamed. Just give it time."

I have often alluded to the fact that I am an exceptionally *impatient* sort of person. Give it time? Oh, please. But the doctors were sure they were right and in essence refused to look for any deeper problem. After three days of non-stop agony, I called my missions doctor in Mossel Bay, and patience had nothing to do with it. Pain definitely did.

The missions doctor and a woman neurosurgeon consulted and decided something was indeed very wrong. "Can you get down here? Oh, and incidentally, Brenda, can you do it flat on your back?"

Jo'burg to Mossel Bay is a fifteen-hour drive halfway across the country. I called MAF in RSA. They had me there twelve hours later, and they did indeed fly me flat on my back. I did mention they're angels, didn't I?

Anatomy lesson: the spine is a stack of cylindrical bones, the vertebrae, all tied together with very strong tendons. As you probably know, the vertebrae are prevented from rubbing on each other by pads of cartilage called disks. It's a tight stack, so the nerves to the arms, legs, and other parts emerge from this stack of vertebrae through holes called foramina (the singular is foramen). Still another MRI showed that a piece of disc was jammed like a cork in a bottle into the foramen where my left leg nerve left the spinal cord.

Back to the operating table. In the first surgery the doctors had cut into the neck of one of the stabilizing bones on the vertebra. This is fairly routine. What the second team of doctors didn't know was that this weakened bone had snapped. It floated loose beside my spine. When the second neurosurgeon made the initial incision, that rogue bone popped out and startled the whole operating room (third lumbar vertebra, for those of you who are really into anatomy). It's a rare complication and a surprise I could have done without. The bit cannot be successfully fused back on.

My doctor did a lot of delicate work; it took her ninety painstaking minutes to remove the "cork" in the bottleneck. As I understand it, this is nearly impossible to do from that angle. I'm sure a host of angels were pushing from the outside to help her get that minute fragment. However, because of that bone damage, my back was no longer stable and might require a fusion if exercises didn't hold it in place. My spine now had to depend solely upon muscles to keep it aligned, since the stabilizing bone was gone. Think how unnerving it would be to know your back could pop out of alignment at any moment, with severe consequences.

Three weeks later, my patience taxed to the hilt, I was allowed to fly back to Jo'burg with Mercy Air. This trip I flew standing up except for the takeoff and landing.

How I longed to get back to Balama! We were ready to build! The dry season, the building season, would be over before we could start. A bazillion things required my attention. And here I sat doing back exercises! Most important to me was the fact that the people up in Balama kept saying, "We need you. When can you get back?"

I was told I could return to Moz on June 27, after nearly two months of medical madness. Finally! Praise the Lord!

I still could not sit, and standing would be difficult and painful for a while. Any slip of the foot or hard jolt could mess me up badly. So I would make this trip via Mercy Air in a single-engine Cessna, a small propeller-driven plane, lying on a bed tied down to the floor next to the pilot. Not fun, but at least I was going home. They loaded the plane with supplies; the pilot, an easy-going fellow named Gideon, did his safety check, they strapped me down tight, and away we went, howling down the runway in Jo'burg.

We had almost reached takeoff speed when my door popped open! Gideon reached out and grabbed it because I couldn't. For a wild moment the plane swerved and swayed as we decelerated. The plane tipped off the edge of the runway *rump-a-dump!* Imagine being strapped down flat and looking helplessly at the ceiling while all this was going on! But we got right again, and the tower cleared us to take off. The flight went very smoothly, and we arrived at Petersburg in less than two hours. There we refueled and continued on to Malawi, another four-and-a-half-hours distant, to spend the night.

In Malawi we picked up orphanage manager Gerald C., who would help me reopen the Balama mission station. The next morning Gerald and Gideon were walking out to prepare the plane when the Holy Spirit prompted Gideon to check the propeller. How did he know it was the Holy Spirit? He couldn't say, but the message was quite clear, and it was not one you could ignore. He inspected the propeller.

He and Gerald saw large scratch marks across the tip of one of the blades. So Gideon got out his tool box to file the scratches lest they cause a problem. As he touched the blade, it rotated a quarter turn in place—in other words, it was completely loose in its attachment. The stabilizing pin holding it at the correct angle had been sheared off.

Unknown to us, when the plane veered off the runway in Jo'burg, the blade had clipped a landing light. The blade was nicked and the pin broken.

Chills! We all knew that a plane's propeller is very, very carefully balanced to spin without the least bit of shimmy. Not only was that balance completely gone, it had been gone for the whole trip until now.

I do not hesitate to tell you that we were still alive *only* because God intervened and miraculously prevented a disaster. Under normal circumstances, the rapidly spinning propeller should have gone askew slightly. Any such imbalance would have wrecked the plane and killed us both. I won't go into all the mechanical details involved, but the bottom line is that a pin that should have fallen out and destroyed the motor did not, even when we landed and refuelled in Petersburg.

Mercy Air was able to divert another plane to us. A big Beechcraft twin-engine cargo plane fetched us for the next leg of the journey, my bed on a pile of lumber, and me horizontal again. The lumber was secured, but there was no way to anchor me down, so Gerald and Gideon sat beside me the whole way, belted in and pinning me down between them for takeoff and landing. We arrived safely in Pemba late that evening, very grateful for God's grace.

The next morning the crew flew me from Pemba to the tiny strip in Montepuez, and Gerald met us there with the Toyota crewcab. I traveled flat in the backseat padded by pillows and a special mattress. Gerald drove the last rough leg very, very carefully, and the thirty-mile trip that normally takes an hour and a half took three hours.

That's not the end of the story. The patience that I had not asked for was not present, naturally, and I was up and out of bed a lot more than I should have been. I admit it. And don't you ever rush things a little too? I mean: there was just so much to get done! I was doing my exercises faithfully and sitting the only way I could, in a reclining lawn chair. I might also mention that not only was my body building tolerance to the pain-killers, I was becoming dependent on them—plain old addicted.

The tenth day, the night of July 6, I got into bed and without warning, the third lumbar vertebra in my back moved with a loud pop. A burning pain hit my back and radiated down the left leg. Again.

Karen, my assistant from Ohio, was there by then. Gerald and Karen prayed for me. The next morning I could not get up. By e-mail my doctor said to stay with the anti-inflammatories and pain meds and maintain five days of bed rest.

Keeping me in bed for five days is like holding a ten-foot cork underwater. I was frustrated. I was angry, confused, disappointed—you name it. The heat was miserable; I sweated constantly; it was stuffy in that mosquito-netted bed...My patience snapped. But there was nothing I could do except endure.

Finally, on day four, I cried out to God, "What is blocking my healing?"

His answer: *unforgiveness.*

"Toward whom?"

The two doctors who did this.

That stunned me. Unforgiving? I had deliberately forgiven the two erring doctors when I was still in RSA. That was behind me. But having all this time to ponder things, I finally understood. Yes, I had forgiven them. But when my back went out here in Balama, I got those angry thoughts all over again. If they had only done it right the first time, I wouldn't be suffering all this.

Resentment leads to bitterness. It might seem the source of my present bitterness was merely impatience, but I could see now it was far more. Bitterness leads to unforgiveness. That's where I was at the moment.

The Lord showed me that in my mind's eye I was seeing them

nailed to a cross. Down deep inside, I was heartily wishing they could suffer the way I was suffering.

The Lord then gave me this: "Forgive them, for they know not what they do."

I felt terrible, and I don't mean my back. Through the years the Lord had forgiven me so much and blessed me so much. Now I was being nasty and vengeful. I repented then and truly forgave them.

That night I got up for supper and ate in my reclining chair. As the Lord had insisted I do, I confessed the whole thing to my friends. Nothing physical changed—I was still in pain—but my heart was so much lighter!

They prayed for me, of course. Three minutes later, as we were praying for someone else, my pain—the constant, intense pain that was breaking through the morphine—suddenly ended. Stunned by the suddenness of this, I went to bed telling no one.

The next morning I felt different, and I can't explain why or how. It was—well, it was just different. I felt absolutely cheery. Yeah. Cheery! And when I got up, there was no pain! I was weak, of course; lying around in bed for five days does that to you. But the pain had abated. I started functioning again.

I told my friends what God had done for me, and now I am telling you.

I see now that forgiveness is not so much for the person being forgiven as it is for the person doing the forgiving. It is a healing action, whether spiritual or physical. I needed spiritual healing as much as the physical. God showed the way. That forgiveness, you might say, was the key to unlocking God's healing power. The power had been there all the time, but out of reach, inaccessible.

How about you? Is unresolved anger, resentment, or just general unforgiveness crippling you in some way? Only you and God can answer that, but I beg you to consider the question carefully.

Forgiveness is essential to wellness.

That is *still* not the end of the story!

On October 5, I headed back for the United States. God had told me a year before that I was to attend this world-wide missions conference in Tulsa, Oklahoma. Surely, having given me such a long lead, he knew what agony I would be in and how difficult—no, impossible—it would be to fly so far so soon. Surely!

My back was still unstable. I could only sit for five minutes at a time. Many are the people who urged me to dump the conference and stay in Balama. But as I constantly remind you, I have learned, sometimes the hard way, that when God says to do something, you do it.

Mercy Air flew me out again, still flat on my back except for takeoff and landing. It took two days to hop down to Johannesburg to catch a British Air flight. I had been sternly warned, fly all the way lying down or don't go. My back couldn't handle twenty-three hours of sitting. So we bought a business class ticket on British Air because they have beds in business class. I was able to lie down all the way, two flights, each nearly twelve hours long.

By the time I reached Tulsa for the conference, I was barely able to walk. X-rays the day I arrived showed the problem. The deformity caused by the missing disk and broken support bone was crushing the left leg nerves. I lived in constant agony. A disc replacement procedure was already scheduled in South Africa for November 10.

Saturday morning as the conference started, women from all over the world, fellow missionaries, joined Pastor B.J. Daugherty to pray for me. As they prayed, the power of God was so strong that I was knocked off my feet by a bulldozer force that hit me from behind. I felt nothing different when I got up, but I knew that God had just done a mighty work of some sort.

What do you do when you know that? You praise him and thank him, of course!

Over the next thirty-six hours, the pain left and I could sit comfortably. Sitting comfortably doesn't sound like much, but I had not been able to do that since June.

Repeat X-rays showed a spine in normal alignment and with a normal disc space
at lumbar three.

"Awesome God" hardly describes my feelings for him. I joyfully returned to RSA on October 27, X-rays in hand, to show my neurosurgeon. How glad my heart was as I told my doctor, "Additional surgery cancelled by Jesus Christ."

41

That's Where all the Money Goes

All around the cobbler's bench
the monkey chased the weasel.
The monkey thought 'twas all in fun.
Pop! Goes the weasel!
A penny for a spool of thread, a penny for a needle.
That's where all the money goes...

Huh? Money? Where? I didn't see it.

You set an ice cube out in the sun on a summer day. In no time at all it has melted and trickled away. Money seems to do that, too, and just about as fast.

Another topic that comes up in question-and-answer sessions wherever I speak, and rightly so, is where do we get our money for the ministry, and, more importantly, how do we spend it?

These are questions every donor should ask any charitable venture before shelling out precious gifts of money. Every charity should be readily accountable. I cannot speak for other ministries in the Third World, because each is unique, with unique needs. But I can explain how we use our resources. Incidentally, the methods we use will almost certainly work for you in your daily life as well. They're pretty much universal principles.

Much of our expense has to do with food.

A minor point that I might have mentioned when talking about culture shock is the seasons. Moz is below the equator—not very far below but below. Our seasons are reversed and there are only three. December to April is the wet hot season, May to August is the cool pleasant season, and September to December is the hot dry season.

When I come Stateside in March and enter the northern spring, I am leaving behind the end of, essentially, summer.

Obviously planting and harvest in Moz must obey the seasons, just as they do anywhere else. Different crops are sown at different times, but usually planting starts in November, which is late spring. The rains are beginning in earnest, and all the seed is in the ground by January. Farmers the world over know that you cannot work the soil when it's too wet, or you'll destroy its structure. So rain more than temperature determines planting. The rain usually lets up in March. Harvest begins in April and extends into June.

Beans, corn, and rice are harvested when they have at least partially dried. They may have to be spread out and sun-dried if they still contain enough moisture to rot in storage. The plumpest grains are reserved for seed. That comes first.

People with any excess beyond projected needs will bring their extra to the market to turn into cash. So if you didn't grow enough, you must buy what you will need and store it in an appropriate warehouse until the next harvest. There is a time constraint. All one's food supply for the balance of the year must be obtained and gathered in by August or September. By then, you see, it's all sold out.

And there's where the money part comes in. For our school kids and all the others we serve, this means tons of food. Yes, tons. Literally. It must all be purchased, for there is not enough land or labor to grow what we need.

In 2001 we bought 100 tons of dried corn and twenty-five tons of dried beans in order to feed the multitudes. It's an awesome thing to find yourself buying in these huge amounts. But when you're feeding 400 or 500 kids, that's what it takes. Basically, we count on two 110-kilo bags—that is 220 pounds—of corn per child. Each child will need about one-fourth that amount in beans. And you'd better be pretty good at estimating what you'll need, for if you run short, the children will suffer.

Budget? What budget? It's like trying to count the number of kernels in a corn popper while they're popping. There is no way of knowing how many kids will be entering the program during the year to come. We always count on buying an excess, and we always end up using it all. So much for cushions. And predicting what the prices will be is strictly a big fat guess.

The two years when those cyclones came through during the growing season, the prices tripled on everything. We paid the equivalent of twenty to twenty-five cents per kilo (2.2 lb.) for commodities that usually run a third of that. But the funds showed up.

First principle: trust the truth that where God leads, he provides.

Understand, he does not just drop goodies in our lap. We have to do our part and work diligently. But it will be there when it's needed. Neither does he trifle with luxuries. He meets needs, not wants. I trust you see the difference there.

Another principle: be a good steward, and he'll take care of the rest.

A neat illustration of that is the pickup I'm driving now.

Now, by good steward I don't mean burying your one talent under a rock like that fellow did in Jesus' parable. I mean using what you have as wisely and as thoroughly as possible. Stewardship? You should have seen the truck I drove before I got this one. It had more dents and bumps than a toad with acne. We had to weld the body back onto the frame three times; the bolts kept breaking off. I drove as carefully as I could because that vehicle was essential to the ministry, not to mention being my lifeline to civilization, but the roads I had to drive it over gave it a pounding. And boy did we ever use it, milking every single bit of worth out of it! That's stewardship.

With the rainy season looming ahead, in September I prayed about my need for a new truck. *I would like four-wheel drive this time,* I prayed. You know, to get around better in the wet. I was at VOL at the time. On my next trip to Lichinga in Niassa province, I met with a man there, a missionary in charge of selling pickups at discount to missionaries. Yes, there really is a job like that, and he did it. The Lord said, *Ask him.*

Okay. So I went up to this fellow and asked him about the availability of four-wheel drive pickups.

"There are five left, but hurry! They're going quickly. Several people who want to buy have said they'll try to get money here in a week."

O-kaaay. I was the next closest thing to penniless. I went off on my errands, one of which was to get my mail at the post office.

My financial statement had arrived. Unknown to me, someone had given $10,000 into my personal account.

The truck cost $9,200 as-is from the factory.

I returned promptly to the agent. "Yes, I'll take one!" Hey, I'm the cautious bunny. I always examine everything before purchasing. This was the first time I had ever made such a massive purchase sight unseen. To take this step of faith, to buy a truck I'd never seen, was a real shock to my system.

I faxed the bank, got the money wired into the right account, and it was all done, one two three.

This one really floored me. When God says *Move!* he provides. The funds were already in place, and I didn't know it.

Another principle: follow the rules.

"Well, duh," you might say. But you'd be surprised how many times I'm tempted to either ignore or circumvent some particularly vexing, petty rule or restriction. Many such rules seem senseless or even mischievous—one of Satan's minions trying to short out the Lord's work. I urge you, stay the course. Dot the i's. Cross the t's. Keep it all official and in good order. The Lord honors that.

We are officially registered as a charitable organization in the United States and in the Republic of South Africa. This is the high road, so to speak. It imposes specific legal restrictions, but it gives us certain freedoms we would not otherwise enjoy. And no one can point to deliberate misdoing and say, "Shut her down! She's illegal."

I suggest that one who might be tempted to cheat on payment of taxes or withhold mention of income when preparing IRS returns ought to consider the consequences. Even if that one is never caught, God knows. Do you really expect God to prosper that one if he or she is being dishonest?

Another principle that works everywhere: as a missionary friend rephrased the old adage, don't put all your eggs in one basket, "Don't put all your begs in one ask-it." We are supported totally by interested Christian companies, individuals, and churches in both countries. We have no single large source of money. It comes in from all over, sometimes a few dollars a month, sometimes a thousand a month. What God puts into the hearts of our supporters is what we get.

So I counsel that anyone getting money—and that is virtually everyone in the world—make the support base as wide as possible. Then if a contributor, even a major contributor, drops out, the ministry is not affected. Cottage industry? Provide a number of products or services. Investments? Scatter them judiciously. Giving? Give as God moves. And don't plug up your ears, hoping you therefore won't hear him say, *Give it away.*

Next principle: set your priorities and serve the first priority first. Our priority is the people, especially the children. In 2001 we were taking care of 400 indigent children in the district. That is, we shouldered the costs of food and clothing, beds and blankets, medical care and school supplies. The total came to $28,000. The Lord provided this.

The children's support costs always come out of our operating funds first. Whatever is left, if anything, goes to growth and expansion. God has always honored that, and I think it is a pretty good rule to follow. For example, in 2000 a friend gave the ministry $5,000 for me to build a house. But that was one of those two cyclone years. We had barely enough money to feed the kids. I couldn't see building a house then. So we invested the $5,000 in food, clothing, beds, etc. Priority: the kids first.

God not only honored that, he multiplied it. In September of 2001, I had $35,000 in the account, *a seven-fold increase,* and we had already built the corn-grinding mill to help make cornmeal that the mothers need and to contribute to the support of the boarding school project. We had the wherewithal to build our three missionary houses, a big warehouse, and a small kitchen with a screened-in area where we could eat and hang out during the long evenings (excuse me, that's "evening fellowship") away from the bugs. What bugs? Malaria-laden mosquitoes, disease-carrying flies. You don't dare sit out at night unprotected.

The lesson to me: if we use the money for his purposes rather than for selfish reasons, he will bless us beyond anything we can imagine.

He will bless you too. You can bank on it.

42

Unity

The partnership between the undisputed Lord of the universe and a humble Christian woman in Africa has never ceased to flabbergast me. He is so vast and so intimate.

For example, he very patiently taught me that forgiveness is essential to wellness. This is the God who forges stars.

And I would point out also God's timing. When he preserved my life and Gideon's, he could have simply called Gideon's attention to the damaged propeller in Petersburg instead of waiting until we reached Blantyre. But there was no backup plane available near Petersburg as there was up north. So his timing was perfect, but it was certainly not what one might expect or predict. To our human eyes, God may do things weirdly, but they are done to his specs nonetheless. I have a brand new respect for his way of doing things, even if those ways are arcane or unpredictable.

There is one other necessary ingredient that helped me in that difficult time. That is Christian unity. Note the huge number of people and organizations who came to my assistance in my time of need. These were diverse members of the body of Christ such as Paul described in Corinthians, each very different, each essential at the moment. Many members, all with unique roles, functioned to one purpose. And that is not to neglect to mention the thousands of prayer warriors. They, too, are an integral part of the whole and just as important as any other part.

To each of you I send my heartfelt thanks. If you had not faithfully provided your piece of the puzzle, I could not have been so effectively rescued and cared for.

Jesus meant for us to be one family without division. He said so. Nowhere is this unity more critical than on the mission field as these end times rush down upon us. It is the source of our strength. Before the worldwide church will be ready for the second coming of Jesus Christ, unity must exist. The body must be complete.

That was the theme of the missions conference I attended in October of 2002. No more Lone Ranger missionaries. We must work together to achieve what must be completed. There is power in numbers when those numbers have one mind and one goal!

But the apostle Paul knew very little about human anatomy when he declared that we are all members of a united body. We know now that the nervous and endocrine systems connect and communicate throughout the body. In other words, we have to hear one another and hear God.

If you're not hearing God, it's not because he's not sending. When we don't hear God, it is because we're not always keying in. I always get an answer. It may not be the answer I want, and it may not come immediately, but always the answer shows up. How do I know God is talking and not Satan? It lines up with the Word of God.

That's a key point. When you pray, you could end up listening to man instead of to God. Your thoughts and the ideas that others have given you intrude, drowning out God. Believe me, you're not getting good information.

We should all be pushing toward a spiritual realm in which we can hear his voice at all times. When he says, *Go here. Do that*, you know who is saying it. And you can also feel when you are being checked in spirit. There is a hesitation; you suddenly feel uncomfortable about going or doing something. Call it intuition.

Even when something unimaginable happens, the voice of God may be there. When the World Trade Center was attacked, a lot of people, some but certainly not all of them Christians, suddenly felt the urge, the idea, to get out. There was a sense of foreboding. They could feel disaster coming even before the first plane hit. I have this as personal testimony from several people.

The Lord was telling them to get out. Those who heeded escaped safely and took a lot of people with them. That's what I mean by listening, being keyed in to hearing God's voice at all times.

I might add one additional observation here. If nothing untoward has happened, and you get the sudden feeling to leave, as those people did, think how silly you sound if you urge others to get out of a perfectly normal building. They could have been laughed at; they could have appeared terribly foolish if they reported their feelings and then nothing happened. They knew that. Listening to God and obeying him was more important to them than how they appeared to the world. It's a critical point to remember.

The Bible says we need to pursue love and desire spiritual gifts. It's the gifts that will get the job done. Revelatory knowledge is a continuous flow revealing what God is saying, and it is backed up by Scripture.

It is my experience that God doesn't just dump some big revelation on you. He starts out by showing us little things. We learn how to hear his voice in little things like taking baby steps when you learn to walk. Then he starts giving us bigger and bigger things, as he's done with me. It started out with little checks. Don't do this or go there. And it can get pretty big.

For example, there was the time in 2001 when I was driving from Montepuez in pouring rain, trying to get back to Balama. This was the time when the ten miles of road washed out in a huge rainstorm, taking five bridges with it. I was driving in when that happened, and several people were riding along with me. We got to a village only twelve miles from being home. But rainwater off the mountains had washed out the road. What was left when we got there was a roaring torrent rushing along a huge trench over four feet wide and four feet deep. You couldn't step into it let alone drive into it; you'd be swept away. Other cars were waiting on higher ground, hoping to cross it if the waters receded.

We waited over an hour. Then I felt in my spirit, *Get out! Get out! Get out!*

I got in the truck and told my traveling companions, "I'm leaving. Come with me if you wish."

I flipped the truck around, which wasn't all that easy. In pouring rain in that gummy mud, I had to wrench it around on a really narrow road with ditches on both sides. I finally managed to get the truck going the other way, and we arrived back in Montepuez safely. I had no idea why the Lord told me to get out other than that I felt a sense of danger. All but one car followed me.

The next morning we went back out to try to get through. The rain had abated, so surely the flood had subsided, right? Hardly. Even before we reached the trenched stretch, we encountered a torrent four feet deep and a hundred yards wide, roaring across the road where there used to be a bridge and a river. Logs and debris tumbled along in the howling water. No way was anyone going to cross that in any form or fashion. We learned that a dam had burst upstream on one of the rivers behind us. We had gotten out the day before through this area that was destroyed hours later.

We ended up staying in Montepuez a second night. On the third day, the water was down to three feet and rolling along more sedately and gently, comparatively speaking.

The administrator himself, the top governmental official in Balama, ventured across in his four-wheel drive. He showed everyone else where the firm, rocky surface was. There is only a narrow ford of solid stony ground. If you venture into the mud on either side, you're stuck. Also, you have to keep moving. If the truck stalls out, the water rushes in and you lose an engine. I have a snorkel on my engine, a pipe that opens up by the truck roof so that the engine doesn't suck water as I enter streams. I can cross water up to the hood, and it doesn't matter.

The other vehicle got across safely. By following the same track he had used, I was able to cross. As long as I kept moving, the water didn't come in over the doors, but it was still three feet deep.

The important point of all this was listening to God's voice and obeying. We were on high enough ground that we would not have been washed away had we stayed where we were, but we would have been trapped for forty-eight hours without sufficient food, water, and clothing for the cold mountain temperatures that prevail after dark.

That was my mistake. I had gone against my own bush rules. My rules are, always carry three days of food and water. But I was only traveling a short distance, so I didn't have my usual supplies.

I do not plan to repeat that mistake.

We continued on beyond that ford and reached the part of the road where the four-foot-deep trench had been. It was still there. So we filled it in with rock and managed to get across. The bridge on the other side had washed out, its planks and logs gone. It took the government men six hours to install enough planks to form a bridge surface that we could get vehicles across. The whole bridge shook as we crossed it. It wasn't a crossing I would care to make again.

And so I managed to get home that third day. But some of the bridges that had been wiped out in the storm could not be fixed, and yet another heavy rain totally took out the route. The shaky bridge we crossed was demolished the very next day.

Having heard God and joined in common cause with my fellow missionaries, I can tell you what our vision for the future is.

Every corporation has its mission statement, its take on what it plans to do, and its vision for the future. Every church, every charitable organization has one. So do we.

But when you write out a mission statement and your vision for the future, somehow that implies that it is set in cement. Static. Unchanging. Down on paper and therefore solid. That could not be further from the truth, at least in our case. Our vision is continuous, ever developing, ever enlarging. And it just keeps unfolding, bigger and bigger.

You will recall how I told in the beginning of this story that God gave me a vision as I was working at that first orphanage in Moz. I was to go north and take care of children in desperate straits. I would build orphanages the African way and keep kids in their culture. These facilities would be as self-sufficient as possible. No details were provided.

About six months later, the Lord showed me a sea of children's faces, revealing to me that I was to bring multitudes of children to him, and he would form up the armies of God for the final days when he would fetch the church.

This was and still is our main goal. But that vision was still woefully scant as regards direction and detail. Incident followed incident, and since 1995 I have been in northern Moz fulfilling the vision. First there was VOL, helping hundreds of refugee children as they came back in from Tanzania and Malawi. That orphanage is still running with trained management. In 1999 I moved on into Balama in Cabo Delgado province to start a new program.

Balama is a more wide-ranging program because more kids there are in such a desperate situation, not just orphans but also others who are severely malnourished or abandoned. And then there are all those children seeking an education and unable to dream because their parent or parents are too poor to help them go on past their village school.

But you see, the details didn't have to be up front there in the vision statement. That's good. It would have overwhelmed us to see it all at the beginning. The vision unfolds as we go along, so long as we are walking in God's will. And how those details expand! I know it is God's vision, because it is so much more than our scanty human eyes could see. That new program I was led to begin in Balama has rapidly become three!

We have the orphan program, but God's vision shot light-years beyond that. Now we also have the malnutrition center to distribute food to abandoned or widowed mothers whose fields fail to grow enough food for the year.

For a moment now, picture yourself as a woman having grown up with no education whatsoever because of the war. I'm not talking only about reading and writing. You had no school at all. That means you know nothing about personal hygiene, health, or financial matters. You have never heard of the outside world. You do not speak

Portuguese, which the rest of your native land speaks, because you have to go to school to learn that. Schools teach what is now called domestic science—cooking and sewing. You didn't get that either. No food pyramid, no mending, no basic arithmetic. Did you learn all that from your parents? No. Chances are great you lost one or both and were raised by others.

God understands those women. His vision encompasses them. We at the Balama mission have come to realize that the well-being of these women is as important to him as is the reign of kings. So we are expanding our facilities into a training center for mothers to teach them the job, sanitation and health skills that their childhood education lacked. We are trying to restore in some way what the locusts have eaten. Can they better care for their children because we shared God's vision? I trust so. Can they make a better living? We'll try! Do their kids face a brighter future? Most certainly.

The projects are so simple, so basic, and these women have never been exposed to them. For example, we can teach them sewing and the preparation of nutritious meals. Not all that goes into the belly profits the body. We can show them what most of the rest of the world knows. They need instruction in how to keep their kids clean, how to take care of their babies, how to maintain better sanitation in and around the house. Sanitation? These women cannot even buy soap for their family.

They have nothing until they can get on their feet. It is difficult to conceive of a person with absolutely nothing. No resources, no fallback, no food, no seed, no tools to work the ground. No matter how hardworking and intelligent they are, nothing is still so very nothing.

Many of these widows and abandoned women either have no house or have a hovel in extreme disrepair. A hut with a grass roof, dirt floor, and bamboo doors and windows can serve if it's well made and strong. Most aren't, so we also assist them with housing when possible. A passable grass house (and grass is a good building material here, remember) costs fifty dollars American. Yes, that fifty will put a family into a house.

Our whole concept is to get them independent again. We provide clothing. We also provide seed. We may supply hoes or machetes. We keep them in the program a year, which comprises one full growing season. Once they get a harvest under their belt, they have food for their family and seed for next year. Do you see what I mean about God's vision being so far beyond what we could imagine? This is all about changing lives.

Our third program is educational support. Our dormitory system houses seventy-two children in the main dorms, and we now have two subsidiary dorms to house another twenty-one. These children completed the fifth grade in their villages. But most come from single-parent dwellings, and their parents are too poor to send them to the next stage of schooling, a boarding situation in Balama, the county seat. Without that resource they cannot continue their education into the sixth, seventh, and eighth grades.

Getting through eighth grade is a real premium. As they complete the seventh grade, they qualify to go to a technical school and learn a skill so that they can get a job locally. But higher education means going into Montepuez, thirty miles away.

And in fact, several of our orphans, exceptional students, will be able to go on. We purchased a house in Montepuez in order to provide them with a place to stay. A housemother oversees the kids so that they're well supervised. But we have neither the funds nor the facilities to send them all on. I wish we could. We have to be content for the moment with our goal of getting as many as possible through the eighth grade.

As God's vision continues to unfold, we are realizing that this rampant expansion isn't the half of it. We have started only two places out of the five that he has shown us that we will start. Now we're waiting on his orders as to when and where to start number three. In the meantime, we are busy expanding the children's evangelistic program to bring in the multitudes of children.

We're starting a youth sports program with soccer, basketball, and games for younger kids. To bring multitudes of anyone in, as I described in the construction chapter, you have to get to know them, explain who Jesus is, tell them stories, show them cartoon evangelistic stories, and bring the children to a saving knowledge of who Jesus is and how much he loves them.

Why the kids? Sixty thousand out of the county's total population of about 103,000 are under the age of fifteen. In short, a children's program reaches the majority of the population. But we serve the adults as well, of course. Our equipment for the Jesus Film has been wonderfully upgraded. Adults and children together all around the county can now watch the film on a massive screen. We can present the film to 5,000 at once, no matter how remote the village, using a video projector, generator, VCR, and a huge screen. The Lord mandated that we show the Jesus Film to all the people in the county. We are on the verge of doing it.

But what good is evangelism if there are no pastors to follow up and plant churches? We have the tools for the outreach. Now we are starting a video Bible school in Portuguese for the training of our pastors. All our pastors are educated to at least the seventh grade and all therefore speak Portuguese. But even if a Bible college or seminary were available, they could not afford it. Now they can learn the Word in their own area. This school will greatly speed up the process of pastoral training. We can then plant churches in strategic areas so that people are in walking distance of at least one.

And what good is it to come to these people with the message of God if their bellies are empty? Jesus loves them as much as he loves you. You know that. They do not. We first take the love of Jesus to people in the way they can see, with the physical help they need. We can show them that Someone out there truly loves them. It is a fact that not enough people know.

Their walk with God, though, remains a totally personal decision. Each man and boy must choose for himself whether to follow Jesus. Each woman and girl must make the biggest decision there is. We cannot do that for them. We wouldn't want to any more than we would like for them to force some sort of decision upon us. God welcomes his children. He does not shove them.

The response from our abandoned and widowed mothers with

all these starving children has been awesome. Basically, they tell us, "Other religions never helped us. They said, 'Do this, do that, and you'll go to heaven.' But they never *did* anything. We can see that this Jesus is different and that his love is real. We see it in how you help us."

I have said many times that these people are not slow. They know that medical, educational, and self-help programs cost money. They know such programs take work. They don't just hold a hand out. They go into this with eyes wide open. Some have shown their gratitude by bringing us some wild fruit or a few eggs if they still have a chicken.

It really brings me to tears when they do that.

What speaks? Actions. No one will listen to our words if they don't see the commitment. How often have you heard, "Put your money where your mouth is?" It's not just an idle statement in America. The world over it's a heart attitude for assessing attitude. If you haven't earned the right to be heard in practical ways, you'll not be heard, no matter how important the message.

God's vision takes that into account. He knows. And because it is his program, we are doing our best to just flow as Jesus tells us. When he says to do something, we will do it.

What we see is an exciting future! Because the end times are so close, a lot is going to happen in the next five to ten years. We must get the Gospel out. We want as many as possible to know about Jesus so they can make the most important decision of their lives. Until they have heard, how can they make a decision?

What an awesome, all-encompassing vision! What an unlimited and loving God!

And finally:

One morning in January of 2002, I was awakened by the Lord, and I was preaching this message. Now I assure you that it is not normal for me to wake up preaching unusual messages. It was impressed upon me that I was to preach this everywhere I went on the 2002 tour. As the end times surge ever closer, we need everybody motivated.

There is an audio-visual aid for this, a gimmick if you will: a jigsaw puzzle in its box. As I speak, I hold up a puzzle piece. Each person in my listening audience, as well as each of you out there reading this book, is a piece of the puzzle.

The assembled puzzle is the end time harvest of souls, the completed plan. God needs all the pieces together and in their proper places so that the end time harvest will be realized. Each piece has a role to play in the picture, a place to be.

That part is simple enough. Easy. The next part is not.

In order to complete your role, you have to step out of your comfort zone. You must leave your own goals and plans behind and ask God what it is that he wants you to do to complete that end time plan. If you accept this assignment and take the part he has given you, he will make you into somebody you never thought you could be. And you will do things you never thought you could do. Most important by far, of course, is that his final plans will be advanced.

But, I repeat, you have to step out of your tidy little security zone in order to move to this higher level. You must build a life by being armed with God's courage, and in order to do that, you have to build faith and trust in him. Then when he sends you forth to do something for him, you will do it, no matter what.

What is his definition of courage? That was given to me also.

Courage is not the absence of fear. Courage is having the trust and faith in Jesus Christ to step forward and do whatever he asks of you even when you are scared out of your gourd.

I am convinced that the time is short. We no longer have time to mess around. He must have his harvest brought in because Jesus is coming very soon.

"Yes," you argue, "but who am I? One person. Limited resources. Zero influence. I can't see that my puny contribution would amount to much when we're looking at masses of people out there, so many millions of puzzle pieces."

Perhaps you heard this in school. "For want of a nail, a shoe was lost. For want of the shoe a horse was lost ... " and it goes up through horses and cavalrymen until the battle was lost, and at the very end, it says that the kingdom was lost for want of a nail. The completed puzzle requires that *every* piece be in place, no matter the size.

And at the very end of things, who made the real contribution here? Jesus died for us, paying a supreme price, and he does not demand that we return in kind. He does ask us to be a living sacrifice, his piece of the puzzle.

If you will follow him, he will truly raise you up into a mighty warrior during these end times. So I invite you, I adjure you, to join him. Join hands with him and with all the other members of his body, helping to bring in the end times harvest.

... So that we can all go to our ultimate home a little bit sooner.

... So that Jesus can come back a little bit sooner.

HOW TO REACH US

Surface mail:

ORPHANS UNLIMITED. INC.

PMB 391

11152 Westheimer Rd.

Houston, TX 77042

Email:

office@orphansunlimited.org

Brenda@orphansunlimited.org

Our Web site:

www.orphansunlimited.org

Donations made to Orphans Unlimited's charitable 501-
C3 account are tax deductible. Please make checks out to
Africa Fund and *not* to me personally. All proceeds from
the sale of this book go directly to the orphanages.

PHOTOS FROM THE BUSH

This photo was taken at sunrise on Christmas morning, 1988, in Sperry, Oklahoma.

At 4:00 a.m. I was walking across my living room when I clearly heard the Lord's voice say, "Photograph the sunrise." It was ten degrees Fahrenheit outside, but I obediently prepared my camera and put on my warmest clothing.

The sky dawned clear blue and cloudless. I noticed a large brown bird with an estimated six-foot wing span flying above the area in which I stood. I thought it strange but was too focused on what I was to photograph to pay it much attention. Suddenly three cloud streams (like streams from a jet engine) shot across the sky as if they had been blown from a cannon. Beautiful pink and yellow colors began to mingle in the sky. I photographed all of this but saw nothing extraordinary, so I decided to go back into the house.

Suddenly I sensed a strong urge to turn around. Through the tree branches I saw the most awesome array of colors. I noticed that the huge bird was sitting in a tall tree right to the left of this magnificent scene. I whipped up my camera and focused. As I took the photo, the bird flew into the scene, but instead of circling back as it had been doing for the last hour, it kept going over the horizon, never to be seen again.

When I developed the film, a man's face was clearly visible with the bird on his right cheek. He was looking down and to the left with an unhappy stern look. I sensed it was God's face, but what was the message?

Two weeks of prayer revealed God's message:
Get ready for the coming of the Son!

Your basic log bridge. Most bridges in the bush use this
log construction. Negotiate carefully or fall through.

The mission station at VOL, showing mudbrick and bamboo construction.

Our orphans at VOL in 1996.

Bush ferry, Luembala River. The canoes are of tree
bark. Fares vary from five to fifty cents.

The crippled leopard that
killed $500 worth of goats.
That's Crispo at the right.

A black mamba. They're
not really black, as you
see. The guard is Joao.

My home for over three years, the rooftop tent on my truck. Note also the mobile radio-operated office.

Eva and her grandmother. We're treating her hands, after she ate the skin off. She's doing fine now.

Our Moz nurse, Roberto, admitting a malnourished baby into the program.
Wait until the upset little guy realizes there is food involved here.

A blind orphan being led by his guide child, in this case
his cousin. They use a stick between them.

The 2001 flood aftermath. That's I in the pink shirt, studying my buried differential. This is when we ventured out to get Les.

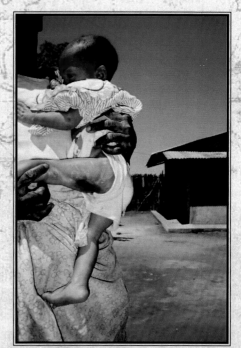

The orphaned baby girl who was grabbed by a pig, stolen right out of her grandmother's hut.

Home. The hut is used for storage. Corn and beans are stored extreme right. Move the corn and you have snakes. The pole is the bush mail radio antenna, the white blob a concrete water storage tank. My rooftop tent is barely visible under the ramada.

Offloading 20 tons of corn. The sacks weigh 50 kilos; that's 110 pounds each. The man is carrying two of them.

Our magnificent tractor/front-end loader and trailer, paid for in large part by the New Braunfels TX Tree of Life church.

Construction crew building the children's center cafeteria and kitchen. It's all hand work.

These are construction crew members who accepted Christ.

LIVE

listen|imagine|view|experience

AUDIO BOOK DOWNLOAD INCLUDED WITH THIS BOOK!

In your hands you hold a complete digital entertainment package. Besides purchasing the paper version of this book, this book includes a free download of the audio version of this book. Simply use the code listed below when visiting our website. Once downloaded to your computer, you can listen to the book through your computer's speakers, burn it to an audio CD or save the file to your portable music device (such as Apple's popular iPod) and listen on the go!

How to get your free audio book digital download:

1. Visit www.tatepublishing.com and click on the e|LIVE logo on the home page.
2. Enter the following coupon code:
   2551-b54e-ff69-fccc-5b6f-cfca-fd8f-042b
3. Download the audio book from your e|LIVE digital locker and begin enjoying your new digital entertainment package today!